Too Much Is Not Enough

Too Much Is Not Enough

INCENTIVES IN EXECUTIVE COMPENSATION

Robert W. Kolb

OXFORD

UNIVERSITY PRESS

OXFORD
UNIVERSITY PRESS

Oxford University Press is a department of the University of Oxford.
It furthers the University's objective of excellence in research, scholarship,
and education by publishing worldwide.

Oxford   New York

Auckland   Cape Town   Dar es Salaam   Hong Kong   Karachi
Kuala Lumpur   Madrid   Melbourne   Mexico City   Nairobi
New Delhi   Shanghai   Taipei   Toronto

With offices in

Argentina   Austria   Brazil   Chile   Czech Republic   France   Greece
Guatemala   Hungary   Italy   Japan   Poland   Portugal   Singapore
South Korea   Switzerland   Thailand   Turkey   Ukraine   Vietnam

Oxford is a registered trademark of Oxford University Press
in the UK and certain other countries.

Published in the United States of America by
Oxford University Press
198 Madison Avenue, New York, NY 10016

© Oxford University Press 2012

Library of Congress Cataloging-in-Publication Data
Kolb, Robert W., 1949-
Too much is not enough : incentives in executive compensation / Robert W. Kolb.
p. cm.
Includes bibliographical references and index.
ISBN 978–0–19–982958–3 (cloth : alk. paper)
1. Executives—Salaries, etc.—United States.
2. Incentives in industry—United States.
3. Incentive awards—United States.
4. Corporate governance—United States.
5. Executives—Salaries, etc.—Government policy—United States.
I. Title.
HD4965.5.U6K65 2012
331.2′164—dc23
2011049486

ISBN 978–0–19–982958–3

1 3 5 7 9 8 6 4 2
Printed in the United States of America
on acid-free paper

To Lori, fully vested and loaded with incentives

{ CONTENTS }

{ PREFACE }

For the typical citizen of the United States, there is nothing more inexplicable and infuriating about corporate America than the high level of executive compensation, particularly that received by the leaders of corporations, the chief executive officers, or CEOs. In many cases, the response is visceral—"It can't be that a CEO deserves four hundred times as much as I make. No one is worth that much!" Merely because the outrage over executive compensation is visceral, it is not necessarily mistaken. One might more charitably characterize the damning of high executive pay as an intuitive one. But these assessments, whether visceral or intuitive, whether entirely mistaken or exactly on target, are not built on solid economic understanding. While the economics of executive compensation is complex, any ultimate judgment about the level and structure of executive compensation should be based on an informed understanding. This book provides that understanding for the educated layperson.

Incentives lie at the heart of the executive-compensation system that dominates corporate America and which increasingly finds favor throughout the world. In the main, corporations act to establish compensation systems that provide their executives with behavior-guiding incentives. However, some executives find their own, often perverse, incentives in the established pay systems. That is, they find their compensation program rife with incentives that they can exploit for personal gain at the expense of the firm and society.

Two main ways of controlling behavior are through monitoring and command, on the one hand, and providing incentives on the other. Monitoring and commanding an individual who is supposed to lead an organization has proven to have severe limitations; although, we will see that effective monitoring can play an important role. This leaves incentives as the chief way to establish framework within which a corporate leader can direct the firm toward increasing profits, building firm value, and benefiting society. Reflecting this line of thought, corporations build executive-pay schemes around incentive compensation, which they deliver mainly in the form of pay related to the value of the firm's shares. The two principal vehicles for providing share-based pay are restricted stock and executive stock options (ESOs).

Perhaps surprisingly, firms provide these incentives mainly to induce CEOs to *increase* the risk level of the firm beyond what they would otherwise choose. The incentive compensation should encourage the CEO to increase risk in the right way, by undertaking riskier projects that create additional firm value. The main purpose of this book is to explain how this scheme of incentive compensation works and to assess its effectiveness. The reader of this book will come to a greater understanding of how executive compensation functions and how well it performs, as well as learn of the considerable deficiencies that infest the system. The book also points the way toward improving the system through improvement in the structure of corporate governance.

This book will disappoint the reader hoping for a manifesto against executive compensation. Instead, this book aims to provide an objective assessment of how executive compensation operates and how well it performs. In doing so, it draws on the tremendous volume of research into executive compensation that has been produced over the last few decades and that continues to expand at a rapid rate. Almost all of this research appears in academic journals, tends to be highly mathematical, often relies on complicated statistical techniques, and is generally invisible to the wider public. This book strives to make the weight of that research intelligible and to use it to guide an assessment of executive compensation, as well as to indicate how to improve the performance of executive pay.

Chapters 1 through 3 provide the necessary background for an understanding of executive compensation. Chapter 1 analyzes the general level of executive compensation and explains the main components of executive pay packages. Understanding the efficacy of executive compensation requires the proper framework, and chapter 2 discusses the two main ways in which economists and public policymakers conceive the system of executive compensation. In chapter 3, the analysis turns to a more detailed consideration of the CEO's pay package and how different elements play, or fail to play, an incentivizing role.

Chapters 4 through 8 constitute the core analytical portion of the book. They further explain the detailed performance of incentives in the compensation scheme and show how the best research further informs our understanding of incentives in executive compensation. Chapter 4 addresses the complications of executive stock options in a way intelligible to the layperson. Once an incentive-compensation program is in place, firms, CEOs, and investors all respond to the system in various ways, some constructively, others less so. Chapter 5 examines how these various constituencies interact with and respond to the incentive-compensation schemes that firms adopt. In chapter 6, we focus on the incentives to increase risk that lie at the very heart of incentive compensation. This is the key question of incentive compensation: Is incentive compensation effective in inducing CEOs to increase the risk of the firms they lead in ways that create more value than would otherwise be achieved? As chapter 6 shows, the system may be generally beneficial, but there are many problems.

Chapter 7 examines how incentive compensation affects many dimensions of corporate management, ranging from the crucial investment and financing behavior of firms, to how firms pursue mergers and respond to takeover attempts, how incentive compensation tilts firms away from paying dividends and toward buying their own shares, and how incentives influence the extent and truthfulness of the way that corporations report their results. The conclusions are both comforting and disturbing. Chapter 8 shows that incentive compensation plays a key role in corporate dishonesty and the commission of felonies by CEOs. For those who favor incentive compensation, this clear evidence of widespread misconduct, in which CEOs lie, cheat, and steal, stands as the greatest reminder that the system of incentive compensation now in place is defective in serious ways and sorely in need of correction. According to these malefactor CEOs, "too much is not enough."

Chapter 9, the final chapter, summarizes the weight of evidence on incentive compensation and shows how it can be improved through the strengthening of corporate governance. However, it presents no grand conclusions or sweeping recommendations. Instead, it characterizes a system of incentives that is generally beneficial, yet plagued by real defects, and it suggests some serious improvements that can occur within the general framework of corporate governance and regulation that has developed in the United States and that is likely to remain in place for the considerable future.

Acknowledgement

I would like to thank the Center for Integrated Risk Management and Corporate Governance at Loyola University Chicago for its support of this project.

Chicago, November 2011

Too Much Is Not Enough

The Magnitude and Structure of Executive Compensation

In public perception, executive compensation has always been high. In previous eras, when most businesses were owned by a single person or a family, the perceived avarice of the owners was already an issue and the stuff of literature. As business enterprises grew, the broadening gulf between workers versus owners and senior managers led to greater resentment and wider misunderstanding. By the middle of the nineteenth century, characters emerged such as Ebenezer Scrooge in Charles Dickens's *A Christmas Carol*, 1843, and it was in the same period that Friedrich Engels produced his classic *The Condition of the Working Class in England*, 1845. Scrooge was both the proprietor and manager of his firm. While Engels does not identify the ownership structure of the sweatshops he describes, it is fair to infer that some were single proprietorships while others were managed for their owners. After all, Engels arrived in Manchester, England in 1842 at the behest of his father to work in the cotton-manufacturing firm of Ermen and Engels, with a view to preparing him for a career as owner-manager. (Needless to say, the young Friedrich was to disappoint to his father.)

Today, when we think of executive compensation, the focus is on executive pay in corporations, particularly the pay of the chief executive officer (CEO), but also on the top management team of the firm, which would typically include the chief financial officer (CFO) and a handful of others. While these top executives often hold a significant fraction of their personal wealth in the shares of the firm they manage, their holdings are almost always well below a controlling interest. As early as 1932, Adolf Berle and Gardiner Means described this separation of ownership and control in their book, *The Modern Corporation and Private Property,* and they realized that this separation of ownership and management would generate conflicts between the goals and desires of owners (the shareholders) and the managers they hired to run the firm in their interest.[1]

As we will see, this inherent divergence of interest between shareholders and managers—the conflict between principals and their agents—remains a driving force in disagreements between the two parties. The pay practices for corporate executives, which also, for the most part, emerged as a function of this separation of ownership and control, are primarily responsible for the current public outrage over the high level of executive pay. Because present-day concern centers on the pay of executives in large firms with separate ownership and management, and because reliable data on executive pay only became available at about the time that Berle and Means were writing, this book considers the period beginning with the Great Depression and then focuses on the current situation and the immediate past, especially from 1992 forward.

The public is clearly repulsed by the widespread reports of what many perceive as extremely high levels of executive compensation. However, the typical consumer of media reports about CEO pay gives little attention to the structure of executive compensation—how the, admittedly large, compensation "pie" is divided into many components—salary, bonus, long-term incentive plans, restricted stock awards, executive stock option grants, pension and retirement benefits, perquisites of office, and postretirement noncash benefits. As this book shows, an understanding of the structure of executive compensation lies, or should lie, at the conceptual heart of the debate over the magnitude of executive compensation.

The two questions "Why is executive pay so high?" and "Why is executive pay distributed across so many vehicles?" cannot be answered in isolation, and there are two basic competing responses that economists give to these joint questions. The "optimal contracting," or "incentive alignment," approach stresses that executive compensation must be structured to provide executives the right incentives to manage the firm in a way that maximizes its value, and this required structure necessarily leads to high levels of compensation. The second dominant approach to understanding executive compensation, the "managerial power hypothesis," asserts that executives capture the pay-setting process and essentially write their own excessive paychecks. On the managerial power view, the complicated structure of executive compensation serves a key purpose by disguising or "camouflaging" just how much that total compensation really is. The next chapter explores these competing theses, but before turning to those theories this chapter offers an overview of the magnitude and structure of executive pay.

The Magnitude of CEO Compensation

From the 1930s to the present, most contemporary observers have regarded executive compensation as "high." Figure 1.1 shows the median total compensation for CEOs and other members of the top-management team at the largest U.S. firms from 1936 to 2005. To make the comparison more meaningful,

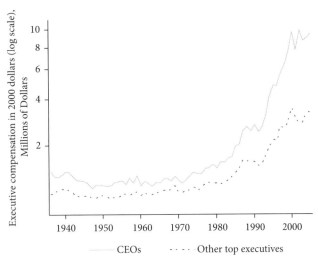

FIGURE 1.1 *Median Compensation of CEOs and Their Top Managers, 1936–2005.*

Source: Carola Frydman and Dirk Jenter, "CEO Compensation," *Annual Review of Financial Economics,* 2010, 2, 75–102. See p. 77.

the graph expresses the amounts in constant 2000 dollars. The marked rise in CEO compensation from around $1 million to $10 million represents a 10-fold increase in CEO real compensation over the 65 years from 1936 to 2000—the increase in compensation is not an artifact of inflation at all. As figure 1.1 shows, the non-CEO top executives also made out quite well, but only about half as well as their bosses. In 2011 dollars, the CEO of 1936 earned about $1.3 million, while his top assistants received about $650,000 each. As we will see in detail later, the CEO of the largest U.S. firms today receive total compensation of around $11 million, while members of the top-management team receive around $3 million each.

Figure 1.2 focuses on the more recent period from 1992 to 2010; the data from this timeframe is much more complete and accurate.[2] It shows the total median and average compensation for CEOs of S&P 500 firms from 1992 to 2010 in nominal dollars—dollars paid at the time and not adjusted for inflation. At least three features of the graph deserve comment. First, we can see a marked surge in compensation during this period, with mean CEO compensation rising from $2.6 to $11.4 million, and median compensation rising from about $2.0 to $9.6 million. Second, there is a marked peak, especially in average compensation, in 1999–2001, primarily due to the dotcom bubble of that era. Third, the graph depicts a significant divergence between the average and median compensation levels from 1992 until about 2000, and then a retreat to a lower ratio of mean-to-median compensation. This reflects a wider divergence of compensation between CEOs and their top assistants during the dotcom bubble. More precisely, the gulf between average and

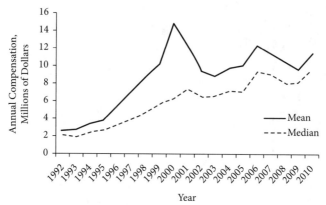

FIGURE 1.2 *Total CEO Compensation, 1992–2010.*
Source: Graph by author, based on ExecuComp data.

median compensation around 2000 is due to a small percentage of CEOs receiving extraordinary compensation packages, which created a skewed distribution.

From 1992 to 2010, compensation for CEOs and top managers rose dramatically in the large firms of the S&P 500. In the earlier portion of this period, CEO compensation accelerated more rapidly than did pay for other managers, but by the end of the period, the ratio of CEO pay to that of top managers returned to a level similar to that which prevailed in 1992. While the median top manager saw a pay increase from about $750,000 in 1992 to $3.1 million in 2010, CEOs made out much better, as figure 1.3 indicates. In both 1992 and in the current period, the CEO makes about 2.5 to 3.0 times their top subordinates.

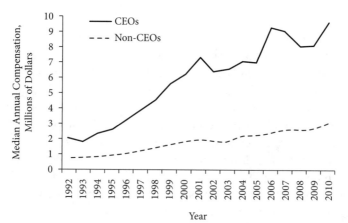

FIGURE 1.3 *Median Compensation of CEOs and Their Top Managers, 1992–2010.*
Source: Graph by author, based on ExecuComp data.

Another useful way of looking at CEO pay is to examine compensation levels without the influence of inflation, so figure 1.4 shows average and median CEO total compensation for S&P 500 firms in constant 2010 dollars. From 1992 to 2000, average CEO compensation rose from about $4 million to a peak of almost $19 million in 2000 (in 2010 dollars). Then from 2000 to 2010, average compensation fell to a level of $11.4 million, dropping by 40 percent. During the same period, median compensation started at $3.2 million, escalated to slightly more than $9 million in 2001, and reached its highest point in 2006 at over $10 million, before falling back near the $9.6 million level. Thus, even though average CEO pay has declined by 40 percent in the last 10 years in real terms, the typical CEO of an S&P 500 company makes about $11 million per year.

Even if the typical median to average CEO might make $9–11 million in 2010, the range of compensation is extreme. Table 1.1 shows total compensation for selected prominent executives for several years: 1992, 2000, and 2009. Many of the executives with the lowest levels of reported pay are firm founders. Perhaps most striking, Steve Jobs served as CEO for Apple in 2009 for a single dollar. Other notable entrepreneurs that stayed with their firms to become CEO include Barron Hilton, William Wrigley, and Leon Hess in 1992; Steve Ballmer and Larry Ellison received relatively low levels of compensation for leading Microsoft and Oracle in 2000, respectively. In spite of his low level of compensation in 2000, Larry Ellison is one of the richest men in the world, with most of his fortune deriving from his firm Oracle—in other years besides 2000, Ellison did very well indeed.

Some of the highflyers on the 2000 compensation table were sentenced to prison terms such as Bernie Ebbers of WorldCom and MCI, Richard Scrushy of HealthSouth (although his legal struggles continue as of this writing),

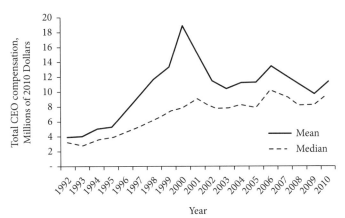

FIGURE 1.4 *S&P 500 CEO Total Compensation, Average and Median 1992–2010.*

Source: Graph by author, based on ExecuComp data.

TABLE 1.1 Sampling of S&P 500 CEOs and Their Total Compensation

Executive	Firm	Total Compensation ($ thousands)
1992 AVERAGE COMPENSATION: $2.59 MILLION		
Michael A. Miles	ALTRIA GROUP INC	18,113.246
John F. Welch, Jr.	GENERAL ELECTRIC CO	14,680.867
P. Roy Vagelos	MERCK & CO	12,935.911
H. Wayne Huizenga	BLOCKBUSTER ENMNT CORP	7,878.126
Ray R. Irani, Ph.D.	OCCIDENTAL PETROLEUM CORP	6,087.217
Lawrence J. Ellison	ORACLE CORP	4,936.621
Roberto C. Goizueta	COCA-COLA CO	4,622.343
August A. Busch III	ANHEUSER-BUSCH COS INC	3,808.334
Paul H. O'Neill	ALCOA INC	3,719.401
John W. Snow	CSX CORP	3,668.257
John Shepard Reed	CITICORP	3,496.784
Maurice R. Greenberg	AMERICAN INTERNATIONAL GROUP	3,413.461
John F. Akers	INTL BUSINESS MACHINES CORP	3,202.280
Laurence Alan Tisch	CBS INC	2,228.331
Andrew S. Grove	INTEL CORP	2,173.157
Rand V. Araskog	ITT CORP	1,724.147
Arthur Ochs Sulzberger	NEW YORK TIMES CO-CL A	1,484.252
Edward A. Brennan	SEARS ROEBUCK & CO	1,431.972
Barron Hilton	HILTON HOTELS CORP	1,104.577
Robert L. Crandall	AMR CORP/DE	1,013.471
William Wrigley	WRIGLEY (WM) JR CO	803.390
Leon Hess	HESS CORP	311.443
2000 AVERAGE COMPENSATION: $14.97 MILLION		
Steven P. Jobs	APPLE INC	600,347.351
Sanford I. Weill	CITIGROUP INC	230,033.652
L. Dennis Kozlowski	TYCO INTERNATIONAL LTD	141,675.569
John F. Welch, Jr.	GENERAL ELECTRIC CO	125,402.914
Sumner M. Redstone	CBS CORP	70,346.064
Stephen M. Case	TIME WARNER INC	68,984.308
Michael S. Dell	DELL INC	40,477.365
Bernard John Ebbers	MCI INC	40,382.528
Carleton S. Fiorina	HEWLETT-PACKARD CO	37,433.273
Maurice R. Greenberg	AMERICAN INTERNATIONAL GROUP	37,391.600
Richard S. Fuld, Jr.	LEHMAN BROTHERS HOLDINGS INC	34,426.505
Michael D. Eisner	DISNEY (WALT) CO	33,546.567
Kenneth Lee Lay	ENRON CORP	30,904.586
James Dimon	BANK ONE CORP	30,855.937
August A. Busch III	ANHEUSER-BUSCH COS INC	16,133.863

(Continued)

TABLE 1.1 (Continued)

Executive	Firm	Total Compensation ($ thousands)
2000 AVERAGE COMPENSATION: $14.97 MILLION		
Charles Robert Schwab, Jr.	SCHWAB (CHARLES) CORP	13,289.010
Eric E. Schmidt, Ph.D.	NOVELL INC	11,605.414
Angelo R. Mozilo	COUNTRYWIDE FINANCIAL CORP	9,578.707
Richard M. Scrushy	HEALTHSOUTH CORP	6,195.765
Howard D. Schultz	STARBUCKS CORP	5,39.476
Joseph P. Nacchio	QWEST COMMUNICATION INTL INC	4,354.690
William Wrigley, Jr.	WRIGLEY (WM) JR CO	3,800.124
Philip H. Knight	NIKE INC-CL B	2,641.427
J. W. Marriott, Jr.	MARRIOTT INTL INC	2,602.735
Richard B. Cheney	HALLIBURTON CO	2,358.505
Steven A. Ballmer	MICROSOFT CORP	633.514
Lawrence J. Ellison	ORACLE CORP	42.945
2009 AVERAGE COMPENSATION: $9.55 MILLION		
John H. Hammergren	MCKESSON CORP	54,584.021
Ray R. Irani, Ph.D.	OCCIDENTAL PETROLEUM CORP	31,401.356
Mark Hurd	HEWLETT-PACKARD CO	30,332.527
Ralph Lauren	POLO RALPH LAUREN CP-CL A	27,700.007
Rex W. Tillerson	EXXON MOBIL CORP	27,168.317
Keith Rupert Murdoch	NEWS CORP	19,887.610
Alan R. Mulally	FORD MOTOR CO	17,916.654
Kenneth I. Chenault	AMERICAN EXPRESS CO	17,398.568
Howard D. Schultz	STARBUCKS CORP	12,109.792
Jeffrey R. Immelt	GENERAL ELECTRIC CO	9,885.240
Stephen A. Wynn	WYNN RESORTS LTD	8,385.831
Jeffrey P. Bezos	AMAZON.COM INC	1,781.840
J. W. Marriott, Jr.	MARRIOTT INTL INC	1,579.599
James Dimon	JPMORGAN CHASE & CO	1,322.094
Steven A. Ballmer	MICROSOFT CORP	1,276.627
John J. Mack	MORGAN STANLEY	1,249.666
Michael S. Dell	DELL INC	963.623
Lloyd C. Blankfein	GOLDMAN SACHS GROUP INC	862.657
John P. Mackey	WHOLE FOODS MARKET INC	710.076
Eric E. Schmidt, Ph.D.	GOOGLE INC	245.322
Edward M. Liddy	AMERICAN INTERNATIONAL GROUP	204.058
Vikram S. Pandit	CITIGROUP INC	128.751
Steven P. Jobs	APPLE INC	0.001

Source: Data drawn from ExecuComp and show the total reported compensation for each indicated fiscal year for each executive.

Note: Amounts reported for individuals can differ markedly depending on the assumptions under which they are computed.

and Dennis Kozlowski of Tyco International. In many years, CEOs of giant financial firms found themselves in the top ranks of the highest-paid CEOs. However, 2009, the aftermath of the financial crisis, showed leaders of some of the largest financial firms in the United States wearing sackcloth and ashes as they garnered relatively modest compensation, including Vikram Pandit of Citigroup, Ed Liddy of AIG, Lloyd Blankfein of Goldman Sachs, John Mack of Morgan Stanley, and Jamie Dimon of JPMorgan Chase.[3] The change in compensation from year to year portrayed in table 1.1 is also striking. Steve Jobs received more than $600 million in 2000 but only $1 in 2009. Similarly, Michael Dell earned more than $40 million in 2000 but received less than $1 million in 2009.

In many instances, knowing the details of an executive's position with respect to her firm can help explain the differences in compensation, although much of the detail may remain a mystery. For example, although Steve Jobs received only $1 in 2009, his ownership position in Apple awarded him huge payoffs as he led Apple from one triumph to the next. The relatively lower level of CEO pay in financial firms in 2009 is almost entirely a consequence of the financial crash. For example, Lloyd Blankfein made $68.5 million as CEO of Goldman Sachs in 2007, less than $1 million in 2009, but by 2010 his compensation was again on the way up, reaching $13.2 million.[4]

The public concern over executive compensation has focused on the pay packages at big corporations, notably the S&P 500. For that reason, and because those firms are the most thoroughly studied and have the most uniform data available, this book concentrates principally on executive compensation in S&P 500 firms. However, it is important to realize that the same features of pay at large firms, closely explored in this book, also pertain to smaller firms but at a reduced scale. Figure 1.5 shows the average compensation of CEOs at firms of various sizes from 1992 to 2010. The three size groups are drawn from the S&P indices. The large capitalization (LargeCap) firms are the biggest in the S&P 500, the next-smaller 400 in size constitute the S&P MidCap Index, while the following group of 600 firms comprises the S&P SmallCap Index (which, in total, makes up the S&P 1500). As figure 1.5 shows, the larger the firm, the greater the pay for CEOs, other factors being equal. Further, the movements in compensation levels among the three groups tend to rise or fall together. Also, CEOs at the large firms enjoy the most dramatic surges in compensation, widening the compensation gap over the MidCap and SmallCap firms. As a final point, the LargeCap firms benefited the most from the market peak of 2000, associated with what proved to be the dotcom bubble.

Yet another measure of CEO compensation is to compare the growth in CEO pay with the growth in the value of firms. Figure 1.6 shows the growth in average CEO compensation for S&P 500 firms compared with the S&P 500 index. On the whole, the two appear to be strongly related, a widely noted

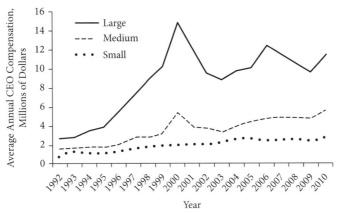

FIGURE 1.5 **Average Annual CEO Compensation by Firm Size,**
1992–2010 *Average compensation in firms of various sizes for each*
year. Large: Made up of the S&P 500. Medium: The next 400 smaller
in size, or MidCap. Small: The following 600 in market capitalization,
or SmallCap.

Source: Graph by author, based on ExecuComp data.

phenomenon.[5] This relationship between pay and the firm's value merely suggests that CEOs are rewarded proportionately for increasing the value of the firm. (We will explore this issue more fully in chapter 4, which analyzes the relationship between executive pay and performance.)

However, the rise in executive pay has clearly outstripped those of ordinary workers, as figure 1.7 illustrates. Ordinary workers have not seen their wages keep up with the increase in the value of the firms they serve. On the face of it, there is no reason why CEOs should be compensated dollar-for-dollar for increasing firm value while other employees of the firm should not. From 1972 until about 1992, the ratio of CEO pay to production-worker pay doubled, from

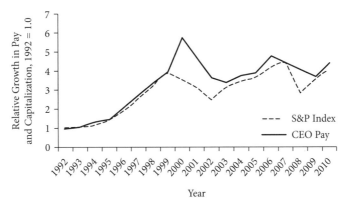

FIGURE 1.6 *Increase in CEO Pay and Stock Market Gains.*

Source: Graph by author, based on ExecuComp data.

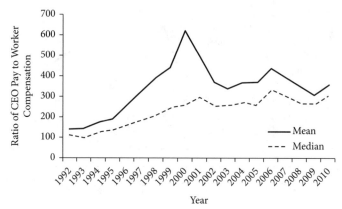

FIGURE 1.7   *Ratio of CEO Pay to Ordinary Worker Compensation,*
1992–2010.

Source: Data for CEO compensation drawn from ExecuComp. The "ordinary worker"
compensation is drawn from the Bureau of Labor Statistics standard table B-2. Average
hours and earnings of production and nonsupervisory employees (1) on private non-
farm payrolls by major industry sector, 1965 to date. U.S. Department of Labor, Bureau
of Labor Statistics, available at ftp://ftp.bls.gov/pub/suppl/empsit.ceseeb2.txt. Annual
worker salary was computed as 50 times the average weekly earnings for each year.

roughly 40 times to 80 times.[6] Thus, while CEO pay was definitely trending
upward relative to production workers, the rate of increase was, in retrospect,
modest. Starting around 1992, however, executive compensation accelerated
radically. Figure 1.7 shows the ratio of average and median S&P 500 CEO salaries to those of ordinary workers during 1992–2010. In 1992 the average CEO
at an S&P 500 firm earned 141 times as much as the representative worker,
while the 1992 median CEO salary was 111 times as large. Because of the huge
surge in CEO compensation from 1992 to 2000, these ratios skyrocketed. In
2000, the average S&P 500 CEO received more than 600 times as much as the
representative worker, while the median pay for the same CEO that year was
259 times as large. In the first decade or so of the twenty-first century, these
ratios dropped, reaching 358 times and 303 times for average and median S&P
500 CEO compensation, respectively, in 2010.

Beyond the belief that, in general, pay for executives is excessive, many have
pointed to the fact that executives in the United States receive significantly
higher pay than non-U.S. executives. While this has been a long-standing
phenomenon, the disparity has widened in recent years. Figure 1.8 depicts
CEO pay levels at several industrialized countries for the years 1984 and 1996
in inflation-adjusted 1998 dollars that are also adjusted for purchasing-power
parity. (The goal of these adjustments is simply to make the cross-country
and cross-time dollar figures more directly comparable. The study also examined firms of comparable size.) As the graph shows, CEO compensation in the
United States was higher in 1984 than in other countries, but the gap soared
from 1984 to 1996. In very recent years, executive pay outside the United

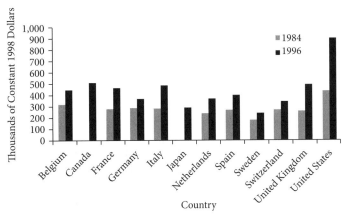

FIGURE 1.8 *Growth in CEO Compensation: International Comparisons, 1984 versus 1996.*

Source: John M. Abowd and David S. Kaplan, "Executive Compensation: Six Questions that Need Answering," *Journal of Economic Perspectives*, 1999, 13:4, 145–168. Adapted from table 1, p. 146.

States has risen rapidly, and there is anecdotal evidence that the international pay gap may be narrowing. However, CEO pay in U.S. companies currently remains substantially higher and U.S.-based executives will probably enjoy this differential for years to come.[7]

We saw in figure 1.8 that compensation for U.S. CEOs has proven to be substantially higher than for CEOs of firms headquartered in other industrialized nations. And figure 1.7 illustrated the gap between CEO pay and compensation for "ordinary workers." Figure 1.9 shows the relationship between CEO pay and the pay of ordinary workers in a variety of countries. In each instance, the CEO earns a multiple of the pay of rank-and-file workers, but the ratio is much higher in the United States than in any other country featured in the graph. While the data is drawn from 1996, this multiple of CEO-pay to worker-pay has increased across the industrialized world in recent years. Yet compared with other countries, CEOs of U.S.-based firms receive excessive compensation relative to ordinary workers.

The Structure of Executive Compensation

To this point, we have focused on the total compensation that executives receive, but this compensation comes in many forms, with different components being related to different aspects of their jobs and performance. Further, the purpose of some types of compensation is hotly debated; some argue that CEO pay is artfully constructed to secure the CEO's best performance—the optimal-contracting, or incentive-alignment, approach. By contrast, the

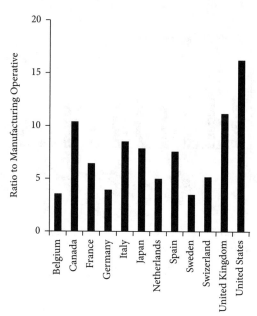

FIGURE 1.9 *Ratio of CEO After-Tax Compensation and Benefits to Manufacturing Operatives, 1996.*

Source: John M. Abowd and David S. Kaplan, "Executive Compensation: Six Questions that Need Answering," *Journal of Economic Perspectives*, 1999, 13:4, 145–168. See figure 3, p. 161.

managerial power approach maintains that the forms of compensation are intentionally kept varied and obscure to provide multiple avenues by which the firm can funnel excessive compensation to executives. We explore those controversies in chapter 2; however, the remainder of this chapter supplies a brief primer on the forms of executive compensation.

SALARY

Salary is the most understandable and transparent part of the CEO's pay package, and it is usually stated as an annual amount. For most CEOs, salary is a small component of overall compensation, a result of federal legislation. In his 1992 campaign for the presidency, Bill Clinton complained of exorbitant CEO compensation, criticizing compensation above $1 million as obviously excessive.[8] After President Clinton took office, Congress passed the Omnibus Budget Reconciliation Act of 1993 (OBRA), which included section 162(m), pertaining to executive pay. This section specified that CEO compensation in excess of $1 million could not be deducted by the firm as a business expense, *unless* the pay over and above $1 million qualified as "performance-based" pay.

The law applied specifically to the top-five executives in a corporation, those typically named in the firm's SEC filings, and the law applied to fiscal years that started on January 1, 1994, or later. Implementation of this law meant that the portion of salaries for these executives that exceeded $1 million would be more costly because the amount over $1 million could no longer be treated as a business expense for tax purposes, in contrast to the treatment of all other salaries. In addition, payments to these executives after retirement were not subject to the treatment of section 162(m). These two features of the new section 162(m) regime—the exceptions for performance-based pay and for postretirement payments—proved to have important consequences, explored later in this chapter.

Table 1.2 provides a quick look at the evolution of CEO salaries for selected years. The year 1993 was clearly unaffected by the law because OBRA's salary regulations applied only for fiscal years that began on January 1, 1994 or later. At the time that Clinton complained about high CEO compensation, the average salary was under $700,000 and more than 90 percent of the CEOs at these largest firms received a salary of $1 million or less. As table 1.2 shows, less than 1 percent of CEOs received a salary of exactly $1 million in 1993. However, following the implementation of the law the occurrence of $1 million salaries increased for 1995, 2000, and 2005. Over the entire period covered by table 1.2, average salaries rose, breaking the $1 million threshold in 2005. The graph suggests that the new law did make the $1 million salary more popular, and that impression has been sustained by thorough studies. One study found, as a result of the law, firms with salaries near the $1 million cap restrained salary growth, and 23 firms actually reduced salaries to under $1 million. However, the same study reported that the main effect of the law was to switch compensation to other forms, such as executive stock options, that qualified as "performance based" or that were deferred—another safe harbor provided by section 162(m). The overall tenor of the study, and the literature on this topic in general, suggests that the law had almost no effect on total compensation growth, but that it augmented the use of qualifying performance-based compensation.[9] While an executive's salary may be the most visible portion

TABLE 1.2 Percentage of S&P 500 CEO Salaries by Year Under, At, or Over $1 Million

	Under $1 Million (%)	Exactly $1 Million (%)	Over $1 Million (%)	Average Salary ($)
1993	89.56	0.84	9.60	691,220
1995	85.48	2.86	11.66	745,804
2000	71.14	6.01	22.85	871,115
2005	54.77	8.71	36.51	1,000,987
2009	46.08	6.86	47.06	1,068,940
2010	43.63	6.91	49.45	1,119,081

Source: Computations by author from ExecuComp data.

of compensation, it plays a relatively minor role for S&P 500 CEOs, currently falling in the range of 10–12 percent of total pay on average.

Bonuses provide a supplement to salaries and come in diverse forms with different time horizons. Bonuses can either be fixed dollar amounts or they can vary based on performance measures. The bonus can be paid in cash or in the common stock of the firm, and if paid in stock, the shares can be *unrestricted* or *restricted*. (Restricted common stock is discussed later. An unrestricted share can be sold immediately if the recipient desires. The recipient of restricted shares must hold the stock for a certain amount time or until the fulfillment of some condition.) Further, bonus plans can be either *qualified* or *nonqualified*. A qualified plan is set up so that it meets the strictures of section 162(m), in that it is sufficiently performance based so that payments under the plan qualify for tax deductibility. If the plan is nonqualified, then payments under the plan must be paid out of the firm's after-tax income.

A common type of bonus is an annual bonus paid in cash. Sometimes the bonus plan is subject to a minimum amount, with an additional range of performance-based bonuses as a further possibility. For example, Citigroup hired Robert E. Rubin, who had just resigned as secretary of the treasury, to start work in 2000. In addition to his salary, he was guaranteed a minimum bonus of $14 million for each year, 2000–2001.[10] Because that bonus clearly did not depend on performance, it did not qualify for tax deductibility.

Qualifying for tax deductibility under section 162(m) also requires that the bonus cannot be discretionary. For example, the board of directors cannot merely meet and discuss the CEO's performance, and then set a bonus based on the board's appraisal of overall performance. Instead, there must be a linkage between objective performance measures and the bonus payout. Designing a qualified bonus plan means that the board loses discretion over the bonus awarded to the CEO once it devises the plan. Many firms decide that the loss of discretion is too severe to justify qualifying a plan merely to capture the tax savings of making the bonus deductible.

Soon after OBRA came into effect, Gillette's board explicitly decided to forgo qualifying its bonus plan, saying in its 1995 proxy statement:

> The [Compensation] Committee has determined that to attempt to amend the Incentive Bonus Plan so that bonuses meet the definition of tax deductible compensation would require changes which would be contrary to the compensation philosophy underlying that plan and which would seriously impede the Committee's ability to administer the plan as designed in accordance with the judgment of the Committee. The Incentive Bonus Plan was deliberately designed so that individual bonuses were not

to be dependent solely on objective or numerical criteria, thus allowing the Committee the flexibility to apply its independent judgment to reflect performance against qualitative strategic objectives.[11]

When the annual bonus is designed to be performance related and thus qualify for tax deductibility, it is typically based on overcoming some hurdle defined in accounting terms; for example, net income rising by 6 percent over last year's figure, total revenues increasing by a predetermined percent, sales growth of a certain percent or dollar amount, and so on. Constructing a bonus with such performance-related contingencies helps ensure the bonus plan is a qualified plan. Almost every firm offers an annual bonus plan, and by 1997, about 40 percent of firms had qualified short-term bonus plans.[12]

Figure 1.10 shows the historical relationship between bonuses and salaries from 1992–2010. The figure portrays a steady increase in salaries, but the evolution of bonuses varies quite dramatically in comparison. Initially lower than the salary level, bonuses escalated rapidly to exceed salaries by 1995. The average bonus reached a peak in 2005, when it was twice the average salary. In recent years, bonuses *as reported*, have fallen, but this may be more appearance than reality. Starting in 2006, the SEC changed the reporting requirements for executive compensation, so some monies that previously would have fallen under bonuses are now counted in a different category.

Many firms also have long-term incentive plans. In most respects, these plans are similar in structure to annual bonus plans. However, instead of being based on the performance for a single year, long-term plans are based on a rolling multiyear or cumulative performance, generally over three- or

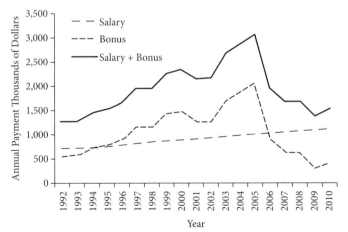

FIGURE 1.10 *Mean Salaries and Bonuses for S&P 500 CEOs, 1992–2010.*

Source: Graph by author, based on ExecuComp data.

five-year periods. Payoffs from these long-term plans can be in cash or stock grants. Grants of stock are usually restricted in some way, as the next section discusses.

RESTRICTED STOCK AWARDS

Firms frequently award restricted stock to their top managers, including the CEO. A restricted stock grant is a commitment of shares to an executive that depends on the executive fulfilling a particular condition. Usually the executive receives full title to the shares if she stays with the firm for a specified period after the date the shares are granted. At that point, the shares are said to be *vested*. If the executive leaves before the shares are vested, then they are usually forfeited and the executive receives nothing.

The grant of restricted stock is subject to section 162(m); that is, the cost of the grant can count as a business expense only if it is tied to the meeting of preestablished performance targets or if vesting occurs when the executive retires.[13] If vesting depends only on the executive's longevity with the firm, it does not qualify as tax-deductible under section 162(m). About 40 percent of restricted stock plans are qualified.[14]

Determining exactly when to count a restricted stock grant as having been made and to evaluate how much it is worth is not as simple as one might expect. For example, assume that the shares of a given stock sell for $100 today, and the firm grants a restricted share to an executive. However, assume the restriction is one of time vesting and that the executive vests only if she stays with the firm for three years. What is the value of the granted share as of the date of the grant? It does not seem quite right to count it as $100, because it certainly cannot be converted into $100 today. Given that the executive does not really receive title to the shares for three years, perhaps one should discount the $100 for three years by some rate of interest? But this cannot be right either, because the shares should be appreciating in value over that time. Similarly, assume that the share vests only if a certain performance target is met by a future date. In this second case, the value of the restricted share depends on the probability that the performance target will be met and that the executive remains with the firm for the requisite period.

In earlier years, 1992–2005, the measure was "the value of restricted stock granted during the year (determined as of the date of the grant)." Based on new SEC-mandated reporting requirements both the frequency and the size of awards are measured as being larger than they were under the old rules. Under the new rules, the focus is on the value of shares that vest in a given year as detailed under the new accounting standard by the Financial Accounting Standards Board *FAS 123R* (which chapter 3 discusses in greater detail). Figure 1.11 reflects these differences by showing the average value of restricted stock grant received by S&P 500 CEOs from 1992 to 2010. This is

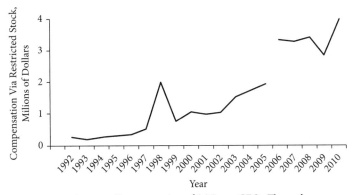

FIGURE 1.11 *Average Compensation of S&P 500 CEOs Through Restricted Stock, 1992–2010.*

Source: Graph by author, based on ExecuComp data.

the average grant across all CEOs, whether they received a grant or not. For all CEOs during 1992–2005, the chance that a CEO received a grant in a given year was 32 percent; with the new reporting requirements, this figure jumped to almost 75 percent for the 2006–2010 period. In sum, restricted stock grants constitute an important element of compensation for the typical CEO, in recent years falling to the $3 to $4 million range.

EXECUTIVE STOCK OPTION (ESO) AWARDS

For many years, executive stock options have been an extremely large and controversial portion of the typical CEO's compensation package. An executive stock option (ESO) is a call option on the shares of the firm that employs the executive—a *call option* is an option that grants its owner the right to buy a share at a certain price during a specified period of time. Thus, an ESO gives the executive the right to purchase a share of the firm at a stated price (the strike price or exercise price of the option), with that right lasting until a particular date (the expiration or termination date of the option).

As an example, assume that the shares of XYZ Corporation trade at $50 today. A firm might award an ESO with a strike price of $50 and an expiration date 10 years from today. If the shares of XYZ Corporation rise to $125, the executive might wish to exercise the option. To exercise the option and convert it to cash, the executive would pay the $50 exercise price, receive the share, and could then sell it in the open market for $125, netting a profit of $75. (If she chooses, she could also keep the share rather than sell it.) Alternatively, if the shares of XYZ stay at $50 or less, the executive can never exercise the option for a profit, because exercise would require paying $50 to receive a share worth less than that exercise price. Thus, the ultimate payoff from an

ESO is a risky proposition, but it is also quite certain that the typical ESO has significant value at the time it is granted, and that ESOs have been a substantial portion of CEO compensation.

They typical ESO has a number of features that contrast with more familiar options, such as stock options that trade on organized exchanges like the Chicago Board Options Exchange. First, exchange-traded call options give the owner the right to purchase an already existing share of a firm. By contrast, when an executive exercises the typical ESO, the firm creates a new share and awards it to the executive. This kind of contract has almost all of the same features as an exchange-traded option, except for the creation of a new share, and the technical term for such an instrument is a *warrant*. However, it has become almost universally customary to refer to ESOs as "options" and to treat them as such, rather than the more technically correct treatment that regards them as warrants.[15]

A second feature of ESOs that makes them different from exchange-traded options is that ESOs are not transferable. The executive cannot sell the option; she can receive value from the option only by exercising it. A critical special consideration about ESOs is a difference between the cost to the firm of granting the option and the value of the ESO to the executive who receives it, and this stems largely from the nontransferability of the option. Like almost all employees, the typical firm executive has her human capital tied to the fortunes of her firm. Ideally, she would like to hold a well-diversified portfolio, but the fact that her income derives from a single source implies a portfolio commitment to her employer that is already too large compared to what she likely desires. Therefore, granting her an ESO that cannot be transferred ties a still higher percentage of her personal portfolio to her employing firm, thus an ever-greater commitment of her portfolio to a single firm has a diminishing personal value to her, just as would be the situation for a person of any rank in the firm. (To understand this intuitively, consider the unfortunate employees of a firm like Enron who held a high proportion of their retirement accounts in the form of Enron stock. When Enron collapsed, these employees not only lost their future employment income stream, but Enron's bankruptcy also eviscerated their retirement savings. Clearly these Enron employees would have been much better off had they held a well-diversified stock portfolio. Having too much of her portfolio wealth tied to her own firm puts a CEO in an analogous situation.)

A third typical and important feature of ESOs is that they generally involve a vesting requirement, such that the executive who receives the ESO does not obtain full ownership of the option until a future date when the ESO vests. A representative ESO might be granted with 10 years to expiration, subject to a four-year vesting requirement. This would mean that the executive could not exercise the option until the vesting date. In this example, the option's life would still extend for six years beyond the vesting date, and the executive could exercise the ESO at any time during those remaining six years. In the typical vesting situation, if the executive departs the firm before the vesting date, the executive forfeits the ESO and receives nothing. Thus, with a four-year horizon to the vesting date, the typical executive has a significant probability of exiting the firm before the vesting date. For example, the executive might receive a better offer at another firm or be dismissed from the firm that granted the ESO. This vesting requirement diminishes the value of the ESO significantly, but an ESO is still undeniably very valuable in the typical situation.[16] If the ESO vests the owner can sell the option or retain it. However, if the option owner departs the firm after the vesting date, she is usually required to exercise the ESO upon departure.

Figure 1.12 shows the average value of executive stock options received by S&P 500 CEOs from 1992 to 2010. This average value ranged from a low of about $250,000 in the early years to a peak above $10 million in 2000, before falling in more recent years. The peak in the graph corresponds to the height of the dotcom bubble. Figure 1.13 shows the large importance of ESOs in the total paycheck of S&P 500 CEOs. In 2000, ESOs constituted almost 70 percent of total CEO pay, but this proportion has fallen quite steadily since then. In 2010, the percentage of pay conveyed through stock options dropped below 20 percent for the only time in the entire period. As we will see in chapter 3, determining the value of ESOs is difficult and subject to considerable debate.

OTHER FORMS OF COMPENSATION

In addition to salaries, annual bonuses, restricted stock, and ESOs, corporations provide their executives with a variety of other forms of compensation. These include long-term incentive payments and multiyear bonus plans,

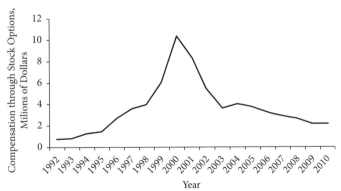

FIGURE 1.12 *Average Annual Compensation through Stock Options for S&P 500 CEOs, 1992–2010.*

Source: Graph by author, based on ExecuComp data.

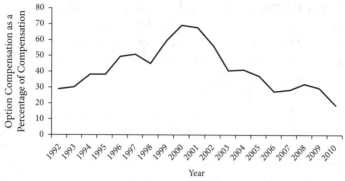

FIGURE 1.13 *Percentage of S&P 500 CEO Compensation Paid through Stock Options, 1992–2010.*

Source: Graph by author, based on ExecuComp data.

which were mentioned earlier. Additional significant payment methods include (or previously included) pension plans, retirement accounts, departure payments, change-of-control payments, alteration of stock and option grants to make the terms more favorable, perquisites while the executives are in office, postretirement perquisites, postretirement consulting contracts, executive loans made on better-than-market terms, and forgiveness of loans once they have been issued. (Loans from firms to executives are now illegal.)

In short, the methods of payment are limited solely by human imagination. Taken together these other payments—beyond salary, bonus, restricted stock, or stock options—constitute a large portion of total executive compensation. Also, the exact magnitude of many of these components can be difficult to measure. Figure 1.14 shows how ExecuComp has measured the various

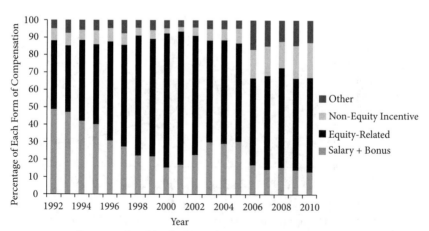

FIGURE 1.14 *Compensation Mix for S&P 500 CEOs, 1992–2010.*

Source: Graph by author, based on ExecuComp data.

TABLE 1.3 Elements of Executive Compensation

Salary + annual bonus:	cash compensation paid in a given year
Equity-related compensation:	value of restricted stock plus ESOs
Non-equity incentive compensation:	long-term bonus plan
Other:	pensions, perquisites, retirement plans, executive loans, etc.

forms of compensation over time as a percentage of total payments.[17] For ease of analysis, table 1.3 divides compensation into four categories.

For all S&P 500 CEOs taken together, these other forms of payment have exceeded $700 million in recent years, with total compensation to these 500 individuals equaling about $5 billion per year. Today, these other forms of compensation comprise about 15 percent of pay for these top executives.

A notable category among these "other" forms of pay is payments associated with retirement, pensions, and assorted retirement accounts. Analyzing current SEC reporting requirements, it appears that about 10 percent of total CEO pay derives from changes in the value of pension plans. With CEO pay averaging more than $11 million for S&P 500 companies, the average compensation deriving from pensions ranges from about $700,000 to $1 million per year.

These pension payments can be even more valuable than these figures suggest. Lucian Bebchuk and Robert Jackson studied a sample of pension arrangements for CEOs who had recently retired or were approaching retirement. Table 1.4 summarizes some key results from the Bebchuk-Jackson study. In their sample, annual pensions averaged about $1.3 million and were to be paid over the life of the CEO (and in some cases over the life of the CEO's spouse as well). This stream of payments can be valued using actuarial techniques to answer the question: "What is the value today of the stream of pension payments extending into the indefinite future?" As table 1.4 shows, Bebchuk and Jackson estimate the average dollar value today of that stream of future payments as $17 million per CEO.

TABLE 1.4 Summary Statistics for the Value of Pension Values (51 CEOs: retired or approaching retirement)

	Annual Pension Amount ($)	Actuarial Value of Pension Commitment ($)
Median	1,132,488	15,002,428
Mean	1,320,938	17,145,984
Standard Deviation	909,569	12,282,278
Minimum	360,000	3,302,733
Maximum	5,760,000	73,377,666

Source: Adapted from Lucian A. Bebchuk and Robert J. Jackson, Jr., "Executive Pensions," *Journal of Corporation Law*, 2005, 30, 823–855, table 5, p. 843.

Particular examples are even more striking. As a case study, Bebchuk and Fried explored the retirement benefits of Franklin Raines, who left his position as CEO of Fannie Mae under pressure in December 2004. (During his tenure, Fannie Mae not only helped to lay the foundations of the housing crisis and Fannie Mae's ultimate bankruptcy, but the firm was also embroiled in accounting scandals from which Raines appears to have benefited personally. He received compensation that relied on reported earnings that proved to be based on misrepresentations. He was never charged with any crime.) At the time of his departure, Fannie Mae promised him a monthly retirement payment of $114,000 for as long as he or his wife lived. According to Bebchuk and Fried, Raines walked away with a retirement package worth $33 million, including retirement payments, medical coverage, life insurance, deferred compensation, and the benefits of immediate option vesting.[18]

TABLE 1.5 Top-Earning CEOs of the First Decade of the Twenty-First Century (millions of U.S. dollars)

Company and Executive	Total	Salary	Bonus	Restricted Stock	Gain on Options	Other Comp.
Oracle Lawrence J. Ellison	1,835.70	6.70	41.60	0.00	1,778.30	9.10
Interactive Corp/ Expedia.com Barry Diller	1,142.90	7.60	23.10	0.70	1,100.10	11.60
Occidental Petroleum Ray R. Irani	857.10	12.80	65.20	206.70	553.80	18.70
Apple Steve Jobs	748.80	0.00	45.80	646.60	14.60	41.80
Capital One Financial Richard D. Fairbank	568.50	0.00	0.00	18.30	549.30	1.00
Countrywide Financial Angelo R. Mozilo	528.60	17.30	93.40	6.70	406.50	4.70
Nabors Industries Eugene M. Isenberg	518.00	6.30	109.40	47.10	350.10	5.10
Yahoo Terry S. Semel	489.60	2.80	0.90	485.80	0.10	0.10
Cendant Henry R. Silverman	481.20	21.20	58.50	0.00	312.40	89.00
UnitedHealth Group William W. McGuire	469.30	13.90	29.10	0.00	420.10	6.20
Lehman Brothers Holdings Richard S. Fuld, Jr.	456.70	6.00	67.50	26.50	356.30	0.50
Dell Michael S. Dell	453.80	9.70	9.00	0.00	429.20	5.90
Percentage of pay from each source		1.22	6.36	16.82	73.34	2.27

Source: Adapted from the *Wall Street Journal*, "The Decade's 25 Top Earners," July 27, 2010.

Critics of current executive-compensation arrangements find these payments that fall in the "other" category to be particularly troubling. Some forms of payment are obvious, or "salient" as these critics often say. Others are less salient. For example, some escape the reporting of standard databases of executive compensation, such as ExecuComp, on which the vast majority of academic research relies. As Bebchuk and Jackson put the point: "Standard data sets of executive pay generally include only those components of compensation for which a precise monetary value has been disclosed in firms' public filings. Estimating pension values requires additional research and financial analysis, and standard databases therefore do not include compensation paid through pension plans."[19] As we will see, critics of executive compensation find the presence of these "non-salient" forms of compensation particularly galling. In some cases, they refer to these types of payments as "stealth compensation" and interpret the presence of such forms of pay as prime evidence of a failed system of executive compensation.[20]

This chapter concludes with a survey of the top-dozen CEO earners of the first decade of the twentieth century. Table 1.5 shows their total earnings and the distribution of reported earnings over the categories discussed in this chapter. Larry Ellison, founder and CEO of Oracle software, led the pack with total compensation of almost $2 billion over the decade. As the table illustrates, over 80 percent of the total compensation was equity related, with most of that derived from ESOs. Salary played a nearly trivial role. It is interesting to note the diversity of firms and CEOs who made the list. It includes entrepreneur CEOs who built firms and created great wealth for their investors. But it also includes the now-failed, and in some cases disgraced, former captains of financial firms.

Corporate Governance, Agency Problems, and Executive Compensation

Chapter 1 explored the magnitude and structure of executive compensation. It was noted that current CEO compensation for those at the helms of the largest firms, the S&P 500, is approximately $11 million per year, typically composed of a variety of compensation forms: salary, annual bonus, multi-year bonus plans, restricted stock, executive stock options (ESOs), pension benefits, retirement plans, and various perquisites that pertain during and after the CEO's time with the firm.

Corporate Governance

In the United States, and in most corporations around the world, corporate charters and the laws of the jurisdictions that allow firms to incorporate assign broad responsibilities of corporate governance to boards of directors. Almost universally, corporate boards have the responsibility to hire, compensate, manage, and dismiss the executives of the firm, including the CEO.

In the dominant understanding of the nature of the corporation, the shareholders own the firm, and the corporation's board has the task of managing the firm for the benefit of those owners. However, the very idea of shareholder ownership is stoutly denied by many specialists in corporate governance, while vigorously defended by others.[1] Nonetheless, the literature on corporate governance and executive compensation has developed over the last 20 years predominately within a framework that views shareholders as owning the firm and acting as principals who retain boards of directors and senior executives as their agents. This, in crudest summary, is the *agency theory* of the firm, and it is particularly dominant in the finance literature: Shareholders own the firm and act as principals to retain managers to act as their agents and operate the firm on the behalf of the owners. Under this model, shareholders charge corporate boards with the general oversight of the firm. One of the board's key duties is to constitute and regulate the top management team. Like corporate board members, the top managers are considered agents of the shareholders as well.

The agency theory of the firm analyzes firm management in those terms, proposing methods for mitigating problems that arise in principal-agent relationships and investigating how well firms perform when evaluated from within the perspective elaborated by agency theory. In their seminal statement of the agency theory of the firm, Jensen and Meckling succinctly describe the essential potential conflict between principals and their agents:

> We define an agency relationship as a contract under which one or more persons (the principal(s)) engage another person (the agent) to perform some service on their behalf which involves delegating some decision making authority to the agent. If both parties to the relationship are utility maximizers, there is good reason to believe that the agent will not always act in the best interests of the principal.[2]

Almost explicit in this quotation is the view that humans are utility maximizers. To conceptualize humans as maximizing their personal utility is already to adopt a theory of human nature, or it at least amounts to adopting a certain view of human nature as a methodological stance. Conceiving humans as maximizing their personal utility or self-interest has been a methodological tool that has dominated the fields of economics and finance for several decades, and it plays a central role in agency theory. Reduced to its essence, this particular methodological assumption is that individuals, in particular the managers of the firm, seek to maximize their personal utility.[3] Traditionally, economists making this assumption about how humans behave have not maintained that it accurately depicts the way people actually think and behave. Instead, they have justified this conceptual framework as providing a parsimonious psychological model of human behavior that yields good predictions about how managers actually do behave. Formally, it is not supposed to provide a normative prescription about how managers *ought* to behave, but it is supposed to be useful in understanding how they behave now and will in the future. As we shall see, conceptualizing human behavior in these terms has strong implications about how a principal should approach agency problems.

The central tension within agency theory is the realization that owners and managers of the firm are persons with their own desires, goals, and ends for which they strive. The perfect agent is one who operates the firm exactly as shareholders would if they were in managerial authority and had the full suite of skills that a professional manager is supposed to bring to bear on the administrative problems that the firm confronts. Particularly, the perfect agent would be just as diligent as the owner-shareholder would be and would strive just as hard to make decisions that would increase the value of the firm. If the firm's owner manages the firm, there is no agency problem at that level. Of course, if the firm hires employees, they will have their own interests and may pursue their own goals instead of being fully faithful servants of the firm. If so, that creates an agency problem at the employee level.

Contrary to following the owners' desires, managers may operate the firm in a way designed to advance their personal agendas and life plans, rather than serving the interests of the firm and its suppliers of capital. This divergence of interests between the owners of the firm and the managers of the firm creates an agency problem or agency conflict—the divergence of interests that arises between the principals (shareholders) and their agents (managers).

As the ultimate principal in a corporation, the shareholder must deal with inescapable agency problems. There are two ways to confront the problem of agency: the principal can monitor the agent and correct the agent's behavior as necessary, or the principal can establish incentives designed to induce the agent to behave in a manner more to the principal's liking. In the typical corporation, the shareholder has little prospect of monitoring and successfully controlling the behavior of board members or top managers. First, the shareholder may have only a small portion of his wealth committed to a particular firm, making it financially unfeasible to devote the resources necessary to monitor effectively. Second, a shareholder owning a minuscule portion of the firm will have little sway over the firm's managers in any event.[4] Third, the laws of corporate governance that prevail in most states in the United States give the board of directors considerable discretion in managing the firm, a situation that essentially impedes direct management by shareholders in an effective way.

Beyond agency conflicts between owners and managers, the key role that the board of directors plays in corporate governance gives rise to further agency conflicts because members of the board of directors are also agents of the shareholders. Just as shareholders and the managers of the firm are persons in their own right, board members have their own interests and life plans that they are almost certain to pursue instead of acting as perfect agents. Just as with owners and managers, agency conflicts are likely to arise between shareholders and the board of directors of the firm that they govern on behalf of shareholders. This potential conflict has been recognized for almost 250 years, going back at least to Adam Smith and his *Wealth of Nations* in 1776:

> The directors of such [joint-stock] companies, however, being the managers rather of other people's money than of their own, it cannot well be expected, that they should watch over it with the same anxious vigilance with which the partners in a private copartnery frequently watch over their own. Like the stewards of a rich man, they are apt to consider attention to small matters as not for their master's honour, and very easily give themselves a dispensation from having it. Negligence and profusion, therefore, must always prevail, more or less, in the management of the affairs of such a company.[5]

Thus, with three parties—shareholders, board members, and managers—the key agency problem in the firm is really triangular in nature. Rather than serving as monitoring bulldogs, many observers allege that boards accommodate the interests of top management to a degree that seriously sacrifices the interests of the shareholders and other stakeholders in the firm.

One key duty of the board of directors is to set executive compensation. If the board functions as the perfect agent of shareholders, then it will set the compensation plan in a manner designed to elicit the optimal managerial performance, such that the management team will act to maximize the value of the firm, net of managerial compensation costs. However, it may well develop that the interests of the board members are served by reaching an accommodation with managers to pay them more than is optimal for the firm and to maintain a good relationship with the top management team, particularly with the chief executive officer. After all, the CEO interacts both professionally and socially with board members, and the CEO often plays a critical role in recruiting and retaining board members. Further, the CEO and the board members may well regard themselves as belonging to a common club, professional league, and social stratum, such that board members tend to be highly appreciative of the CEO's merits and tend to view the CEO's compensation in terms very much as the CEO might see them. For all these reasons, board members may find it congenial to sacrifice the interests of shareholders, who are, after all, remote from and unknown to the board's members, in favor of an enhanced relationship with the firm's top managers.

While the triangular relationship among shareholders, boards, and managers certainly presents a rich set of potential agency problems, the focus of this book is on executive compensation. Therefore, the book considers conflicts between shareholders and boards only through the lens of executive compensation. As we will see, some have argued that a key problem with executive compensation arises from boards acting as less-than-faithful agents, and we will consider those issues fully. Nonetheless, the prevailing structures of corporate governance establish the board of directors as the key operators of the corporation, including being the agent of the firm's owners and having the duty to monitor the managers that the board puts in place. This means that the focus of executive compensation should be on the relationship between the board of directors and the firm's top managers, particularly the CEO. Because the CEO plays such a dominant role in most firms, this book concentrates on the issue of CEO compensation and CEO performance.

Agency Theory and Incentive Alignment

From the standpoint that the board of directors acts as the agent of shareholders, the question that must be faced is, "How can the firm regulate managerial behavior so that managers act as truer and more faithful agents of the shareholders?" As we have seen, agency theory offers two main techniques for bringing the behavior of the manager into better alignment with the interests of the principal: monitoring the agent's behavior and aligning incentives between the shareholders and the manager.

Consistent with the monitoring approach, the firm's board may expend resources to monitor the manager's performance. The effectiveness of this approach differs widely depending on the context. If an employer hires a worker to stack bricks, for example, monitoring is fairly easy: Count the number of stacked bricks and inspect the bricks to ensure that the brick-stacker has kept the rate of damage to an acceptable level. In other contexts, monitoring is much more difficult, as is the case of monitoring a CEO's performance. Corporate boards are remote from the daily operations of the firm, typically meeting for part of one day each quarter. By contrast, the CEO has day-to-day control of the firm, creates and manages the firm's financial records, and supervises the firm's employees. As a result, the CEO almost certainly will possess much more information than the board and would find it fairly easy to deceive the board if she or he so desires.

Beyond monitoring, the second main method of influencing the behavior of an agent turns on the establishment of incentives. Setting proper incentives for an agent should bring the agent's behavior more into line with the principal's desires. If incentives could be set perfectly, they would establish *incentive alignment* between principal and agent. However, it is generally recognized that no incentive scheme is likely to achieve perfect incentive alignment, thus agents will likely behave in some ways that sacrifice the interests of their principals. Accordingly, it will be impossible to escape agency problems altogether, and no matter how carefully principals craft the incentives they put before their agents, there will always be some residual agency cost—the loss of value to the principals that results from the manager pursuing personal interests instead of acting as a perfect agent for the principals.

In the corporation, the board of directors has the primary responsibility for setting the compensation terms for managers, so they have the main role in attempting to align incentives. The ideal executive compensation contract induces the entirely self-interested, utility-maximizing manager to operate the firm exactly as the shareholders desire. Of course, as with all principal-agent relationships, the incentive alignment between managers and shareholders can never be perfect. Even the staunchest advocates of the agency-theoretic approach to executive compensation are well aware of this problem and acknowledge it explicitly. For instance, in their survey of issues of executive compensation, Jensen, Murphy, and Wruck state:

> While remuneration can be a solution to agency problems, it can also be a source of agency problems. However well intentioned, boards and remuneration committees are not spending their own money, so there is an agency problem between boards and the company that they are there

to represent. In addition, even the best-designed plans contain exploitable flaws, and because they have a huge information advantage clever executives can inevitably manipulate the remuneration process to benefit themselves at the expense of the company if they choose to do so.[6]

From this perspective, the ideal (or, as economists like to say, "first-best") contract can never be achieved. There will always be some degree of imperfection in incentive alignment between the principals and agents.[7] Faced with this reality, the optimal contract available is one that is "second-best"—the best that can be achieved given the prevailing realities, but one that inescapably admits of some degree of inefficiency.

In contrast to a straightforward, or even naïve, approach to executive compensation that expects to set a wage and get an executive's best effort, agency theorists ask: "Can the compensation package be set to align the incentives of the utility-maximizing CEO with the interests of the shareholders to create as much shareholder value as possible?" Incentive alignment will never be perfect, so there will always be a gap between the ideal and actual CEO performance. However, the goal is not to extract every increment of service from the CEO for every incremental penny of compensation. The agency theorist knows that there will be some waste in compensation—or residual agency cost—because it is impossible to achieve perfect incentive alignment. The agency theorist quite willingly accepts this inefficiency in compensation if it creates more net shareholder value than other possible pay structures would provide.

For example, assume the board of directors hires a CEO for a straightforward annual salary of $1 million. A responsible professional that is so handsomely rewarded would strive to do a good job because she takes professional pride in her work and wants to earn her compensation, as would any ethical person. Being well-paid, she would also like to keep her present lucrative position and expand future job opportunities by performing well in her current role. So described, the CEO with an attractive salary resembles most professionals.

Consider now the same hypothetical person that the board of directors compensates with an enhanced pay package—the same $1 million annual salary, plus stock options that cost the firm a second $1 million. The stock options are structured so that they become extremely valuable if the firm's share prices move up appreciably, but the options become worthless if the firm's share price fails to rise.[8] In setting this richer compensation package, the board bets that the incentive structure of the new pay package will encourage the CEO to greater effort and diligence that will pay off for the firm. For that to happen, the CEO must manage the firm to produce results under the second pay package that more than offset the extra cost to the firm of the stock options. This is not to say that the CEO would do a poor job with the straight

$1 million salary. However, almost all of us in any job *could* produce a little more or perform our jobs a little better if we tried a little harder, even if we are presently doing a fine job and fully earning the compensation we receive.

Of course, there is a limit to how much one can produce. Also, the ordinary worker is not in a position to change her behavior to create a great deal of additional value—the scope of the typical job is too limited to allow a radically different economic impact for the firm as a whole. For a CEO in command of billions of dollars of corporate resources, by contrast, a little more effort or a little better management can make a huge economic difference. Realistically, a CEO who gets an extra tenth of 1 percent of corporate performance generates an economic benefit that completely dwarfs her salary. As an example, consider Hewlett-Packard Company. In mid-2011, its earnings-per-share (EPS) stood at $4.07 per year and the firm's price-earnings (P-E) ratio was 8.82, consistent with the firm's share price of $35.89. The company had 2.15 billion shares outstanding. Assume the CEO made an extra effort and increased the firm's earnings by just one-tenth of 1 percent to $4.07407 per share. This extra $.00407 per share translates into an increased total share value of more than $77 million, given the P-E ratio of 8.82 and the 2.15 billion shares outstanding. As this example shows, because the CEO of Hewlett-Packard commands about $120 billion of total assets, the slightest increase in percentage performance translates into many millions of dollars of extra shareholder wealth. Thus, any responsible board should try to set the CEO's compensation to encourage that enhanced marginal performance. As economics teaches, to maximize the value of the firm, the board should increase the CEO's incentives ever higher, so long as an additional dollar of compensation generates an increase in firm value, net of the additional payment to the CEO.

This kind of reflection highlights an essential conflict in the points of view between an economist and a representative member of the public. While this discussion of CEO incentives is quite simple, it is still at variance with the popular conception of CEO compensation. In the popular press and in the public imagination, the question is not how to incentivize executives to achieve better performance. Rather, among the public at large, the great question about executive compensation is, "Why are executives paid so much, and how can we stop it?" It may well be that executive compensation is wildly excessive. Compared with ordinary workers, the pay levels of CEOs and other top corporate managers are extremely high, as almost everyone seems to agree and as chapter 1 documents.

It was hinted that for economists in general, and for agency theorists in particular, one cannot merely look at the huge salaries and conclude that executive compensation is immoral, out of control, or even problematic. Instead, logically prior questions must be addressed before concluding that rapacious CEOs are looting firms for personal gain. First, economists, in general, approach the issue of compensation by thinking in terms of a market for labor services. There is a supply of and demand for CEO talent, and it might be costly to secure the services of a good one. The example of Hewlett-Packard reinforces a second consideration. Assume that a corporate board wants to maximize the value of the firm by hiring and incentivizing a good CEO, and they do this acting fully in good faith as agents of the shareholders. Their problem is to maximize the value of the firm. If the CEO happens to become rich in the process, that is immaterial. It would be easy for the board to hire a bureaucratically oriented CEO at a salary that would raise no political problems inside or outside the firm. But, the board's task is to hire and incentivize a CEO who can maximize firm value, not to hire a time-serving bureaucratic manager.

Having the talent to be an excellent CEO is extremely valuable and quite rare, judging from general corporate-performance results. A truly gifted CEO at the helm of an S&P 500 firm, for instance, commands billions of dollars of corporate resources, which can be deployed well or poorly. An excellent CEO will be able to create many millions or even billions of dollars of shareholder value, over and above that which could be achieved by a merely adequate manager. Therefore, the difference in value to the firm of the best CEO versus a merely mediocre CEO is huge, and that difference in corporate performance would render the CEO's compensation trivial by comparison. From this perspective, it is at least possible that the market for executive talent performs well, and that it really is costly to acquire the services of executives with the talent to run a large firm in a highly successful manner, and it is additionally costly to incentivize the manager to strive harder to create a better result for the firm. If that is the case, and if corporate boards can successfully distinguish talented from mediocre managers, we might expect to find a strong correlation between executive pay and shareholder returns. (We examine this pay-performance relationship in chapter 4. To foreshadow, we will see that study results of the pay-performance relationship are not reassuring.) From this perspective—which goes beyond a visceral response to admittedly huge executive paydays—the truly infuriating aspect of executive compensation erupts when paychecks are enormous and performance is miserable.

In summary, from this general agency-theoretic perspective the main issue concerns whether the job market for executive talent is efficient in the sense of achieving additional shareholder value for each incremental dollar of pay, given that there will always be some divergence of interests between the executive and the firm. This leads to the critical question of executive compensation from the perspective of agency theory: "How well do executive compensation packages perform in aligning principal-agent incentives and, thereby, increasing shareholder wealth net of executive compensation?" This book is devoted to answering that question by assessing an overwhelming mass of evidence pertaining to the performance of firms in setting incentives for executives and how executives respond to those incentives. Incentives are powerful factors in stimulating human behavior, and, as we will survey, they have become a tool more and more self-consciously deployed in many aspects of contemporary life. Problems develop, however, when the incentives are too powerful, as well as misdirected, leading to a variety of perverse results. As we will examine in detail, incentives have worked powerfully in executive compensation, but the ultimate effect of those incentives often led to bad behavior and unfortunate results.

Corporate Governance, Incentive Alignment, and the Managerial Power Hypothesis

While the agency theory offers an elegant and a convincing depiction of how corporate governance might work, other corporate-governance scholars have mounted a powerful attack on the actual practice of corporate governance. Some of these scholars have designated their view as the "managerial power hypothesis."

Managerial power theorists do not criticize the conceptual framework of setting incentives to induce managers to perform in an optimal manner. Instead, the managerial power hypothesis maintains that the actual practice of corporate governance does not resemble the ideal world portrayed by agency theorists, where corporate boards act as the generally faithful agents of shareholders in setting executive compensation. Instead, these critics of contemporary corporate governance argue that top managers, and CEOs in particular, gain undue influence over the pay-setting process. In bluntest terms, according to the managerial power view, powerful CEOs effectively set their own pay, and they devise pay packages for themselves that ensure large rewards no matter how well they perform as managers and without regard to the financial results of the firm. In the view of managerial power theorists, the corporate executives have turned the tables on the board, by controlling the board instead of being controlled by the board. Further, these powerful executives camouflage the magnitude of their pay by conveying compensation to themselves through obscure channels that are reported to the public in a less salient manner. For example, instead of having the board pay them a higher salary, CEOs receive valuable postretirement benefits that appear only in the footnotes of the firm's public disclosures.

The most outspoken critic of executive compensation and the chief protagonist of the managerial power hypothesis is Lucian Bebchuk, who has written extensively on the topic, most notably in his book (with Jesse Fried) *Pay Without Performance: The Unfulfilled Promise of Executive Compensation.*[9] Bebchuk and Fried state their position as follows:

> Financial economists studying executive compensation have typically assumed that pay arrangements are produced by arm's-length contracting, contracting between executives attempting to get the best possible deal for

themselves, and boards trying to get the best possible deal for shareholders. This assumption has also been the basis for the corporate law rules governing the subject. We aim to show, however, that the pay-setting process in U.S. public companies has strayed far from the arm's-length model.

Our analysis indicates that managerial power has played a key role in shaping executive pay. The pervasive role of managerial power can explain much of the contemporary landscape of executive compensation, including practices and patterns that have long puzzled financial economists. We also show that managerial influence over the design of pay arrangements has produced considerable distortions in these arrangements, resulting in costs to investors and the economy. This influence has led to compensation schemes that weaken managers' incentives to increase firm value and even create incentives to take actions that reduce long-term firm value.[10]

THE LEVERS OF MANAGERIAL POWER

How do CEOs obtain such power over the very boards that are supposed to be *their* supervisors? Bebchuk and Fried adduce a variety of techniques through which CEOs can influence and even control their boards.[11]

Being a director is a good deal. A seat on the board brings with it considerable prestige and generous compensation, so board members may be reluctant to alienate a CEO by constraining her pay. Generally, management puts forward a slate of directors and shareholders approve that slate. Therefore, placement on the slate for election is the key to acquiring or retaining a seat on the board. The CEO has considerable influence on the construction of the slate presented to shareholders; thus, the CEO has considerable influence on whether the "bosses" on the board actually get the job to begin with and whether they get to keep it.

The CEO can act to benefit directors in a variety of ways, and this ability to help a board member gives the CEO influence. First, the CEO has a substantial say regarding pay increases for directors. If the board is generous with the CEO, then the board might reasonably expect the CEO to reciprocate. Bebchuk and Fried make the point: "At a minimum, generous treatment of the CEO contributes to an atmosphere that is conducive to generous treatment of directors."[12] In addition, the CEO has the ability in many instances to direct her firm's business to firms she favors. If the CEO has good relations with a director who manages another firm, the CEO might direct business to the director's firm.

Frequently, a variety of personal relationships connect CEOs with their board members. First, the CEO often plays an important personal role in recruiting a board member. Given that a director's relationship with a firm might begin with a personal relationship with the CEO, we might expect a director to enjoy a friendship with the CEO and also to feel a certain degree of loyalty. This may especially be the case when the director's worth has been validated by the very act of being recruited to the board by the CEO. Given the CEO's initial vote of confidence in a director, the CEO can probably expect the director to display an attitude of loyalty and appreciation toward the CEO.

In many respects, the CEO and the directors of the board are drawn from the same pool—one might say that they are members of the same club. Or to make the point even more invidiously—board members and CEOs are all drawn from the same tight class. In many cases, board members are themselves CEOs. Often directors and CEOs have an assortment of mutual professional acquaintances and may be connected through a nexus of interlocking boards. For example, the CEO of company A may serve on the board of company B, while a director of company A sits on the board of company C. There may well be individuals who sit on the boards of both companies B and C, providing the CEO and directors of company C with an indirect relationship connected by a single degree of separation. In essence, a CEO and board member may be drawn from the same small class of company executives and may see the world from a common perspective, with strong affinity to, and a high appreciation of, that particular view of the world. As Bebchuk and Fried argue:

> Because individuals have a tendency to develop views that are consistent with their self-interest, executives and former executives are likely to have formed beliefs that support the type of pay arrangements from which they themselves have benefited. An executive who has benefited from a conventional option plan, for example, is more likely to resist the view that such plans provide executives with excessive windfalls. Further reinforcing such cognitive dissonance, an executive who serves as a director in another firm might identify and feel some solidarity or sympathy with that firm's executives. She naturally would be inclined to treat these executives the same way she would like to be treated.[13]

As a final consideration, awarding generous pay to a CEO costs a board member very little. After all, it is the company's money that is spent—we have already noted that board members have their own agency problems.

While the CEO-board relationships just outlined may provide reasons that boards may be willing to grant large pay packages to CEOs, they are principally only suggestive. However, advocates of the managerial power hypothesis make a positive argument for the claim that CEOs gain influence over the pay-setting process. According to the managerial power point of view, there is considerable evidence that CEO pay is higher when CEOs are stronger relative to their boards. Bebchuk and Fried note the following relationships based on a variety of research findings.[14] CEO pay tends to be higher: if the CEO is also chairman of the board; if members of the board's compensation committee own less stock (i.e., less of the board member's own funds are paid to the CEO); if boards are large (making coordination among board members more difficult); if the CEO has appointed many of the board members (strengthening bonds of loyalty and affection); if board members serve on several boards (diffusing their attention); and if the firm has antitakeover provisions in place (thereby making the CEO's position more secure). CEO pay is lower: if there is a large outside shareholder (who has a financial stake sufficient to motivate monitoring); and if a significant portion of the firm is owned by institutional investors (such that their larger stakes provide motivation to monitor the firm's performance and the CEO's compensation). In summary, the managerial power view asserts that CEOs have considerable power over their own pay, and the greater the power, the greater the pay.

LIMITS TO PAY IN THE MANAGERIAL POWER HYPOTHESIS

Why is CEO pay what it is? After all, if the managerial power hypothesis is correct, why isn't CEO pay even higher? A successful theory of CEO compensation has to explain not only why it is as high as it is, but also why it is subject to any limits at all. The optimal contracting, agency-theoretic approach explains CEO pay by depicting a board that, on the whole, acts in good faith to secure managerial services for the firm and structures managerial pay to provide incentives for managers to increase shareholder wealth. As such, the agency-theoretic approach sees pay as determined principally in a market for executive talent in which market forces of supply and demand predominate in the determination of the CEO's pay level.

By contrast, the managerial power approach emphasizes the power that CEOs have over their own pay. In such a setting, what could limit pay? According to the managerial power approach, the main constraint on CEO pay is the presence of "outrage costs." These outrage costs include embarrassment and reputational harm to directors and managers, the chance of shareholder uprisings, and a greater shareholder willingness to see the firm taken over by an outside party. A textbook example of outrage occurred during the financial crisis of 2007–2009, when a loud public outcry erupted over high executive compensation at failing financial firms, many of which received government rescues. Consequently, at many of those firms, compensation levels fell, while at others the rate of increase slowed—at least temporarily.

According to the managerial power approach, another piece of evidence in favor of the hypothesis is the prevalence of so-called stealth compensation— compensation that takes a form less visible to public view and less related to CEO performance. Types of "stealthy" compensation include pension plans, deferred compensation, postretirement perks, and postretirement consulting contracts. Now illegal, previously firms would grant loans to executives at favorable below-market rates, another form of stealth compensation according to managerial power theorists. These kinds of compensation *are* reported, but they are usually disclosed in the notes to financial statements and in a manner that makes them less "salient" to the public and to investors.[15]

These forms of compensation can be substantial. As we saw in chapter 1, the erstwhile Franklin Raines of Fannie Mae received a generous post-departure compensation package worth $33 million. In the estimation of Bebchuk and Fried's case study of Raines, much of the $33 million consisted of "stealthy...camouflaged," and "non-salient" forms of compensation—retirement payments, medical coverage, life insurance, deferred compensation, and the benefits of immediate option vesting.[16]

The package Raines received was not an isolated instance, as Bebchuk and Jackson document in another study, a key finding of which was presented in table 1.4. Using a sample of 51 executives who had retired in 2005, or were approaching retirement, Bebchuk and Jackson found that the average annual pension receipt was $1.3 million, with the present value of the entire pension promise averaging more than $17 million, with one pension promise having a present value in excess of $73 million. Because these payments were outsized and obscure, especially considering the efforts required to document them, Bebchuk and Fried take their findings as additional evidence of the use of stealth compensation and camouflage to enlarge and disguise the real magnitude and nature of CEO pay.

Assessing the Conceptual Conflict Between the Agency-Theoretic and Managerial Power Views of Executive Compensation

While both the agency-theoretic and managerial approaches have additional nuances beyond those captured in this chapter's brief synopses, how can we assess the key differences between the two views? It is important to realize that, whatever their apparent disagreement, the agency-theoretic and managerial-power-hypothesis views share a fundamental, common outlook. In fact, even the most ardent adherents of the agency-theoretic approach consistently acknowledge that the incentive-alignment approach leads to only a second-best contract and that perfect efficiency is impossible. Thus, those economists who emphasize the agency-theoretic approach generally recognize that there is some inefficiency in the pay-setting process. For example, in the quotation from Jensen, Murphy, and Wruck previously mentioned, they explicitly acknowledge that "even the best-designed plans contain exploitable flaws," and that "clever executives can inevitably manipulate the remuneration process to benefit themselves at the expense of the company if they choose to do so."

Even Bebchuk and Fried, the two most prominent exponents of the managerial power approach to executive compensation, do not propose to discard the baby of optimal contracting and incentive alignment with the bathwater:

> Although the managerial power approach is conceptually quite different from the optimal contracting approach, we do not propose the former as a complete replacement for the later. Compensation arrangements are likely to be shaped both by market forces that push toward value-maximizing outcomes, and by managerial influence, which leads to departures from these outcomes in directions favorable to managers. The managerial power approach simply claims that these departures are substantial and that optimal contracting alone cannot adequately explain compensation practices.[17]

Part of the apparently radical difference between the agency-theoretic and managerial power views stems from different standards of excellence in contract results that the two approaches expect or require. The incentive-alignment approach acknowledges that real-world contracts will always be "second-best," thus agency costs will always remain. Beyond that, incentive-alignment theorists try to determine the extent to which contracts succeed in generally aligning the interests of principals and agents, and they stress the incentive alignment that their research reveals.

Those who emphasize managerial power stress the gap between perfect contracts and real-world executive compensation contracts. For example, Bebchuk and Fried construe the problem of excess pay and poor contracts in the following terms: "Let's start with the excess pay that managers receive as a result of their power—that is, the difference between what managers' influence enables them to obtain and what they would get under arm's-length contracting."[18]

But defenders of the incentive-alignment view do not maintain that executive compensation contracts are the result of arm's-length bargaining. In their review of Bebchuk and Fried's book, Core, Guay, and Thomas respond to this demand for an "arm's-length standard":

> Arm's-length contracting amounts to a standard of theoretical perfection, and such a contract would only exist in a perfect world without frictions such as contracting costs and transactions costs. As such, it is not a relevant benchmark. Saying that there is something wrong with a contract because it is not arm's length is akin to saying that there is something wrong with a tank that does not perform well on a racetrack (where there are small frictions) because it has been designed to operate in the desert (where there are large frictions).[19]

In essence, Core, Guay, and Thomas believe that the managerial power critique attacks a straw man:

> Bebchuk and Fried do not directly critique optimal contracting theory, but instead critique the lack of arm's-length contracts, which are a very

restrictive subset of optimal contracts. Because contracts will only be arm's length when *there are no contracting costs and no transactions costs,* the arm's-length standard is a questionable benchmark, and is not typically used by economists, who prefer to examine whether contracts are optimized to maximize share value net of contracting and transactions costs.[20]

In effect, elaborating this point, Core, Guay, and Thomas also state:

> When we argue below that many contracts with managers may in fact be optimal, we are not claiming that U.S. corporate governance is perfect, or as economists sometimes say, "first best efficient." Nor are we claiming that contracts meet Bebchuk and Fried's standard of arm's-length contracting. What we mean is that U.S. corporate governance may in fact be extremely good given the existence of information costs, transactions costs, and the existing U.S. legal and regulatory system. Conceivably, improved regulation or other changes to the contracting environment could lower contracting costs and improve overall governance by, for example, making boards more independent and effective monitors.[21]

But isn't this approach merely saying that the executive compensation system performs well, except for the factors that make it perform poorly—information costs, transaction costs, the legal system, and the regulatory structure? If the optimal-contracting defenders exclude the problems with executive-pay contracts, then of course they find that the contracts perform well in aligning incentives.

This leads to the crux of the managerial power critique. Those who emphasize the power that managers exert over their pay are criticizing the results of the overall system: asserting that the contracts are too far from optimal, claiming they are too distant from an arm's-length result, maintaining that the institutional arrangements that govern executive compensation allow too much excess pay, and thus demanding the system undergo extensive reform. Speaking to what they see as pervasive and systemic problems, Bebchuk and Fried assert:

> To begin with, flawed compensation arrangements have not been limited to a small number of "bad apples"; they have been widespread, persistent, and systemic. Furthermore, the problems have not resulted from temporary mistakes or lapses of judgment that boards can be expected to correct on their own. Rather they have stemmed from structural defects in the underlying governance structure that enable executives to exert considerable influence over their boards. The absence of effective arm's-length dealing under today's system of corporate governance has been the primary source of problematic compensation arrangements. Finally, while recent reforms that seek to increase board independence will likely improve matters, they will not be sufficient to make boards adequately accountable. Much more needs to be done.

Thus, the real difference between the incentive-alignment approach and the managerial-power critique concerns how well the overall system functions. However, the two analyses essentially agree on the importance of incentive alignment through compensation arrangements.

As the name suggests, the incentive-alignment approach sees setting compensation incentives as the key tool for resolving the problem of agency costs. Bebchuk and Fried agree on the centrality of equity compensation and the key role of incentive alignment as well. After all, they title their book *Pay Without Performance*, and the central link between pay and performance runs through equity compensation by linking the manager's pay to the stock price—the clearest measure of the firm's performance. Bebchuk and Fried assert: "We strongly support equity-based compensation, which in principle can provide managers with desirable incentives. In practice, however, the design of executives' stock options has enabled executives to reap substantial rewards even when their own performance was merely passable or even poor."[22] They also say: "We wish to emphasize our strong support for the concept of equity-based compensation which, if well designed, could provide managers with very desirable incentives. The devil, however, is in the details."[23]

At a conceptual level, then, there is really very little disagreement between the approaches of the optimal-contracting/incentive-alignment school of thought and the view expressed through the managerial power critique. Both accept a model in which the problem of executive compensation is to create a system in which managerial behavior is regulated and controlled by incentives. The optimal-contracting/incentive-alignment school of thought maintains that the system works pretty well, although with some problems. The managerial power analysis believes that the entire system is rife with agency problems that leave corporations subject to plunder by the executives and boards who are supposed to manage them.

What About Ethics, Duty, and Justice?

Of the two accounts of executive compensation—the optimal-contracting/incentive-alignment view and the managerial power perspective—the managerial power critique is more aligned with public perception. However, the public outcry over executive compensation has not been directed toward renewing the system of corporate governance as the managerial power view demands. Instead, the public outcry has been a normative argument against what is perceived as the injustice of huge pay differentials between CEOs and ordinary workers, against CEOs being rewarded even though their firms are faring poorly, against CEOs walking away from destroyed firms with their wealth intact or even enhanced, and against CEOs of floundering firms receiving readjusted pay packages to help them do well in the future even if their firms do not recover. Neither the optimal-contracting/incentive-alignment view nor the managerial power approach addresses the moral dimension of CEO compensation directly. (However, as discussed in subsequent chapters, both interpretations of executive compensation provide insights that are directly relevant to normative critiques of executive compensation.)

The lack of focus on the ethical dimension of human interaction is inherent in the moral psychology that dominates the economics profession, and the same perspective flows through the optimal-contracting/incentive-alignment literature and the managerial power critique of executive compensation. As noted earlier in this chapter, the methodology of economics largely views humans as maximizers of their personal utility. For many, such a view of human nature simply implies that humans are selfish and immoral actors. Thus, from that particular point of view, the economics profession assumes universal immorality—if selfishness is truly immoral—and therefore hae little or even nothing to say about the ethical dimension of human life.

The managerial power view focuses almost exclusively on institutional arrangements of corporate governance, and Bebchuk and Fried plainly state that their critique is not an ethical critique of individuals or their behavior:

> Before proceeding, we want to emphasize that our critique of existing pay arrangements and pay-setting processes does not imply that most directors and executives have acted less ethically than others would have in their place. Our problem is not with the moral caliber of directors and executives, but rather with *the system* of arrangements and incentives within which directors and executives operate. As currently structured, our corporate governance system unavoidably creates incentives and psychological and social forces that distort pay choices. Such incentives and forces can be expected to lead most people serving as directors to go along with arrangements that favor their firms' executives, as long as these arrangements are consistent with prevailing practices and conventions and thus not difficult to justify to themselves and to others... If we were to maintain the basic structure of the system and merely replace current directors and executives with a different set of individuals, the new directors and executives would be exposed to the very same incentives and forces as their predecessors and, by and large, we would not expect them to act any differently. To address the flaws in the pay-setting process, we need to change the governance arrangements that produce these distortions.[24]

Thus, we cannot expect either the optimal-contracting/incentive-alignment or the managerial power school of economic thought to address the moral dimension of executive compensation in a specific way. However, as we follow the economics of incentives, we will see that the economic analysis does provide an important and necessary background to understand the ethical issues involved in executive compensation. However, before pursuing the economic analysis, we can consider two main ethical critiques of executive compensation.

FIDUCIARY DUTY

In accepting their positions, members of the boards of directors and CEOs accept positions that carry with them fiduciary duties—they are accepting positions that involve promising to act on behalf of others. This is related to the idea of boards and managers acting as agents for their principals, and it is generally conceded that there are moral as well as legal fiduciary duties.[25]

If board members have fiduciary duties to act on behalf of shareholders, then why is incentive compensation necessary or even an issue? These corporate officers accept the positions and receive what most would reckon as very handsome compensation. Surely shareholders and society have a reasonable moral expectation that board members and top managers will fulfill the duties associated with their positions as do other members of society who have jobs and receive compensation. Instead, the economic mode of analyzing executive compensation appears to be quite different and seems to be addressed toward answering a question of the form: "Now that we have a director (or CEO), how are we going to structure his compensation so that it will be in his interest to fulfill the duties associated with his position?"

Given the clear power of incentives, it would be self-defeating to structure a job or its compensation in a way that presented a person with strong incentives to behave in the wrong way. Thoughtful employers try to ensure that the incentives of a position run with, instead of against, the employer's goals for the employee. However, to drop the idea of a position's duty from consideration altogether and to focus only and immediately on providing incentives seems to leave the key concepts of ethics and duty entirely out of consideration. However, such is the mode of economic thought, and one may well wonder if the economic analysis of compensation arrangements omits the key factor of positions of trust having both legal and moral duties associated with them.

EXECUTIVE COMPENSATION AND DISTRIBUTIVE JUSTICE

Distributive justice is concerned with the justness of the methods by which the goods in a society are distributed and with the justness of the resulting distribution.[26] Typically, the focus is on wealth or income, and in the context of executive compensation, it is most relevant to express the ideas of justice in terms of income. Traditional views of distributive justice can each be characterized in a single sentence. *Egalitarianism* asserts that a just society is one in which each person receives the same income. *Utilitarianism* holds that a just distribution of incomes is one that maximizes the well-being of the entire society—so it doesn't really matter if one person receives more than another. *Libertarianism* focuses on the process by which the allocation of incomes might be decided and holds that whatever income distribution results from free agents contracting without deceit, force, or fraud is a just distribution, simply because it is the distribution that arises from just procedures.

Clearly, the present level of executive compensation offends those who hold an egalitarian theory of justice. As noted in chapter 1, the average CEO makes several hundred times as much income as the ordinary worker. The same is true of top entertainers and sports figures as well. If egalitarianism is true, CEO compensation truly is unjust. In contrast, libertarian and utilitarian views of executive compensation present more interesting cases.

The debate between the optimal-contracting/incentive-alignment advocates and those who take a managerial power approach makes direct contact with a libertarian theory of justice. Libertarian approaches to justice generally favor market-driven solutions, and the freer the markets the more sure libertarian thinkers are that market outcomes are just. But how are we to understand the director-CEO interplay that determines the CEO's compensation package? If incentive alignment is working well, with boards fulfilling their fiduciary duties and representing the interests of shareholders as honest agents, then CEO compensation arrangements may well be just, or at least nearly so, on the libertarian conception. On the other hand, from the point of view of a theory of libertarian justice, we can read the managerial power theorists as saying that the system of executive compensation that prevails in the United States fails to meet the key condition for the CEO compensation contract being just. If the CEO has undue influence over the pay-setting process, as managerial power advocates insist, the CEO's exercise of this power violates the key libertarian condition that a contract must be reached without force, fraud, or deceit.

On the utilitarian view, all that matters is that society's total welfare be maximized by the distribution of income. If we were to reduce CEO compensation and transfer those funds to others with the result that the CEO lost less utility than the others gained, then such a transfer would increase the justness of society. Given the general view that there is a marginal decreasing utility associated with additional compensation, it might appear that utility could be increased by reducing the compensation of a rich CEO in favor of transferring some wealth to a poorer person.[27] However, this line of argument implicitly assumes that the CEO's job performance would not be altered. If the CEO truly were being incentivized to perform, and without that compensation, her job performance would be seriously diminished leading the firm to create substantially less wealth, then such a transfer of income away from the CEO to others might well diminish total utility. At this point, the argument runs up against the typical problem of utilitarian theories—the apparent impossibility of measuring an individual's utility relative to others and in aggregating utility across individuals.

A final and extremely influential view of distributive justice seems worthy of consideration. In one of the most influential works of political philosophy in the twentieth century, *A Theory of Justice*, John Rawls propounded a nuanced theory of distributive justice that attempted to take account of basic rights while favoring a general egalitarianism.[28] Rawls propounded two basic principles of justice, with the first having absolute priority. As a first principle, a just society must preserve certain basic individual rights, such as the right of free speech and the right to participate in political processes. (In articulating this principle, Rawls consciously rebelled against utilitarianism, which would view all other values, such as rights, as being subject to the utilitarian calculus.) Second, subject to the protection of the rights articulated in the first principle of justice, there should be a generally egalitarian distribution of a society's goods. However, departures from an equal distribution can be justified if, and only if, allowing some individuals to have more of society's goods benefits those in the society who are the least well-off.

Rawls seemed to have in mind a truly gifted person with the talent for creating immense wealth or other benefits for society, such as a great artistic talent, a brilliant scientist, or a gifted entrepreneur. Assume that the talented person is unwilling to deploy her special gift unless she receives more than the average compensation. In a society governed by strictly utilitarian principles it would be just to force her to exercise her talents for the benefit of others if the net increase in utility of others more than offset the loss of utility she would suffer due to her enslavement. For Rawls, however, such force would violate the first principle of justice and therefore cannot be permitted. Instead, it would be just on Rawls's view to offer incentives to this person on the grounds that the exercise of her talents would make the worst-off members of society better.

Rawls did not appear to have CEOs in mind as candidates for this exception from the generally egalitarian distribution of wealth and income. But the application is nonetheless quite straightforward. Imagine a truly gifted person capable of leading a firm to the creation of a great increase in wealth. Such a person might be unwilling to work as hard as such an effort would require unless granted highly incentivizing compensation. If the creation of that new wealth would benefit the least well-off in society, granting the CEO incentive compensation sufficient to call forth the wealth-creating effort appears to be justified on Rawlsian grounds. If this interpretation does not do too much violence to Rawls's views, it may be a way of justifying sharp differentials in compensation, especially if those differentials are organized to create wealth in a way that benefits the least well-off in society.

Contrasted with this excursus into ethical theory, both the optimal-contracting/incentive-alignment view and the managerial power theory are firmly rooted in economics. Neither camp wishes to propound their views as articulating moral principles. However, both approaches have implications for assessing the justice of executive compensation. For example, if the manage-rial power view is true, then executive compensation does not meet the condi-tions of a libertarian theory of justice. By contrast, if the optimal-contracting/ incentive-alignment view accurately describes the market for CEO services, then the practice of corporate governance is broadly consistent with the pre-conditions of a libertarian theory of justice. In addition, some who defend current corporate governance and executive compensation practices do so on utilitarian grounds. The claim that current corporate-governance practices generally succeed in allowing firms to maximize wealth creation, or at least to approximate that ideal, amounts essentially to a defense of current practice on utilitarian grounds. From that perspective, both approaches to executive compensation attempt to substantiate views with significant and conflicting implications for assessing the justice of corporate-governance practices.

The Incentive Structure of Executive Compensation

The most important development in economics in the last forty years has been the study of incentives to achieve potential mutual gains when the parties have different degrees of knowledge.

—*KENNETH J. ARROW, 1972 NOBEL LAUREATE IN ECONOMIC SCIENCES*

The unintended and unimagined consequences of man's enterprise have been and will always be more potent, more widespread, and more influential that those he intended.

—*DANIEL BOORSTIN*

The Incentive Revolution and Executive Compensation

Incentives have become a governing paradigm of the economic understanding of human behavior, and the incentive way of thinking has become a way of life. A quick Internet search of "Obama AND incentives" makes the president appear as the "Incentivizer in Chief" with headlines such as:

"Obama: Schools Can Improve with Right Incentives"
"Obama Is Focusing on Tax Incentives"
"Obama Announces Middle Class Incentives"
"Economy: Obama Announces Incentives for Businesses"
"Obama Offers Incentives to Stimulate Auto Sales"
"Obama Proposes 'Green Tax' Incentives"

The list of similar items goes on and on. We tend to think of "getting the incentives right" as a solution to all of our public policy problems, whether the current problem is securing the correct patent policy, improving higher education, rewarding efficiency, or reducing medical errors.

The long-recognized, unwelcome consequences of setting incentives are the "unintended consequences" of human actions. On happy occasions, these unintended consequences can be beneficial. Perhaps the most famous passage in Adam Smith's *Of the Wealth of Nations* calls our attention to the beneficial effects of the "invisible hand":

> As every individual, therefore, endeavours as much as he can both to employ his capital in the support of domestic industry, and so to direct that industry that its produce may be of the greatest value; every individual necessarily labours to render the annual revenue of the society as great as he can. He generally, indeed, neither intends to promote the public interest, nor knows how much he is promoting it. By preferring the support of domestic to that of foreign industry, he intends only his own security; and by directing that industry in such a manner as its produce may be of the greatest value, he intends only his own gain, and he is in this, as in many other cases, led by an invisible hand to promote an end which was no part of his intention. Nor is it always the worse for the society that it was no part of it. By pursuing his own interest he frequently promotes that of the society more effectually than when he really intends to promote it.[1]

This awareness of unintended consequences grew, and in 1936 there appeared Robert K. Merton's influential article, "The Unanticipated Consequences of Purposive Social Action," in which he identified five sources of unanticipated consequences.[2] So widespread has the presence of unintended consequences become that a website was spawned: "The Museum of Unintended Consequences," which categorizes the many ways we frustrate ourselves by setting incentives.[3]

Given the prevalence of incentives and unintended consequences in current social policy and modes of thought, it might appear that this way of thinking is of long standing. However, it is only fairly recently that the setting of incentives has come to dominate discourse. As Ruth Grant explained persuasively, "incentive" gained its current meaning in economics in the middle of the twentieth century, when "incentive" was used in the context of stimulating better job performance during the middle of World War II.[4] Incentives are as old as human behavior, of course, but the modern explicit conceptualization as a primary wellspring of human activity suggests that incentives played a relatively minor role for earlier thinkers, as technical terms usually develop to express the key ideas of theories.

While the idea of incentives as a crucial factor in economics, generally, and in discussion of compensation, particularly, may have had a delayed beginning, it has quickly come to dominate the conversation. This is especially true in the area of executive compensation, where scholars have studied the idea of providing incentives to secure a desired behavior. Through the twentieth century and to the present, the setting of incentives has developed an ever-larger role in the economic understanding of human behavior, and the incentive way of thinking has spilled over into our political and personal discourse as well.

The virtual obsession with incentives in compensation stems mainly from a famous 1990 article by Michael Jensen and Kevin Murphy, "CEO Incentives: It's Not How Much You Pay, But How." In the article, Jensen and Murphy called for a method of paying executives that would encourage them to take additional risk and make greater effort. In an idealized system, corporate boards would structure executive compensation such that "they would reward managers for the increased success fostered by greater risk taking, effort, and ability," but boards would also organize compensation in a manner such that "the threat of dismissal for poor performance can be made real."[5] The 20 years following the publication of the article witnessed great intellectual attention to incentives in executive pay and a great practical emphasis on incentives in executive pay packages, implemented largely through executive stock options (ESOs).

In the aftermath of the financial crisis and given the long, steep ascent of executive pay (documented in chapter 1), two features of the Jensen and Murphy article are particularly striking. The essay essentially called for increases in executive pay, albeit structured in a manner that would induce CEOs to take additional risks to increase firm value:

> These increases in compensation—driven by improved business performance—would not represent a transfer of wealth from shareholders to executives. Rather, they would reward managers for the increased success fostered by greater risk taking, effort, and ability. Paying CEOs "better" would eventually mean paying the average CEO more. Because the stakes are so high, the potential increase in corporate performance and the potential gains to shareholders are great.[6]

Put even more starkly, Jensen and Murphy portrayed CEOs, circa 1990, as un-incentivized paper pushers, rather than as corporate buccaneers: "On average, corporate America pays its most important leaders like bureaucrats. Is it any wonder then that so many CEOs act like bureaucrats rather than the value maximizing entrepreneurs companies need to enhance their standing in world markets?"[7] Along the same lines, some studies have found that CEOs, when sheltered from competition and constrained by state laws from engaging in truly entrepreneurial approaches to firm leadership, are apt to enjoy the "quiet life." That is, rather than engaging in value-maximizing firm leadership or even in building their own corporate empires for the consumption of perquisites and privileges, managers in such positions succumb to the temptation of laziness.[8]

In contrast to the situation that Jensen and Murphy perceived in 1990, the cry today is that executive compensation is too large and that CEOs take too many risks. One of the most popular explanations of the cause of the financial crisis of 2007–2009 has been that financial executives, predominately motivated by self-enrichment, led their firms to take excessive risk.[9] Much of the financial regulation advanced in the aftermath of the crisis aims to constrain risk-taking in the financial sector. For example, the Federal Reserve Board's October 2011 *Incentive Compensation Practices: A Report on the Horizontal Review of Practices at Large Banking Organizations* begins its executive summary with the bald assertion: "Risk-taking incentives provided by incentive compensation arrangements in the financial services industry were a contributing factor to the financial crisis that began in 2007."[10] Starting from that position, much of the document is devoted to a discussion of getting the incentives right.

There is little doubt that during the 20 years after Jensen and Murphy's article appeared, 1990–2010, executive pay skyrocketed and has come to consist more strongly of elements that are at least plausibly related to providing incentives to executives to maximize firm value. To this point, we have seen that the pay of corporate executives is large and consists of several elements. However, whether the magnitude and structure of executive pay is oriented toward aligning the CEO's incentives with maximizing the value of the firm is a subject of great controversy. This chapter considers key elements of the pay structure and how those diverse components might succeed or fail in inducing the CEO to maximize the value of the firm. The four most prominent elements of the CEO's pay package are salary, bonuses, restricted stock, and stock options, and we consider the power of each to create and shape the incentives facing the CEO. As we will see, equity compensation—consisting of restricted stock and executive stock options—is the prime vehicle through which the firm can incentivize its CEO.

SALARY

We begin with a brief consideration of salary. As demonstrated in chapter 1, salary typically makes up a relatively small component of executive pay—in recent years it ranged between 10 and 20 percent of total compensation. If there is any incentive in incentive compensation, it must be that compensation varies with performance. If we think of salaries in society at large, they very seldom fall over time. The contrary is actually the case: salaries tend to rise in normal times, and widespread salary cuts occur only in conditions of serious economic distress. The same appears to be true for CEO salaries. Equilar, Inc. studied changes in CEO pay and its relationship to total shareholder return (TSR) for all S&P 1500 firms over the three-year period from 2006–2009, producing some interesting, but not particularly surprising, results: "Nearly all of the companies studied for the three-year timeframe increased their CEO's base salary over that period, even if overall CEO pay decreased in the same period."[11] As far as CEO salaries are concerned, they may differ in size compared with those granted to the rest of us, but like salaries of ordinary workers, they seldom fall.

The scarcity of salary cuts and the prevalence of salary increases prevailed no matter how the firm performed. If total pay increased over the three-year period, 87–92 percent of salaries rose as well. Even in the most unlikely case—when both overall CEO pay and the firm's TSR fell—73 percent of CEOs still enjoyed an increase in their base salary.[12] If incentives arise by varying pay based on firm performance, those incentives are not carried by salary fluctuations, and we must look elsewhere for the kind of compensation that might carry incentives.

BONUSES

We have seen that most CEOs receive bonuses and that these can be structured as annual bonuses or as multiyear plans. Figure 3.1 shows the typical structure of a performance-based bonus plan. Key to the plan is a "performance measure" such as the firm's net income or earnings-per-share. To qualify for a bonus based on the performance measure, the measure must achieve at least the "performance threshold," at which point the CEO earns the minimum bonus. As the performance measure exceeds the threshold, the bonus increases linearly until the bonus reaches the bonus cap. Performance above the bonus cap yields no further increase in bonus. The most typical performance measures are based on earnings or sales.[13]

The performance measure is one of the most critical factors in the design of bonus systems. The first question is whether the measure is to be an internal or

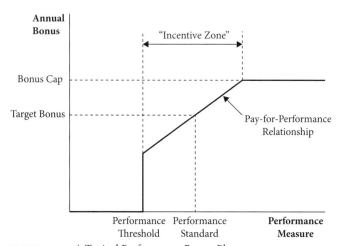

FIGURE 3.1 *A Typical Performance Bonus Plan.*

Source: Closely adapted from Kevin J. Murphy, "Performance Standards in Incentive Contracts," *Journal of Accounting and Economics,* 30, 2001, 245–278, figure 1, p. 251. See also Kevin J. Murphy, "Executive Compensation" (June 1999, working paper), figure 5, p. 80; and Michael C. Jensen and Kevin J. Murphy, "Remuneration: Where We've Been, How We Got to Here, What Are the Problems, and How to Fix Them" (2004, working paper), figure 10, p. 70.

external measure. The key difference is the extent to which the party receiving a bonus has control over the performance measure. Consider a division manager who receives a bonus based on shipments of a product produced by her division in a given fiscal year. If shipments fail to meet the performance threshold of figure 3.1, she receives no bonus. After meeting the performance threshold, she receives a bonus that is a linear function of the units the division ships, but only up to a point. If shipments exceed a number corresponding to the bonus cap of figure 3.1, she receives no bonus associated with the shipments beyond the level of the cap. As a straightforward example, assume the performance threshold is 10,000 units and that the bonus cap kicks in at 20,000 units.

As the end of the fiscal year approaches, assume that the division has shipped 9,500 units and has an order for 475 units in hand, with no time left to receive and ship additional orders. In this situation, the division manager has a strong incentive to delay shipment to the next fiscal year or even to ship in the current year and record the shipment in the next fiscal year. If those 475 units are recorded in the current fiscal year, they will not generate a bonus, but if delayed for accounting purposes to the next fiscal year then they may contribute to achieving a bonus in the next year. Similarly perverse incentives kick in as the number of shipments nears the bonus cap. Assume now that the division has shipped 20,000 units as the end of the fiscal year draws near and has an order in hand for an additional 1,000 units, which she could ship this year and book in this year's results. But, the division manager has an incentive to withhold those units and "save" them until next year. Having already maximized her bonus for this year, shipping the additional 1,000 units now will not contribute to the bonus, but if she ships them next year they might increase the bonus for that period. Different circumstances could give the manager the incentive to move shipments from the next year to this year to capture a bonus. For example, assume that the division has shipped 19,000 units, and that a reliable customer orders 1,000 units every month. The division manager might be tempted to immediately ship 1,000 units to the customer in anticipation of the order not yet received.

The perverse incentives to withhold or accelerate shipments (or just to manipulate the accounting records associated with shipments) that arise are indicated by the "kinks" in the line of figure 3.1 that show the division manager's bonus. Over the linear portion of the graph, the "Pay-for-Performance" region, there are no such perverse incentives. A CEO might face a similar situation if the bonus is based on a typical accounting measure such as the firm's reported earnings. There are many accounting tricks that the CEO might be tempted to deploy to fatten a bonus; for example, delay this period's earnings to the next period, or to advance anticipated earnings from the next fiscal year to the present one. As the preceding example shows, incentive plans must be designed carefully to obtain the desired behavior while avoiding perverse incentives. (Some plans fail to provide meaningful incentives at all.)

While figure 3.1 pertains most clearly to an annual incentive plan, multiyear bonus plans are more complicated. Campbell and Wasley present an interesting case study of a 10-year incentive plan implemented at the Ralston Purina Company.[14] In 1986, the Ralston Purina Company (hereafter Ralston) instituted a bonus plan for 14 top managers. It was multiyear plan encompassing 10 years with an external standard based on the stock price, and the bonus was to be paid in the form of shares of the firm. The plan, adopted in March 1986, awarded a total of 491,000 shares to the managers, but the award was contingent on the shares of Ralston closing at $100 or above for 10 consecutive trading days within 10 years of the initiation of the bonus plan. Different managers received awards of different sizes, with the largest being a 160,000-share grant to the CEO, which would be worth $16,000,000 if the share price met the target.

While the terms of the Ralston plan are somewhat complex, the payoffs for the managers are very simple: collectively, the managers receive nothing if the stock price fails to meet the target; they receive $49,100,000 if the stock price does meet the target. This is a binary, or all-or-nothing, payoff structure as figure 3.2 depicts. In March 1986, when the plan was adopted, Ralston's shares traded for $63.375. In order to receive the bonus, the managers had to elevate the stock price to $100, a gain of 57.8 percent. (One might less charitably say that the managers did not have to raise the stock price, they just had to be employed when the stock price met the target.)

While a 57.8 percent stock price increase sounds formidable and an achievement worth rewarding, it must also be viewed in the context of the

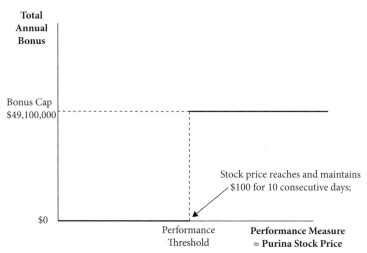

FIGURE 3.2 *Ralston Purina's 1986 Bonus Plan for 14 Top Executives.*

Source: Based on Cynthia J. Campbell and Charles E. Wasley, "Stock-Based Incentive Contracts and Managerial Performance: The Case of Ralston Purina Company," *Journal of Financial Economics*, 1999, 51, 195–217.

long period of 10 years granted to reach this goal. If the stock price grew at a mere 4.67 percent over the 10-year period, the goal would be reached in exactly 10 years. However, Ralston's paid a 3.1 percent annual dividend at the time the plan was instituted. With this as a continuing policy, this dividend represents a 3.1 percent annual "leakage" of value from the stock price. (In the normal event, when a stock pays a dividend, the value of a share of stock falls by the amount of the dividend.) This means that the value of Ralston's shares had to increase by 7.77 percent annually to cover both the necessary increase in the share price plus the dividend payment. In March 1986, when Ralston put the bonus plan into effect, the 10-year U.S. Treasury bond yield was 7.5 percent. This meant that Ralston's managers could earn their bonus by increasing the value of the firm at a rate that was just a hair (27 basis points) above the risk-free rate for the same period.

Every corporation has to secure capital to finance its operations by issuing bonds or selling stock. In their detailed study of Ralston, Campbell and Wasley estimate that Ralston's cost of capital was 11.6 percent, after adjusting for the dividend.[15] If Ralston met the lowest of reasonable targets over the bonus period, by exactly earning its cost of capital over 10 years, the stock price would reach $189.92. As Campbell and Wasley evaluated the situation: "Thus, if the hurdle price is met in exactly ten years, manager[s] *could* actually destroy $98.92 per share of shareholder value and still receive the contract's payoff."[16]

Another way of looking at the bonus contract is to ask how long it would take for the share price to reach $100 if Ralston exactly earned its cost of capital. Campbell and Wasley calculated that the stock price would reach $100 in 51 months if the stock price grew at exactly the cost of equity capital. In fact, on February 22, 1991, Ralston closed above $100 for the 10th consecutive day. This was 59 months after the bonus plan was instituted, so Ralston earned less than its cost of capital over this period. Even though Ralston lost actual value by earning less than its cost of capital, the managers captured their bonus.

At the time the bonus plan went into effect, Ralston was a very mature business, having been in operation almost 100 years, with a well-established brand and operating policy. The bonus plan gave Ralston's managers strong incentives to merely plod ahead with the firm's current plans. In essence, all the Ralston managers had to do was keep the ship on a steady course and avoid any icebergs along the way to their bonus. Thus, far from incentivizing the managers to undertake value-creating investments or to embark upon worthwhile risky projects, the terms of the bonus contract rewarded a steady policy of stewardship rather than one of creativity.

In addition, the bonus plan furnished managers with a reason to alter the firm's long-standing dividend policy in a manner that would not benefit shareholders. Given the terms of the bonus plan, one easy approach the managers might have adopted in trying to reach the target stock price would be to reduce or even eliminate the dividend. If Ralston eliminated the dividend, all of those dividend payments, which flowed out of the value of the stock, would remain impounded in the stock price. Perhaps not surprisingly, Ralston did reduce the dividend yield after 1986 from 3.1 to 1.8 percent, helping to boost the stock price. It appears that the bonus plan may have encouraged the managers to change the dividend policy of the firm to benefit them and not the shareholders.

Given these features, the Ralston bonus plan has become a classic example of a poorly designed plan. It rewarded an outcome that was likely to occur without a superior managerial performance; it discouraged creative risk-taking investments; and it encouraged gratuitous changes in the firm's dividend policy. Figure 3.2 reflects some of these key features, particularly the discontinuity in payoffs resulting from the all-or-nothing character of the bonus. This feature encouraged a total focus on getting the stock price to $100, but gave no reward for pushing the stock price beyond $100. This characteristic created a situation in which there were no rewards to managers for creative investment or risk-taking. Also, the managers were effectively able to reduce the performance threshold depicted in figure 3.2 by reducing the firm's dividend yield, thereby artificially boosting the stock price. Thus, as we have seen in our discussion of bonus plans, the kinks in payoffs shown in figure 3.1 and the radical discontinuity of figure 3.2 create problems in plan design that can provide managers with perverse incentives. In the light of these difficulties we now turn to a consideration of restricted stock, an incentive tool that has an ultimately linear payoff structure.

RESTRICTED STOCK AND PERFORMANCE SHARES

Restricted stock comes in a variety of forms, but all varieties ultimately grant shares or share equivalents in the employing firm. In a simple restricted stock grant, the firm awards shares to an executive but the shares have some restriction, usually requiring a vesting period. After the vesting period, the executive has full title to the shares and can sell them for her personal account. Closely related, is the *restricted stock unit*. This is a promise to grant shares upon meeting a condition, such as the executive remaining with the firm through a specified vesting period, at which time the firm grants shares that are fully the property of the executive. In the Ralston Purina bonus plan, considered in the preceding section, the bonus promise consisted of restricted stock units of a particular type.

Another form of restricted stock is a performance stock grant. This is a grant of restricted stock, but instead of the restriction being merely a period of time until the stock vests, the restriction on the shares is removed when some performance target is met. A *performance stock unit* is a promise to grant shares at some future date conditional upon some performance target being met. Thus, the Ralston Purina bonus plan involved the granting of performance stock units to the managers conditional upon Ralston's stock price reaching and maintaining a closing price of $100 within a 10-year horizon.

Restricted stock in all its various forms has become more popular in recent years. As figure 3.3 shows, the percentage of S&P 500 firms granting restricted stock to their CEOs has increased from about 20 to 80 percent over the years from 1992 to 2010. The percentage was essentially stable in the early years, but accelerated around 2000, concurrent with the dotcom boom. Not surprisingly, this increasing percentage of firms granting restricted stock has led to a significant increase in the number of restricted shares granted and the number of restricted shares outstanding. (A restricted share that is outstanding is one received by the original recipient that has not yet been sold.) From 2006 to 2010, the granting of restricted shares among all S&P 1500 firms accelerated from 275,600 to 450,200 per year. Over the same period, the average number of restricted shares outstanding increased from 550,000 to slightly more than 1 million.[17]

Unlike the bonus plans considered in the previous section, restricted stock has only linear payoffs. (The Ralston Purina plan used restricted stock, but the discontinuity in the plan was a feature of the conditions under which the stock would be granted. Once the stock is granted, the payoffs are linear.) Figure 3.4 shows the payoffs from a grant of a share of restricted stock, granted with the firm's stock price at $50 per share. Such a grant has two very important features. First, it consists of a very significant amount of compensation. This is especially true in contrast with stock options, considered in the next section of this chapter. Second, the grant has important incentive effects. Once the grant is made, the recipient potentially has a significant stake in the

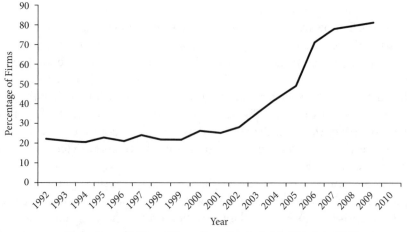

FIGURE 3.3 *Percentage of S&P 500 Firms Granting Restricted Stock to CEOs.*
Source: Graph by author, based on ExecuComp data.

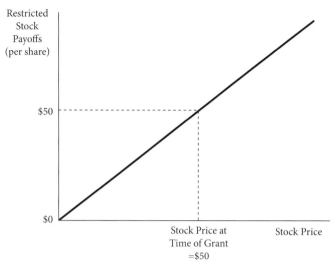

FIGURE 3.4 *Costs and Payoffs from Restricted Stock.*

Source: Graph by author, based on ExecuComp data.

success of the firm. However, the cost of creating the incentives is very high. For example, assume the firm wishes to create a situation in which increasing the value of the firm's shares by $20 would imply a reward of $1 million to the executive. Creating this incentive by using restricted shares would require a grant of 50,000 shares, with a total cost of $2.5 million. Thus the cost of the restricted stock itself, plus the cost of the payoff on the incentive would reach $3.5 million.

By contrast, a grant of performance shares could create the same incentive at a much lower cost. For example, the firm could grant 14,286 performance shares, with the performance condition being that the share price must reach $70 by a particular date. Note however, that this is very much like the structure implemented by Ralston Purina with all of its attendant problems. To mitigate the problems of a single hurdle and the binary payoff, the firm could issue smaller batches of shares with stepped performance conditions. For example, the performance conditions could be met with a stock price of $55, $60, $65, and $70. This type of structure has a payoff shape that combines the features of figures 3.1 and 3.2. Assuming that the 14,286 shares are divided into four tranches of an equal number of shares, figure 3.5 depicts the payoff structure. Notice, however, that this payoff structure still has kinks similar to the problem depicted in figure 3.1, but by partitioning the grants into small increments, some of the perverse incentives are reduced, even though not fully eliminated.

As a final point, it is important to note the risk-reducing incentives inherent in the grant of restricted stock. Consider a firm that grants shares of

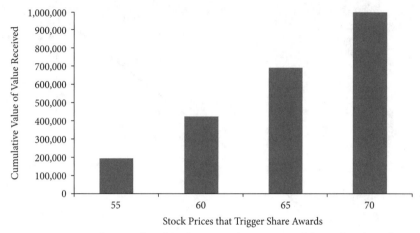

FIGURE 3.5 *Cumulative Value of Performance Shares Received for Each Achieved Stock Price.*

Source: Graph by author, based on ExecuComp data.

restricted stock to a CEO, with those restricted shares scheduled to vest in five years. If the value of the firm's shares goes up, the shares the CEO hopes to receive will have greater value. However, if the shares fall in value, so does the value of the grant to the CEO. Thus, restricted shares offer a reward for an increasing stock price, but a penalty for a falling price. As a result, restricted stock has only a limited value as an incentive to take risks. Also, if the CEO does take a risky course of action in an effort to raise the stock price, but the risky projects fails, not only will the value of the CEO's restricted shares fall, but the CEO might face dismissal before the five-year vesting horizon is reached.

EXECUTIVE STOCK OPTIONS

Of all financial derivatives, options are the most interesting and complex. All executive stock options are call options, giving the owner the right to buy a share of the firm at a specified price (the exercise price), with that right lasting a specific length of time (until the option's expiration date). Plain vanilla options come in two forms, European and American. A European option can only be exercised on the expiration date of the option, while an American option can be exercised whenever the owner chooses. Plain vanilla options also have a single underlying good that determines the exercise value of the option, such as a share of stock. If an option is not a plain vanilla option, it is classified as an exotic option. Some exotic options are fairly simple, while some are extremely complex.

Almost all ESOs are issued with a vesting requirement—they can be exercised at any time after the vesting date. For this reason, the typical ESO is an exotic option. Some classify them as Bermudan options—halfway between European and American options, in that they can be exercised before expiration, like an American option, but not before the vesting date. After the vesting date, an ESO becomes similar to an American option but with one important difference.

For almost all ESOs, the issuing firm requires that if the owner leaves the employment of the firm, the option must be forfeited, or surrendered as worthless, if it has not yet vested. If the employee leaves the firm after the option is vested, and if the option is "in-the-money"—with the stock price above the exercise price—then the departing employee must exercise the option, receiving a value equal to the difference between the stock price and the exercise price. If the option is vested, but is "out-of-the-money"—with the stock price equal to or less than the exercise price—then the departing employee must surrender the option as worthless.

In spite of the complexity of options, Fischer Black and Myron Scholes devised an option pricing model that revolutionized finance in 1973. They proved that the value of a plain vanilla European option on a stock that paid no dividend could be expressed as a function of five variables: the stock price, the exercise price, the time until expiration, the risk-free rate of interest (such as the interest rate on a treasury bill), and the standard deviation of the underlying stock's rate of return. The Black-Scholes model was soon extended by Robert Merton to give a formula for a European option on a stock that pays a dividend at a continuous rate. (Most actual dividend payments are not continuous but are paid quarterly.) In subsequent years, other researchers have devised formulae to price many more complicated options. However, no formula exists to price many complex options, such as ESOs. Even in the absence of a formula, the value of these very complex options can be computed by more sophisticated methods, most notably by using binomial "trees" or lattice methods.[18]

Under current regulations, companies that issue ESOs must report the value of those options in their regular financial statements. They are allowed to make this computation using either lattice methods or the Black-Scholes model, but to use the Black-Scholes model the reporting firm must estimate the expected life of the option, and they must make and report some assumption about the prospective standard deviation of returns for firm's stock. Today, a typical ESO might be issued with 10 years to expiration and a four-year vesting period. Typical assumptions are that the option will either be exercised or forfeited about five years from the date of issue and the prevalent assumption about volatility (the standard deviation of the firm's stock returns) is to assume that the volatility of the firm's shares is about 40 percent per year.

Consistent with those assumptions, figure 3.6 shows the value of an option computed according to the Black-Scholes formula, assuming the stock price

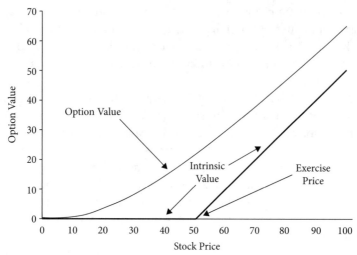

FIGURE 3.6 *The Value of a Call Option as a Function of the Stock Price.*
Source: Graph by author, based on ExecuComp data.

is $50, the exercise price is $50, the time until expiration is 10 years, but the option's expected life (the number used in the computation) is five years, that the standard deviation of the firm's returns is 40 percent per year, and the risk-free rate is 5 percent per year.[19] The figure also shows how the value of the option varies as a function of the stock price. The intrinsic value of an option is the difference between the stock price and the exercise price at a particular moment, and it equals the profit the owner of the option would capture by exercising the option immediately. (As we noted, it is not always possible to exercise an ESO due to vesting restrictions.) The graph also shows the exercise price, which is always at the inflection point in the intrinsic value of the option. Thus, the intrinsic value of an option is zero if the stock price is at or below the exercise price.

Figure 3.7 shows a close-up view of a portion of the same information contained in figure 3.6. As figure 3.7 depicts, the price of the option is $21.44 with the current stock price of $50 per share. Assuming the other factors remain constant, a stock price of $60 corresponds to an option price of $29.41, while a stock price of $70 gives an option value of $37.86.

With our assumptions about the option, including a current stock price of $50 and an exercise price of $50, the value of the option is about 40 percent of the price of the stock. This is a fairly typical relationship between a newly issued ESO and the value of the underlying stock. When section 162(m) became law, restricting deductible executive salaries to $1 million, it also exempted incentive-based pay, including ESOs, from that restriction. In addition, accounting rules provided that ESOs could be issued without having an impact on the firm's reported earnings if the exercise price were set to equal

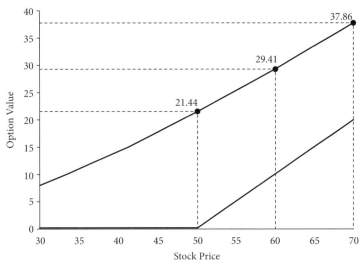

FIGURE 3.7 *The Value of a Call Option as a Function of the Stock Price (enlarged section of figure 3.6).*

Source: Graph by author, based on ExecuComp data.

the firm's current stock price. As a result, almost all ESOs have been issued to meet that condition, at least until recently. Therefore, the sample option of figures 3.6 and 3.7 is fairly representative of actual market practice.

As the graphs of figures 3.6 and 3.7 indicate, ESOs at the time of issuance are quite valuable. However, they cannot be converted into cash any time soon because of vesting restrictions and because the option has no intrinsic value at the time of issue. If the stock price never goes up, the option never has any intrinsic value and can never be converted into cash. If the stock price remains stagnant or drops below the exercise price of the option, the ESO will lose value over time. By contrast, if the stock price rises, the ESO pays off handsomely. As shown in figure 3.7, a sudden 20 percent rise in the value of the stock from $50 to $60 gives a 37 percent increase in the value of the option from $21.44 to $29.41. This surge in the option value for an increase in the stock price illustrates the inherent leverage in the value of options—the price of an option changes more in percentage terms than does the underlying stock.

While figure 3.7 illustrates that an executive receiving an ESO has a strong incentive to increase the stock price, an example emphasizes the point. Consider the executive who receives the ESO of figures 3.6 and 3.7. Assume the firm's stock price increases at an annual rate of 9 percent for the four years of the vesting period, so after four years, the stock will be worth $70.58. The option will vest at that time, and the executive could exercise the option and realize its intrinsic value of $20.58. However, exercising before expiration discards some of the value of the option. In this particular example, at the time of vesting the option still has six years remaining until it expires. The value of the option at that time depends on assumptions we make about its expected life. If the executive, now in full possession of the vested option, expects to stay with the firm for the remaining six years until the option expires, the option's value is $40.73, with the stock price of $70.58. Exercising the option as soon as it vests will only net the intrinsic value of $20.58, so early exercise (exercise prior to expiration) discards a tremendous portion of the value of the option.

These features of ESOs make them an interesting proposition from the firm's point of view. Granting an option conveys very significant value to the recipient, but it involves no cash outlay at the time the firm grants the options. For start-up firms, ESOs are particularly seductive because option grants can serve as partial substitutes for salaries in cash-starved businesses. This practice of granting options in partial lieu of salary pervaded pay practices at high-tech firms in the dotcom boom, as the next chapter discusses more fully. From the perspective of providing incentives, ESOs have attractive features as well. As just noted, granting an ESO requires no immediate cash outlay, and granting an option with an exercise price equal to the current stock price only turns into a real cost to the firm if the stock price rises and the option is exercised. Even if the option is exercised, the firm suffers no cash outflow, because it merely creates and issues a new share of stock to meet the exercise. However there is real cost to the firm at that point, because issuing the new share of stock increases the number of shares outstanding. This increase in the number of shares dilutes the ownership of the firm and causes the stock price to fall commensurate with the increase in shares.

If the executive really can act to increase the value of the firm, the ESO provides an extremely strong incentive. The executive captures her payday only if the stock price rises, while a stagnant or falling stock price eventually will render her initially valuable options worthless. Thus, from the point of view of the firm, granting ESOs provides powerful incentives for creating firm value, which is exactly what the firm desires, but if that increase in value does not materialize, there is no ultimate cost to the firm.

Figure 3.8 shows the history of option grants to CEOs of S&P 500 firms from 1992 to 2010. The solid line shows the average number of options granted in each year per CEO, while the dashed line shows the average number exercised by each CEO. As the graph illustrates, option granting and exercising hit a peak in 2000, at the height of the dotcom bubble. In recent years, there have been fewer options granted and much fewer exercises. The diminished exercise activity has been due in large part to low stock prices in the aftermath of the financial crisis of 2007–2009, which made exercise impossible or unattractive if the intrinsic value was actually negative or if the intrinsic value was quite low.

As figure 3.8 also shows, exercises are a high proportion relative to grants. This implies that the process that has evolved is a repeated granting of options followed by exercises and yet more granting of options. This is a very important feature of incentives to the executive and regarding the cost to the firm. When an executive exercises an option, she receives a share. But historically,

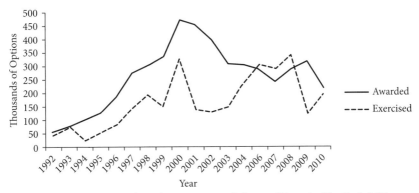

FIGURE 3.8 *Average Number of Options Awarded to and Exercised by Each S&P 500 CEO, 1991–2010.*

Source: Graph by author, based on ExecuComp data.

the executives sell the shares immediately upon exercising. From the point of view of the firm concerned about incentives, this is problematic as exercise followed by sale of the share leaves the executive lacking the incentive that the options provided. To restore the incentive dimension of compensation provided by having the executive hold options on the firm's stock, the firm must then reissue new options.

As we saw in figure 3.7, ESOs contain substantial real value at the time of issue. And as figure 3.8 shows, the number of options granted to and exercised by S&P 500 CEOs is sizable. These facts imply an extremely large transfer of value from these firms to their CEOs. Figure 3.9 shows the average value of options awarded to each S&P 500 CEO annually from 1992 to 2010. In every year from 1994 to the present, the value of those grants has averaged more than $1 million per CEO. The average annual value per CEO peaked at $8.1 million in 2000.

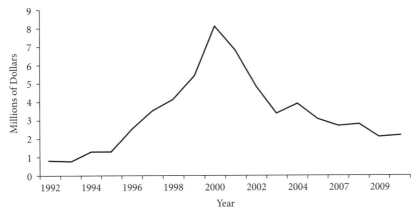

FIGURE 3.9 *Average Value of Options Awarded to Each S&P 500 CEO, 1992–2009.*

Source: Graph by author, based on ExecuComp data.

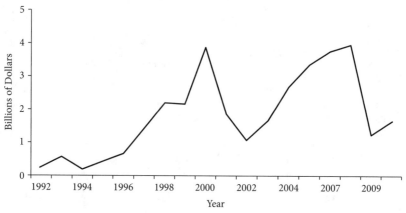

FIGURE 3.10   *Total Value of Options Exercised by All S&P 500 CEOs, 1992–2009.*
Source: Graph by author, based on ExecuComp data.

While grants of ESOs typically have very substantial value, we have seen that they do not involve an immediate cash flow from the firm or an immediate cash receipt by the executive who receives the option. Only at exercise does the executive receive full ownership of the share, and only on the sale of the share does the executive actually receive cash. Figure 3.10 shows the total exercise value captured by all S&P 500 CEOs annually. Over the 1992–2010 period, this aggregate exercise value has reached billions of dollars, with peaks of just under $4 billion dollars in 2000 and 2008. This is clearly a tremendous transfer of value from these firms, and from society at large, to a handful of individuals. (Actually, figure 3.10 slightly understates the total value, because the ExecuComp database is missing a few observations.) The real question about the social value and corporate wisdom of ESOs is whether the incentive effects created by these option grants are sufficiently unique and valuable to justify this very substantial transfer of wealth.

Evaluating the incentive effects of ESOs requires a more complete understanding of the intricacies of ESOs and an evaluation of the empirical evidence about how those incentives have performed. However, before turning to those issues in subsequent chapters, this chapter concludes with a comparison of the costs and incentive effects of bonuses, restricted stock, performance shares, and ESOs.

Equity Compensation: Retaining the Employees You Have and Attracting the Ones You Want

On August 24, 2011, the legendary Steve Jobs resigned as CEO of Apple Computer, and Tim Cook, the firm's chief operating officer, was appointed to assume the title. The firm filed an 8-K report with the SEC the same day, which included the following simple lines:

> In connection with Mr. Cook's appointment as Chief Executive Officer, the Board awarded Mr. Cook 1,000,000 restricted stock units. Fifty percent of the restricted stock units are scheduled to vest on each of August 24, 2016 and August 24, 2021, subject to Mr. Cook's continued employment with Apple through each such date.

That day, Apple's closing stock price was $376.18, making this grant of restricted stock potentially worth $376 million *if* Cook stayed with the firm for the full 10 years and assuming no change in the stock price. If the stock price were to rise at 10 percent per year, an ambitious but not unreasonable possibility given Apple's apparent golden touch, Cook's entire package of stock would be worth $976 million ten years hence. For many workers, this grant of restricted stock would provide a powerful incentive to remain a faithful employee. Similarly, it would give almost any CEO a strong incentive to make the stock price grow.

ESOs have similar potential to encourage good employees to stay with the firm. With a typical vesting horizon of 10 years on the date of issue, they hold out the possibility of a huge payoff, but at a distant date. As we will explore in detail in the next chapter, options have inherent leverage, so Apple might have offered a package of options with a similar incentive effect at a lower anticipated cost to the firm. However, restricted stock and options are also importantly different in other ways, as we will also explore in detail. Here we will note just one important difference. ESOs are almost always awarded with an exercise price equal to the current stock price. Assume that Apple had awarded ESOs to Cook with an exercise price of $376, but that Apple's stock price fell by half, to $180. The restricted stock package would still have tremendous evident value—after all 1,000,000 shares at $180 is still worth $180,000,000. However, the chance that the options would actually pay off would be much reduced, because they will only yield a positive cash flow if the stock price exceeds the exercise price.

There is considerable research on the effectiveness of equity compensation as a tool for retaining employees. In general, the weight of research indicates that both restricted stock and ESOs are powerful tools for retaining employees.[20] However, as the stock price falls significantly below the exercise price of an ESO, this kind of "underwater" option loses much of its power to retain good employees. As a result, many firms engage in the controversial practice of "repricing" or "resetting" the exercise price of the underwater option to the then current and reduced stock price, a controversial practice discussed in more detail in the next chapter.[21]

The firm wants to hire the right kind of executive with respect to optimism, self-confidence, and a willingness to take risks. Pay packages with the same economic cost to the firm can be structured in different ways to attract different kinds of employees. For example, in the latter part of his career, Steve Jobs received only $1 in annual compensation. However, he held an enormous position in Apple's shares, which might have provided ample financial motivation. (Of course, Jobs was a special case as far as executive motivation is concerned, as illustrated by the famous story of how Jobs recruited John Sculley away from Pepsi. Sculley reports: "And then he looked up at me and just stared at me with the stare that only Steve Jobs has and he said do you want to sell sugar water for the rest of your life or do you want to come with me and change the world and I just gulped because I knew I would wonder for the rest of my life what I would have missed."[22])

Thus a pay package consisting only of a salary might attract a time-serving and bureaucratically oriented CEO, but a pay package with the same cost to the firm that contains a substantial equity component will tend to attract executives with much more of an entrepreneurial outlook. As Arya and Mittendorf put the point: "We demonstrate a complementary benefit of option-based compensation: options also prove efficient in matching managerial pay to ability. Options are useful because they force a manager to put his pay on the line."[23]

Different Instruments as Tools of Incentive Compensation

These different tools for incentivizing executives have their own particular features, both beneficial and detrimental. Bonuses provide an effective incentive to achieve a particular goal. But they can induce various destructive games directed toward achieving the bonus rather than benefiting the firm, contradicting the firm's aim of the bonus plan. Performance shares function similarly, with a sudden and singular payoff for achieving a targeted stock price. Both bonuses and performance shares have the benefit of ultimately costing nothing if the bonus condition is not met or if the targeted stock price is not achieved. Executive stock options share the feature of having no ultimate cost if the firm's stock price does not increase, but ESOs avoid the perverse behavior of attempting to meet an artificial bonus condition. This is reflected in the graph of smooth payoff function for ESOs in figure 3.6, contrasted with the kinked payoff function for bonuses in figure 3.1. However, as we will explore in the next chapter, ESOs may have their own problems with providing the incentives that the firm wants to create.

Granting restricted stock has the disadvantage of making an irrevocable transfer of wealth to the recipient. Even if the share price falls from the time of the grant, the restricted shares will still retain significant value. Restricted stock has the advantage of having an extremely smooth, even linear payoff function, which helps to mitigate the game-playing behavior associated with bonuses that utilize thresholds. Restricted stock involves two conceptual components: an immediate transfer of value similar to paying a salary or bonus on the award date, plus an incentive effect. However, the cost of achieving a forward-looking incentive effect is quite high. Just as an example, consider a stock selling for $50 and assume the firm would like to incentivize the CEO to increase the stock price to $60 per share. Further assume that the firm would like to create an incentive that would reward the CEO with $1 million for this achievement. To create this incentive through restricted stock, the firm would have to grant 100,000 shares at a total immediate cost of $5 million dollars, a value transfer that is final and may not ultimately pay off for the firm.

These reflections help to explain the vast popularity of ESOs. They require a zero initial cash outlay, and they pay off only if the share price increases. Further, they have a smooth payoff function that avoids the problems with the kinked payoff functions of typical bonus plans. In spite of these clearly attractive features of ESOs, they have peculiarities that may make them quite problematic in many ways, as the next chapter explores in detail.

Executive Stock Options and the Incentives They Create

As discussed in chapter 3, the typical executive pay package consists of many elements with disparate effects on the executive's incentives. Of the various elements of pay, salary, bonus, and so on, the equity portion is the main vehicle through which the firm seeks to give the executive incentives for long-term value maximization. Further, as we have seen, the two principal equity vehicles are restricted stock and executive stock options. Of these, restricted stock is fairly straightforward and familiar in design, with a purely linear payoff structure. By contrast, ESOs are much more complicated. As figure 3.6 showed, the payoff of ESOs has a complex curvilinear shape.

The most salient feature of ESO payoffs is this curvilinear shape, which means that issuing an ESO ultimately costs the firm nothing unless the stock price rises above the exercise price of the option. For stock prices well above the exercise price, these options pay off very handsomely for the executive. This chapter explores the nature of ESOs and their incentive effects more closely, particularly because we have not fully considered some of the complications inherent in ESOs over and above plain vanilla stock options. These additional feature of ESOs—particularly their long lives, the vesting restriction, the possibility of forfeiture if the executive leaves the firm before vesting or while the options are out-of-the-money, and the requirement that any vested and in-the-money options be exercised upon departure.

ESO Incentives, Firm Practices, and the Effect of Accounting Rules

The development of ESOs as a major component of executive compensation and the development of firm practices surrounding the treatment of ESOs has turned in important ways on the accounting rules that govern the granting of ESOs. In recent years, ESOs have been governed by three distinct accounting regimes. The first was the Accounting Principles Board Opinion APB 25, promulgated in 1973. Second, came the *Statement of Financial Accounting Standards No. 123, Accounting for Stock-Based Compensation* (or *FAS 123*), issued in 1995, which recommended some changes to APB 25 but allowed key practices of APB 25 to continue if the firm desired. *FAS 123* was supplanted in 2004 by the *Statement of Financial Accounting Standards No. 123 (Revised), Share Based Payments* (or *FAS-123R*). These statements, APB 25, *FAS 123* and *FAS 123R*, have been extremely influential in determining corporate accounting practices regarding stock options, and these accounting choices have had real economic effects.

APB 25 required firms to show the granting of ESOs as a business expense and stipulated that the expense should be recorded as the intrinsic value of the option—the excess of the firm's stock price over the exercise price of the option. As we saw in chapter 3, and as we explore more fully in this chapter, ESOs are typically much more valuable than their intrinsic value. In the ESO of figure 3.6, for example, the intrinsic value was zero, because the firm granted an option with an exercise price equal to the firm's existing stock price. However, the computed economic value was $21.44. This is a representative differential between the true value of an ESO and the ESO's intrinsic value. With APB 25 in place, firms could issue these valuable ESOs and would not need to show any associated expense in their accounting statements. Under the directive of APB 25, it was the nearly universal practice of firms to issues ESOs with an exercise price equal to the firm's current stock price and to show no expense in the firm's income statement.

Clearly, ESOs can constitute an important portion of executive compensation. As demonstrated, in some years the economic value of ESOs made up more than half of total executive compensation. In economic terms, showing no expense for the issuance of ESOs is analogous to not showing wages as an expense to the firm. The dictates of APB 25 had two important associated incentive effects. First, paying executives with ESOs granted with an exercise price equal to the firm's current stock price buoyed firm's reported earnings because the reporting left out some of the firm's true employee-compensation expense. Second, APB 25's accounting practice reduced the apparent level of executive-compensation cost. This practice relates to the managerial power hypothesis and its claim of the importance of stealth compensation. If firms seek to pay executives through less than transparent means, the accounting mandates of APB 25 provided a potent vehicle for paying stealthy compensation.

FAS 123 aimed at correcting the problems of APB 25, but it proved to be a half measure at best. It featured two key measures related to accounting for ESOs: a recommendation and a requirement. *FAS 123* recommended that firms treat the value of ESO grants as an expense, and that they reflect that expense in the firm's income statements. *FAS 123* required that firms disclose the value of the options that they granted, but the rule allowed firms to present that value in the notes to financial statements. According to many, this treatment made the grants much less salient and less visible to the firm's shareholders and to the investment community as a whole. After examining the choices presented by *FAS 123*, almost all firms continued to prepare their income statements under APB 25.[1] That is, they continued to issue ESOs with a strike price equal to the current stock price, and they used a zero option-value in their formal income statements. In requiring firms to disclose the value of the options—in the notes to the financial statements at least—*FAS 123* offered some guidance about how that fair value was to be computed:

> This Statement requires a public entity to estimate the fair value of an employee stock option using a pricing model that takes into account the exercise price and expected life of the option, the current price of the underlying stock, its expected volatility, the expected dividends on the stock, and the current risk-free interest rate for the expected life of the option.[2]

To many, *FAS 123* was inherently unsatisfying, and it embodies a clear intellectual inconsistency. If the economic value of the option that is granted to an executive can be measured, and the firm gives that option to an executive, then accurate financial statements should reflect that conveyance of value. Instead, the outcome of *FAS 123*—firms identifying the value of the options they grant but only in the footnotes, while continuing to present income statements that imply that the options are costless—was clearly the result of a political process rather than the outcome of disinterested reason.

In the years after the issuance of *FAS 123*, controversy over the issue raged, with a hefty number of academic studies and industry analyses devoted to the topic.[3] Much of the controversy was resolved with *FAS 123R* in 2004. The new rule required that firms estimate the economic value of ESOs and recognize this cost in their income statement by amortizing it over the period of service associated with the option grant, which is usually the vesting period.

Because the value of an ESO depends so clearly on the key factors that *FAS 123* correctly identified (expressed in the earlier quotation), it raises two sets of incentives, one for the issuing firm and one for the receiving manager of the option. From the firm's point of view, there may well be an incentive to estimate the option parameters in a way that reduces the reported value of the option the firm is granting. For example, estimating a short expected life for the option or estimating a low volatility for prices of the firm's share will reduce the estimated cost of the option. In simplest terms, a firm that wants to minimize the impact of ESOs on reported earnings has an incentive to provide low estimates of ESO values. The executive who receives an ESO grant has incentives to increase the economic value of her options by changing the way the firm operates. After all, the CEO holds the levers of firm power and can initiate financing and investing policies that boost the options' value. To understand the incentives of both firms and their executives with respect to these option factors, we need to consider option pricing in more detail. The next section provides a nontechnical introduction to option pricing, after which we return to examining the behavior of firms when shaping their option grants. Subsequent chapters are mostly devoted to examining how executives respond to their incentives when shaping the operating policies of their firms.

Option Pricing Models

There are two basic kinds of option models: analytical models represented most notably by the famous Black-Scholes-Merton (BSM) model, and lattice or binomial models in which one uses dynamic programming to find the value of the option. Models from the two families calculate the same option prices because of the same underlying assumptions about the terms of the options (except for some minor discrepancies due to technicalities that need not concern us here).[4]

FAS 123 and *FAS 123R* recognized the existence of these two families of pricing models when it allowed firms to use one of the two different approaches—a variant of the Black-Scholes-Merton (BSM) option pricing model or a lattice model. Most firms use a model based on the BSM approach; only about 10 percent choose a binomial model.[5] However, most economists agree that a lattice approach offers a better way of assessing the complexity of ESOs.

The BSM model and the binomial model require the same key inputs: the stock price prevailing at the time the value is computed, the exercise price of the option, the volatility of the underlying stock, the risk-free rate of interest, and an estimated dividend rate. In addition, every model faces uncertainty about how long the option will last before it terminates due to exercise or the departure of the owner from the firm.

As originally developed, the BSM model applied to plain vanilla options, which have a known and certain expiration date. At the time it is issued, the termination date of an ESO is unknown. The actual life of an ESO depends on the vesting period, whether the recipient leaves the firm before or after vesting, or the possibility that the option recipient will choose to exercise the option before its expiration date.

The uncertain life of the option presents a problem for both the BSM and binomial models. However, the BSM model applies, strictly speaking, to only European options—those that can be exercised only at expiration. European options contrast most clearly with American options—those that can be exercised at any time at the owner's discretion. However, ESOs are technically not American options either because they can be exercised only after they vest, and they must be exercised before expiration if owner of the options departs the firm.

As we saw in chapter 3, one way of using the BSM model to estimate values of ESOs is to adjust the input for the time to expiration by selecting the expected life of the option as an input variable instead of the time to expiration as contemplated by the model's developers. In the context of lattice models, a similar adjustment occurs by estimating the probability that the owner of the option exits the firm in a given period. For example, an executive who is starting her career might move from firm to firm until she becomes established in a senior position. On reaching a secure position in the prime of her career, it is likely that she will remain with her firm for a considerable horizon. As an executive approaches retirement, each year, the probability of leaving the firm usually becomes higher. There are numerous other personal considerations that can affect how likely an executive is to leave the firm, including her health, wealth, and so on. The great advantage of lattice models is that they are sufficiently flexible to handle these considerations.

Option Valuation Effects of Individual Option Parameters

To illustrate how the various factors that affect the price of options tie in with incentives, this section uses the results of a lattice model to compute representative ESO values for varying input parameters. The model uses a lattice with 500 periods. That is, the life of the option is divided into 500 equal time-units.

For each year, the model takes as an input the probability that the executive will depart the firm in a given period. To keep things fairly simple, we will consider an example in which the probability of the executive departing the firm in each period is constant, and we will measure this as the probability of departure in each year. In addition, the model takes account of the vesting restriction and computes the price of the option under the assumption that the option cannot be exercised until it vests. (See the appendix for more technical detail on the model.)

Aside from the peculiarities of ESOs, there are six parameters that affect the value of an option, each with positive or negative influences on the price, as shown in table 4.1.

The price of an ESO always changes in accordance with the table, but the option value is more sensitive to some of these parameters than to others. Also, even when we focus on how a single parameter affects the price of the option, the option price can be more or less sensitive to the same change in the parameter depending on the other factors as well. Therefore, the best way to explore the effect of these parameters and the incentives they create is to consider an example in some detail.

We will now define a "base-case" ESO to price using the binomial model and to serve as a reference as we explore the effect of changes in these input factors on the value of the ESO. To maintain a parallel with our example of the BSM model in chapter 3, we focus on an ESO issued when the firm's stock

TABLE 4.1   Option Input Parameters and Their Influence on ESO Values

Input Parameter Increase	Effect on ESO Value
Stock Price	+
Exercise Price	-
Time until Expiration	+
Volatility of the Share Price	+
Risk-free Rate	+
Dividend Rate on the Stock	-
SPECIAL ESO PARAMETERS AND THEIR INFLUENCE ON ESO VALUES	
Vesting period	-
Chance of departure	-

price is $50. In accordance with the prevailing custom of issuing ESOs with exercise prices equal to the current stock price in order to avoid showing an ESO-related expense, we assume that the exercise price is also $50. We also assume that the stock's volatility is 40 percent per year, that the risk-free rate of interest is 5 percent per year, and that the firm pays a dividend at a rate equal to 2 percent of the share's value in each year. As input parameters that are peculiar to ESOs, we use a base-case vesting period of four years, and we assume that the executive has a constant chance of departure of 7 percent each year. Under these assumptions, the ESO will have a value of $16.85. This "base-case" ESO is constructed to have parameters and characteristics that are fairly representative for most ESOs issued by major firms.

Table 4.2 summarizes this base-case information and shows these input parameters as the center column. For our analysis, we consider single departures from the base-case for each input parameters. However, we assume that the time until expiration of 10 years remains constant. Panel 1 of table 4.2 focuses on a change in the stock price. If the stock price falls from $50 to $40, the value of the option declines dramatically. With other base-case parameters held constant, but with a $40 stock price, the value of the option falls from $16.85 to $11.82, a decrease of 29.9 percent. Similarly, if the stock price rises to $60, the option price jumps to $22.26, for a 32.1 percent increase. Thus the option price elastically responds to changes in the stock price: a 20 percent stock price fall causes a 29.9 percent option price fall, and a 20 percent stock price increase causes a 32.1 percent option price increase.

Panel 2 of table 4.2 considers the effect of differing exercise prices on the value of the option. Once an option is granted, the exercise price cannot change. (However, the exercise price can be *misrepresented*, a practice in ESOs that has been amazingly widespread as we explore in chapter 8.) Also, the firm can cancel an existing ESO, with the ESO owner's consent, and replace it with an otherwise similar option that has a different exercise price. This is called *restriking* or *repricing* (addressed later in this chapter). If the exercise price of

TABLE 4.2 Base-Case ESO and the Influence of Changes in Input Parameters

Decline to	Base-Case Values	Increase to
Panel 1		
$40	**Stock Price = $50**	$60
Resulting Price: $11.82		Resulting Price: $22.26
−29.9%		+32.1%
Panel 2		
$30	**Exercise Price = $50**	$70
Resulting Price: $21.50		Resulting Price: $13.73
+27.6%		−18.5%
Panel 3		
0.20	**Stock Volatility = 0.40**	0.60
Resulting Price: $10.84		Resulting Price: $22.17
−35.7%		+31.6%
Panel 4		
2.0 years	**Vesting Period = 4.0**	6.0 years
Resulting Price: $18.49		Resulting Price: $14.99
+9.7%		−11.0%
Panel 5		
No dividend	**Annual Dividend Rate = 2.0%**	4.0%
Resulting Price: $21.34		Resulting Price: $13.82
+26.7%		−18.0%
Panel 6		
5.0%	**Chance of Departure = 7.0%**	10.0%
Resulting Price: $18.50		Resulting Price: $14.67
+9.8%		−12.9%

Base-Case Option Value = $16.85.

Values for Base-Case Option Variables: Stock price = $50; Exercise Price = $50; Time until Expiration = 10 Years; Vesting Period = 4 years; Stock Volatility = 0.40; Risk-free Rate of Interest = 5.0%; Annual Dividend Rate = 2.0%; Chance of Departure Per Year = 7.0%

this option were $20 lower, at $30 instead of the original $50, the ESO would be worth $21.50 rather than $16.85, an increase of 27.6 percent. By contrast, if the exercise price were higher, say $70, the resulting option price would be lower, at $13.73, a decrease of 18.5 percent. These changes in the exercise price are twice as large as the stock price changes that we considered in the first column, but the change in the option prices is about the same in percentage terms. Thus, the price of this example option is much more sensitive to a change in the stock price than it is to a change in the exercise price.

The third panel of table 4.2 shows the effect of changing stock price volatility on the value of the option. A decrease in volatility leads to an option price decrease, and a higher volatility results in an option of greater value. This may seem counterintuitive, but a call option effectively includes an "insurance policy" against a falling stock price. A call option allows the owner to participate in stock price increases, but limits losses from a falling stock price to the value of the option, rather than the entire amount of the fall in the stock price. If the volatility of the stock price falls from the base-case value of 40 percent to 20 percent, the option price falls from $16.85 to $10.84, a loss of 35.7 percent. If the volatility of the stock price increases from 40 to 60 percent, the option value goes up by 31.6 percent to $22.17.

A key feature of ESOs is the vesting period, which prohibits exercise until the vesting date. If the holder of the ESO leaves the firm before the vesting date, her ESO expires as worthless. As a consequence, the longer the vesting period, the lower the value of the ESO. If the vesting period were two years instead of four years, the value of the ESO would be $18.49, instead of the base-case value of $16.85, an increased price of 9.7 percent, as shown in panel 4 of table 4.2. Alternatively, if the option were granted with a six-year vesting period, the price of the option would be $14.99 or 11.0 percent less than the base-case price. The longer the vesting period, the greater the chance that the executive will depart the firm before the option vests. If that occurs, the executive cannot exercise her ESO, and she receives nothing for it.

For a plain vanilla option on a stock with no dividend, it is never optimal to exercise before the expiration date. However, if the option is written on a dividend-paying stock, it can be optimal to exercise the option and capture its intrinsic value before the expiration date. Thus a plain vanilla European and American option on a no-dividend stock will have the same value, but for otherwise similar options on a dividend-paying stock, the American option can have a higher price.

Panel 5 of table 4.2 shows the effect of the annual dividend rate on the price of the option. If all the characteristics of the base-case option remain constant, except the firm eliminates the dividend, the ESO price jumps from $16.85 to $21.34, a dramatic price increase of 26.7 percent from this factor alone.[6] If the dividend rate were 4 percent instead of 2 percent, the option price would be $13.82, for a loss of 18.0 percent. Thus, the amount of the dividend can be a significant factor in determining the value of the option. We can think of the dividend as a "leakage" of value from the price of the stock. Other factors being equal, paying a dividend of 2 percent, as in the base case, will cause a fall of 2 percent in the stock price. As this is repeated year after year over the life of the option, these dividend payments reduce the stock's ultimate terminal price when the exercise occurs. This reduces the exercise value from where it would otherwise have been—or the option could finish out-of-the-money and expire as worthless.

In table 4.2, panel 6 shows the effect of the probability of departure on the value of the option. If the executive owning the ESO departs before the vesting date, she is prohibited from exercising and must sacrifice the option as worthless. If she vests and then leaves the firm before the option's expiration date, she must exercise if the option is in-the-money, or allow the option to expire worthless at that time if it is out-of-the-money. Thus, the higher the chance of departure, the lower the value of the ESO. If the chance of departure is 10 percent instead of the base-case 7 percent, then the value of the ESO is $14.67, rather than the base-case value of $16.85, a reduction of 12.9 percent. However, if the chance of departure is only 5 percent, the value of the option is $18.5, a 9.8 percent increase over the base-case value.

The chance of departure affects the price of the ESO by interacting with the vesting period and the dividend rate. If the chance of departure is high and the vesting period is long, then the two operate together to seriously reduce the value of the option compared with what it would be otherwise. After the option vests, the ESO is akin to an American option—the only difference for a vested ESO is the requirement that the option be exercised or forfeited upon departure. If the firm pays no dividend, then it would be optimal to delay exercise until the expiration date—a forced exercise before then could be costly. By contrast, if the dividend rate is high, then the forced exercise at the executive's departure will be less costly.

The Option Pricing Model and Incentives

We have seen, in the previous section, how changes in individual option parameters can have a large impact on the value of an ESO. In this section, we consider the effect of those option parameters when several change concurrently and the overall incentives that these option features imply for both the firm's reporting choices and the prospective management decisions of executives.

Table 4.3 shows the pricing effect for the base-case option, plus four different pricing scenarios. Of these scenarios, two are oriented toward the preferences of the firm, while two reflect the perspective of the option recipient. Four factors are held constant from the base case: the stock price of $50, the exercise price of $50, the time until expiration of 10 years, and the risk-free interest of 5 percent. The stock volatility, vesting period, dividend rate, and the executive's chance of departure are allowed to vary to create the different scenarios.

These different scenarios are labeled according to the perspective of the firm and the executive. Before turning to those different points of view, consider first the joint-valuation effects of these changes in parameters. In the Firm's Hope column of table 4.3 a slight reduction in volatility and a small increase in the estimated chance of departure for the executive, coupled with a small increase in the dividend rate results in a substantial 22.1 percent drop in the value of the option from $16.85 to $13.13. The more ambitious Firm's Ideal column moves those same variables even more in the direction favorable for the firm, reducing the price of the option to $10.49, a 37.7 percent drop

TABLE 4.3 Effect of Multiple Parameter Changes on the Price of an ESO

Option Parameter	Firm's Ideal	Firm's Hope	Base-Case	CEO's Hope	CEO's Ideal
Stock Volatility	0.30	0.35	0.40	0.50	0.60
Vesting Period	4.0 years	4.0 years	4.0 years	3.0 years	2.0 years
Annual Dividend Rate	3.5%	3.0%	2.0%	1.0%	0.0%
Chance of Departure	9.0%	8.0%	7.0%	5.0%	2.0%
Resulting ESO Price	$10.49	$13.13	$16.85	$24.49	$34.33
Percentage Change	−37.7%	−22.1%	N/A	+45.3%	+103.7%

Constants: Stock Price = $50; Exercise Price = $50; Time until Expiration = 10 years; Risk-free Rate = 5.0%

from the base-case value. Changing these same variables in the other direction (that is, increasing the volatility, shortening the vesting period, dividend rate, and chance of departure) results in a large increase in the value of the option. A modest change in these variables, as shown in the CEO's Hope column gives an increased option price of 45.3 percent, while the more ambitious changes chronicled in the CEO's Ideal column, give an option value of $34.33, an increase in value of 103.7 percent over the base-case option.

Of course, these parameter variables cannot be changed willy-nilly—they are tied to an underlying economic reality. However, the firm can report something different than reality, and the CEO can act to alter the reality of the firm's operations. Let us assume that a firm issues an option with the economic reality described by the base case, so the option it issues is actually worth $16.85. Now consider a firm that wants to reduce the reported costs of its option grants. Under APB 25, there was no requirement to report a value. But *FAS 123* required a disclosure in the notes to financial statements, and *FAS 123R* requires reporting that actual affects the firm's disclosed net income. The firm might be tempted to fudge the reporting to make the report more favorable than the economic reality. The motivation might be wanting earnings to look as good as possible. Also, if the managerial power hypothesis is correct, the fudged reporting might be an attempt to disguise the stealth compensation it is granting to its CEO.

The parameters we have held constant are visible to others, so the reporting of these needs to match reality. (We will see that this is not necessarily true for the exercise price, however, when we discuss the practice of "backdating" options in chapter 8.) In preparing its financial statement, the firm must estimate the volatility of the stock, the dividend rate over the life of the option, and the executive's chance of departure. A firm desiring to minimize the impact of the option grant on the firm's finances has a clear incentive to provide a favorably skewed estimate of these variables. So consider the impact of a firm that issues an option consistent with our base case, but that provides estimates of those variables shown in the Firm's Hope column of table 4.3. That is, the firm's best genuine forecast is consistent with the base case, but it chooses to use modestly more favorable estimates for its reporting requirements. Specifically, the firm reports a volatility of 0.35 instead of 0.40, an annual dividend rate of 3 percent instead of 2 percent, and a chance of departure for the executive of 8 percent rather than 7 percent. Based on those estimated parameters and the other values of table 4.3, the resulting option price is $13.13, which is 22.1 percent less than the $16.85 value of the "base-case" option. In this scenario, the firm reduces its reported grant cost by $3.72 per option. If the firm is truly ambitious, it might report those values listed under the Firm's Ideal column, with a resulting option price of $10.49, resulting in a reported cost of options that is 37.7 percent less than reality. Thus, table 4.3 shows that fairly small changes in the actual parameter values of options can have a large joint effect on the actual value of the option, while a falsified report of those parameters can have the same large effect on what the firm reports.

The CEO receives an option grant from the firm with certain characteristics. Let us continue to assume that the base case accurately characterizes the option that the CEO receives. The CEO cannot change the variables that we held constant in table 4.3: the stock price at the time of the grant, the exercise price (more on this in chapter 8), the time until the option expires, or the risk-free rate.

However, other parameters are under the influence or even control of the CEO. First, there is the future stock price. If the CEO acts as a good corporate steward, then she may be able to increase the stock price to the benefit of the firm as well as to her own ESO-based wealth. Table 4.2 showed that an increase of the stock price from $50 to $60 would, by itself, increase the value of the option by more than 30 percent. Second, we have seen that part of the revolution in executive compensation that began around 1990 and moved the mix of compensation toward equity-based pay was largely stimulated by an explicit desire to induce managers to undertake more risky value-creating projects. From this perspective, the CEO has marching orders to undertake riskier projects and doing so is in her financial interest. Increasing the volatility of the firm's stock price will boost the value of the ESO whether the increase in volatility is associated with good or poor risky projects. So the CEO with an option grant has a clear incentive to increase the risk of the firm, even if good risky projects are unavailable.

As a third factor, although the CEO seldom has absolute control over the dividend policy of the firm, she usually has some influence over the dividend decision. With a large option grant in hand, the CEO has a clear incentive to steer the firm toward reducing the growth in dividends or even in substituting a policy of share repurchases as a replacement for dividends. Either approach will both stop the leakage of value from the stock that dividends represent and have a beneficial effect on the CEO's option position. Fourth, there is the CEO's chance of departure. Every employee in good standing has control over when she leaves the firm. Ironically, one of the key motivations for granting ESOs with a vesting period is to retain executives. The CEO who receives an ESO grant has a new reason to stay with the firm, thereby reducing her chance of departure. Further, CEOs often become entrenched. That is, their position becomes so secure that there is little encouragement or motivation for them to depart the firm.

As a fifth and final factor, there is the vesting period to consider. The firm grants an ESO with a specified vesting period. However, the firm can reduce or eliminate that vesting requirement if it chooses.[7] If the CEO can induce the board to accelerate the vesting of her options, she can capture additional value from them. (A firm accelerates vesting by allowing them to be regarded as vested earlier than the vesting requirement specified in the original option grant.) As we will see in subsequent chapters, there is considerable evidence regarding how CEOs actually respond to these incentives in managing their firms.

The last two columns of table 4.3 show the effect of joint changes in these variables on the value of the ESO from the CEO's perspective. As the CEO's Hope column shows, if the CEO can modestly increase the stock volatility from 0.40 to 0.50, reduce the vesting period from four to three years, reduce the dividend rate from 2 to 1 percent, and change her probability of departure from 7 to 5 percent per year, the option increases from the base-case value to $24.49, a gain of 45.3 percent. If the CEO acts more ambitiously as the CEO's Ideal column shows, the option value jumps from $16.85 to $34.33, a gain of 103.7 percent. With typical option grants near the 300,000 per-year level, only a CEO of the highest moral rectitude could ignore the effect of her managerial behavior on the value of her own portfolio, especially as so many policies also desired by the firm contribute to her further substantial enrichment.

Executive Stock Option Design, Management, and Incentives

Almost all ESOs are granted with an exercise price that equals the current stock price. This is mainly due to an idiosyncratic provision of APB 25 and *FAS 123*—that the issuance of such options requires no impact of the firm's income statement. That practice changed, of course, with *FAS 123R*, but the tradition of granting ESOs with exercise prices equal to the current stock price still continues. There are many other ways the option portion of compensation could be constructed. One widely popular idea is that ESOs should have an exercise price that rises over the life of the option. For example, the exercise price could be set initially at the current stock price and then be allowed to rise in tandem with general returns on the stock market or at a rate approximating the firm's cost of capital. Such an option is an *indexed option*, because the exercise price is indexed to some other observable variable. Indexed options potentially filter out increases in the general level of the firm's stock price that are not really due to the CEO's effort but that occur when the rising tide of the equity market lifts all boats, including the shares of firms managed by able or incompetent CEOs.[8]

To further see the attraction of the idea, recall the bonus contract for Ralston Purina discussed in chapter 3. This contract paid a fat bonus for executives even if the firm underperformed the market as a whole and earned less than its cost of capital, thereby destroying firm value. To many it seems reasonable to create an incentive package in the form of ESOs that pays off little or nothing for a mediocre performance but that provides ample rewards for a truly exemplary job performance.

For example, consider our base-case ESO, with a value of $16.85 per option at the time of the grant. Assume that the issuing firm has an 11 percent cost of equity capital and the stock price goes up at exactly that rate for five years. At this point, the stock price will be $84.25 and the base-case option will be fully vested. An option with the exercise price indexed to the 11 percent cost of capital would be just at-the-money. It would still be quite valuable, worth $24.24 per option, but it would not be exercisable as it would have no intrinsic value.

If the same firm issued our base-case ESO—that is, the base-case option with no indexing—the option would already be vested and exercisable immediately, and the executive could realize $34.25 in cash for each option. Because the option has five remaining years until expiration and there is still plenty of time for the stock price to rise, the base-case option value at this point— with five years remaining until expiration—is $42.63. Typical option grants are sized at 300,000 options in a given year (see figure 3.8)—this is generous compensation for an average job of stewardship, or at least it has seemed so to many. Others, however, point out that an option grant has at least two components, an incentive component and a compensation component. To those with only an external view of the firm, disentangling the compensation and incentive components is difficult or impossible. Further, it is not even clear that the board itself generally thinks of a specified portion of the option grant being a kind of compensation, with the remainder being an incentive.

Figure 4.1 shows how the prices of three options vary with the stock price. One is our base-case options with a constant exercise price of $50, while the others have the same features as the base-case option, except that one is indexed at a rate of 5 percent, while the other is indexed at 11 percent. The graph illustrates that the three options are similar in the way their prices respond to a change in the stock price, although the indexed options are worth considerably less. (With the assumed stock price of $50 at the time of issue, the base-case option is worth $16.85; the option with an 11 percent index rate has a value of $9.91; and the option with a 5 percent index rate is worth $13.51.) One note is of some importance however. Figure 4.1 shows how the

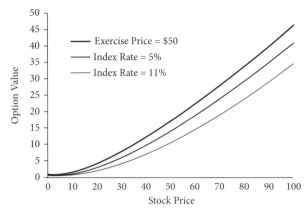

FIGURE 4.1 *Comparison of Indexed and Nonindexed Option Values (in dollars).*

Source: Graph by author.

price of the option varies for different stock prices, all measured at the time of issuance. As time passes, each option's characteristics will change as the vesting date nears, as the executive goes for a longer period without departing the firm, and as the stock price changes. In their study, Johnson and Tian point out that as the firm becomes takes on more risks, an indexed option has lower incentives to increase risk that may already be too high, so that may prove to be a beneficial incentive effect, especially in the view of those who consider firms as already too aggressive in taking risk.[9]

There are other kinds of specialized options with different risk, return, and incentive profiles. For example, a reload option allows the executive to exercise an existing ESO by paying the strike price with shares the executive already owns. The firm then issues new options to replace (reload) the options that were just exercised. This allows the holder of the reload option to lock in the benefits of any price rise. While there are many other complex options that may have beneficial features, they are seldom if ever used, and there is controversy over their reputed benefits in any case.[10]

What Exercise Price?

We noted that it has been the almost universal practice for firms to issue ESOs with an exercise price set equal to the stock price at the time of issuance, and that this practice was driven in large part by the features of the accounting regimes APB 25 and *FAS 123*, which held sway for many years. (Both allowed the firm to show no option-related compensation expense in their income statements if they issued options with exercise prices equal to the stock price at the time the option was issued. However, *FAS 123* required firms to disclose the value of those options in the footnotes to the financial statements.) With the new accounting regime of *FAS 123R*, which requires that firms show option-related compensation expenses in their income statement, there is no particular accounting reason why firms should necessarily issue at-the-money options, although they continue to do so.

The firm could issue options with an exercise price below, at, or above the current stock price. Such options would be in-the-money, at-the-money, or out-of-the-money, respectively. Let us consider again our base-case options, with an exercise price of $50 issued when the stock price is also $50. We have seen that this option will have a value of $16.85. The firm might have preferred to issue an option that was in-the-money, say with an exercise price of $30, with other features of the option held constant. Alternatively, it could have issued the base-case option, except with an exercise price of $70, so the option is out-of-the-money. These three options have very different values due solely to the difference in exercise prices. The base-case option, with an exercise price of $50 is worth $16.85, but the option with an exercise price of $70 is worth only $13.73, and the option with an exercise price of $30 is worth $21.50, all measured when they are issued and assuming the stock is trading for $50.

Let us assume that the firm decides to make an option grant worth $3 million and it is considering which of these three options to issue. To make the grant worth $3 million for each option, it will have to grant differing numbers of options in each case. If the exercise price is $30, $50, or $70, a grant worth $3 million at the time of issuance will consists of 139,535, 178,042, or 218,500 options, respectively.[11] Figure 4.2 shows that these three grants are all worth $3 million when the stock price is $50, but the values diverge when

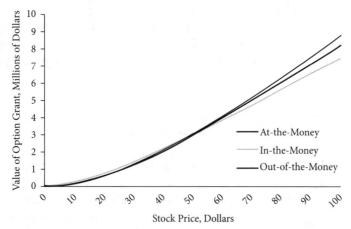

FIGURE 4.2   *Value of $3 Million Option Grants as a Function of the Stock Price.*

Source: Graph by author.

TABLE 4.4   Sensitivity of Option Grant Values to Changing Stock Prices (initial value of each grant: $3,000,000)

Exercise Price	Option Value	Number of Options Granted	Dollar Effect of a 1% Increase in Stock Price Measured at:		
			$30	$50	$70
$30	$21.50	139,535	$22,326	$41,861	$62,791
$50	$16.85	178,042	$21,365	$48,071	$72,997
$70	$13.73	218,500	$24,035	$50,255	$80,845

the stock price moves away from $50. For higher stock prices, the out-of-the money grant is worth more, but for stock prices below $50, the in-the-money grant is more valuable, with the at-the-money grant always occupying the middle ground.

The graph shows this divergence, but it appears modest. Table 4.4 summarizes the situation and shows how the value of the three grants change in dollar value for a 1 percent increase in the stock price measured at $30, $50, and $70—this is essentially showing the elasticity of the option grant values with respect to changes in the stock price. The dollar change in the value of the grants can be radically different depending on the level of the stock price when the 1 percent increase in stock value occurs, ranging from $21,365 to $80,845. However, the results of table 4.4 confirm the initial impression of the graph in figure 4.2—the values of the three grants behave similarly when evaluated under the same circumstances.[12]

Repricing and Reloading Executive Stock Options

Of all the features of executive compensation that annoy the general public, the repricing features of ESOs must surely be near the top of the list, at least for those who have heard of the practice. Repricing an ESO occurs when the firm's stock price has fallen below—usually significantly below—the stock price that prevailed at the time the option was granted. To reprice the option, the firm cancels the existing option and replaces it in the executive's portfolio with a new option that is similar, except that the new option has a strike price that equals the now-prevailing lower stock price.

Consider our base-case option issued when the stock price was $50 and with an exercise price of $50. Assume that the stock price immediately falls to $30. With a stock price of $30, the base-case option has fallen in value from $16.85 to $7.30, a loss of more than 50 percent. If the firm decides to reprice the option, the executive effectively surrenders the base-case option and receives in its place a new option with an exercise price matching the current stock price of $30, an option which would be worth $10.11, assuming it was issued with a 10-year expiration. This is a windfall for the executive, equal to the difference between the new option received less the option surrendered, or \$2.81 for each option.

What offends many is that the executive, who received the initial option grant when the firm's stock price was \$50, has led the company to a \$30 stock price, and for that "effort" receives a windfall from the option repricing. To many, this is clear evidence that there is little accountability for executive performance and even a negative relationship between pay and performance. If this is not a clear reward for failure, then what is?

When the stock price falls below the level at which options were granted, the first question the firm must face is whether to fire the executive. This decision would rationally turn on the extent to which the board judges the fall in stock price to be due to the CEO's stewardship. For example, if the CEO has strongly urged the introduction of a risky new product line with a high investment cost and that new product fails, then the firm might well decide that it is time for new leadership. Alternatively, if the firm's stock has dropped along with a massively falling tide of stock prices, as in the financial crisis of 2007–2009, then the board might judge that the decline in stock price was not really the CEO's fault, and the board may still have confidence in her leadership ability.

Firms sometimes offer such an account as a justification for their repricing policy. For example, the HealthSouth Corporation proxy statement of October 28, 1994 includes the following passage:

> The Board of Directors has determined from time to time that it is desirable to reprice certain outstanding options to bring their exercise prices into line with the then-current market price of the Company's Common Stock. Typically, this has occurred when market conditions have, in the view of the Board of Directors, artificially depressed the market price of the Common Stock for a protracted period, so that outstanding options are significantly out-of-the-money for reasons not related to the Company's performance.[13]

If the board decides to retain the executive, whether wisely or foolishly, it faces a new compensation challenge. If the CEO is capable, as the board has judged by deciding to retain her, she may have an opportunity to move to another firm. One function of granting long-term ESOs is to bind executives to the firm—to encourage them to remain until the options vest and pay off through exercise. If the current stock price is now well below the exercise price of the CEO's options, those options provide little incentive for the executive to stay with the firm and hope that the stock price eventually recovers. In the market for CEO services, it would not be unusual for another firm to offer the executive a value replacement for her existing option package. With the ESOs well "underwater"—the stock price below the exercise price, or out-of-the-money—the hurdle for attracting the executive to the new firm is low, and the power of the existing option package to retain the CEO at the first firm is weak.

As a second consideration, if the options are far out-of-the-money, there is a reduced chance of the stock price ever exceeding the original exercise price, and a correspondingly reduced chance that the options will deliver a cash payoff to the CEO holding those options. A dim chance of a payoff on the options is a poor incentive to stay with the firm. If the incentive story of equity compensation has merit, then the need to restore incentives provides a logical rationale for a repricing.

These two grounds for repricing options—incentivizing retention and incentivizing future performance—are often brought forward by firms to justify their actions. Consider the option repricing granted to the founder and CEO of Comverse Technology, Inc., Jacob Alexander. In December of 2002, Alexander surrendered 2.3 million ESOs, with various exercise prices, some as high as $85. At that time, Comverse was trading for $10.52 per share. The board then issued 1.9 million shares with a strike price of $10.52, the current stock price. The compensation committee of the board explained its action by saying that it had implemented the repricing "because the compensation committee has determined that the exercise prices of the canceled incentive stock options limited their effectiveness as a tool for employee retention and as a long-term incentive."

Graef Crystal, the famed CEO-compensation consultant opined on that it was a "deft maneuver" that "transformed what would have been a paper loss of $58 million into a paper profit of $13 million." He further noted, "If you have an $85 strike price and the current [stock] price is just $10.52, I suppose it is fair to say that particular option doesn't offer much in the way of either a retention incentive or a long-term incentive."[14]

Even if option repricing can be justified in some cases, the public does not understand or accept the rationale. As a result, some firms have abandoned their prior policy of option repricing. For example, about six months after justifying their option-repricing policy, HealthSouth created a new compensation plan, a feature of which prohibited any repricing:

> The 1995 Plan prohibits any reduction of the exercise price of outstanding options granted under the plan except by reason of merger, business combination, recapitalization or similar change in the capitalization of the Company. The 1995 Plan likewise prohibits the cancellation of outstanding options accompanied by the reissuance of substitute options at a lower exercise price.[15]

The practice of repricing options has never been particularly widespread. One might even say that option repricing has become as rare as it is abhorred. While repricing was a common practice in the 1970s and following the market crash of 1987, it has faded from view. The Securities Exchange Commission required detailed disclosure in 1993 and the Financial Accounting Standards Board "imposed punitive new accounting rules" for option repricings in 1998.[16] Previously, option repricings had been fairly common, say 4 percent of companies in the S&P 1500 repricing each year. But by 2001 this practice had faded—less than half of 1 percent of firms were repricing. The same was true of smaller firms outside of the S&P 1500.[17]

Is prohibiting option repricing a wise policy? There is a tremendous volume of research on this practice.[18] On the whole, the research supports the view of option repricing as having a rationale of retaining mobile executives and of restoring diminished incentives. However, repricings do appear to occur more in firms with weaker governance, suggesting that the ultimate motivation for the repricing is the simple conveyance of additional compensation to the executive, consistent with the managerial power hypothesis.

As a final and important dimension, firms that have abandoned repricing appear to have often found surrogates for the practice. Some firms merely issue higher levels of new at-the-money options, leaving the old out-of-the-money options in the hands of executives.[19] This can grant the same retention and performance incentives as a repricing, and it can also be a way of increasing compensation. Other firms issue additional restricted stock after large stock price drops drive existing options out-of-the-money.

The policy of repricing is bound to remain as controversial as the fundamental conflict over executive compensation and the battle between an agency-theoretic explanation or the managerial power alternative. Mark Chen summed up the question rather well after recounting some of these considerations: "Therefore, repricing policy is perhaps best understood not in simple terms applicable to all firms, but rather in terms of individual firms' incentive systems, governance structures, and operating environments."[20]

We close our examination of repricing by considering a somewhat ambiguous case that could be interpreted as an instance of executive aggrandizement or as a stroke of incentivizing genius. Apple Computer granted Steve Jobs options on 20 million shares in January 2000, at a strike price of $43.59. This was the largest option grant "made on a single day in the history of mankind," with an estimated value of $471 million.[21] Apple had tumbled, along with almost all other stocks, in the dotcom crash, and by October 19, 2001, Apple was trading at only $18.30. That day, Apple granted Jobs 7.5 million new ESOs with an exercise price of $18.30. By March 20, 2003, Apple was trading at $14.91. On that day, Apple extinguished Jobs's 27.5 million options in exchange for 5 million shares of Apple stock worth $74.6 million.

These brute facts are consistent with an account of Apple's wisely incentivizing the retention and future performance of a talented executive, but they point equally to a windfall for a failed executive. Perhaps the wisdom of Apple's move can only be assessed in light of Apple's subsequent success or failure. The 5 million shares worth $74.6 million that Jobs received in 2003 were worth $1.78 billion in mid-2011, and Apple was still writing one of the greatest corporate success stories in U.S. history, with Steve Jobs, one of the richest people in the world, still as CEO. (In the next few months, Apple became the most valuable corporation in the world, but then Steve Jobs resigned as CEO and died shortly thereafter in October 2011.)

The CEO's Utility and the Desire for ESOs

There is a great paradox surrounding executive stock options. We have seen that they are extremely valuable in many cases, and executives give every appearance of avidly pursuing ESO grants. If the managerial power hypothesis is correct, ESOs are one of the important ways that companies shovel stealth compensation into the pockets of their CEOs. Nonetheless, in most cases, stock options are not what CEOs desire.

Consider the typical CEO of an S&P 500 firm. Almost without exception, these individuals possess extraordinary wealth compared with almost all other members of society. Financial theory teaches us that risk-averse individuals should want to hold their assets in the market portfolio—that is, they want their assets diversified across the spectrum of assets in a society. The typical CEO may be rich, but she does not have the luxury of fully diversifying her portfolio. First, her employment is tied to her specific firm. Second, she will very often hold an extensive number of shares in her firm, sometimes in the form of restricted stock and sometimes in her personal portfolio. Third, firms that behave in a way that is consistent with the agency-theoretic approach to executive compensation seek to further tie her wealth to the fortunes of the firm by intensifying her investment in the firm by compensating her with ESOs.

Let us assume that an executive receives a typical option grant of $3 million, with the normal 10-year expiration and four-year vesting requirement. This $3 million value can be computed by using the Black-Scholes or binomial pricing approaches discussed earlier in this chapter. However, this $3 million valuation is for a future cash stream that is extremely risky and that the executive may never receive. Our intuition suggests, and much research confirms, that the typical executive would gladly sacrifice the $3 million option grant for an immediate cash payment of much less. The minimum certain and immediate payment that she would except in exchange for the option grant is called the grant's *certainty-equivalent*. Another way of putting the same point is to say that a certain cash value less than the computed $3 million value of the grant that is added to her holdings would leave her just as well off, or with the same utility, as the option grant itself. Thus, an ESO is an inefficient form of compensation—the cost to the firm of issuing the option ($3 million in our example) is greater than the value of the grant to the executive (the certainty-equivalent she would accept in place of the ESO grant).

Some critics of executive compensation note this admitted inefficiency of ESO compensation and take this inefficiency, coupled with the widespread use of ESOs as a form of compensation, as providing more evidence in support of the managerial power hypothesis. If firms were merely interested in acquiring CEO services with the lowest-cost pay package, they would pay in the cheapest way to get the executive they desired and would structure the pay package to have the absolute lowest cost—which almost certainly would not feature ESOs as a significant component. But, as seems always to be the case, there is another side to the story. Those who defend current equity compensation practices point out that there are two components to an ESO grant. First, an ESO plays the role of pure compensation. After all, the option grant really does have a significant value. Second, at least in theory, the option grant is designed to incentivize a certain behavior. If paying with an ESO elicits the desired behavior, the firm may be better off even when it pays its executives with inefficient compensation. From this perspective, the real question is whether the incentivized behavior will lead to an increase in firm value that more than fully offsets the inefficient form of compensation that the ESO grant represents.

These reflections also help to explain why executive compensation packages tend to be packages, that is, why they have so many different elements. If the only goal in constructing a pay package was to incentivize the recipients, then one might expect top managers to be paid only with equity. But there are various tradeoffs between the managers desire for consumption, desire to participate in the potential success of the firm, and an unwillingness to hold a completely undiversified personal portfolio.

Much economic thought exploits the concept of utility, but utility is ultimately only a conceptual construct or even a mere metaphor for what proves to be ultimately some immeasurable index of pleasure, well-being, satisfaction, or happiness. Economists have long acknowledged that there is no suitable measure of cardinal utility; that is, there is no numerical measure of utility that can be compared between individuals. For instance, we cannot say that person X is experiencing 110 "utils" while person Y is only at 100 "utils," and that person X is therefore 10 percent happier (more satisfied, better off, etc.) than person Y. In fact, interpersonal utility comparisons have proven to be essentially impossible. Instead, the best that seems possible are ordinal measures of utility for a single person, and these are usually expressed through preferences. Thus, an individual might be able to say whether she prefers one basket of goods to another, so the preferences are ordered, but they are not measured on an index or scale.

Nonetheless, even against this common background understanding of the conceptual limitations of utility, economists find it useful in many areas of their research to develop mathematical utility functions and apply them to their studies. That has certainly proven to be the case in the exploration of executive compensation. A good mathematical utility function should possess certain desirable properties. For example, if the utility function is expressed in terms of wealth, the function should be monotonic in wealth; that is, more wealth should always increase utility, never reach a maximum and then decline. Also, such a function should be consistent with diminishing marginal utility, reflecting the fact that increasing wealth from $19 billion to $20 billion does not increase utility as much as moving from bankruptcy to the first billion dollars of wealth. Finally, utility functions should reflect the risk aversion that economists believe to characterize most people.

In the field of executive-compensation research, the vast majority of economists choose to work with a power utility function that exhibits the desirable feature of constant relative risk aversion, reflecting a view that people generally gain more utility by avoiding a loss of a given magnitude than capturing a gain of the same amount. This function exhibits constant relative risk aversion, in which utility is a function of only two elements, wealth, W, and the degree of risk aversion, RA, such that:

$$U(W) = \frac{W^{1-RA}}{1-RA}$$

We can think of the CEO's wealth in this equation, the W, as itself being composed of two parts, a fixed portion and the executive's ESO grant. The fixed portion would be the wealth that the CEO holds outside the firm plus the value of the fixed portion of her compensation, such as salary.[22]

For our purposes, we can leave the mathematics of utility functions behind at this point. The important idea about utility functions is that much of the economic research about the behavior of executives with respect to risk taking and the way they value options relies on this kind of conceptual approach. Thus, the study of ESOs is very much organized around a framework that has the following features. First, the executive is presumed to act to maximize her personal utility, as opposed to being the selfless and perfect agent of the firm. This assumption reflects the dramatic agency problem that is presumed to be at the heart of the problem of executive compensation. Second, the executive is presumed to be risk averse. Third, the executive's utility is presumed to be a function of wealth, some of which is held outside the firm and some of which is subject to variability as the firm's fortunes rise and fall. Within this framework, economic theory finds that the risks the CEO will take with her firm varies with her degree of risk aversion, that CEOs with greater wealth will generally tend to be willing to take greater risks, that holdings of ESOs generally increase the CEO's willingness to take risk, and that very large holdings of restricted stock can lead executives to be unwilling to take risks. Much of the study within this framework has confirmed these broad conclusions.[23]

A number of studies use the utility framework just described and similar approaches to value ESOs with formal models.[24] Lisa Meulbroek, for example, finds that executives tend to value their ESOs from 30 to 50 percent less than the options would be worth if they were fully tradable.[25] Lambert, Larcker, and Verrecchia estimate that the value executives place on their options is lower than the value of a tradable option as well, with the executive sometimes placing only a very small value on the options, especially for a manager who has a high degree of risk aversion and a large percentage of personal wealth tied to the stock price of the firm. Kulatilaka and Marcus find that, using reasonable measures of executive wealth, option holdings, and risk aversion, the value of an ESO to an executive can be less than half an otherwise similar tradable option.[26] For their part, Hall and Murphy estimated that the executive values options at only about 50 percent of the cost incurred by the firm to issue them.[27]

These studies rely predominately on a framework exploiting a utility function designed to describe the tastes and preferences of managers. However, virtually all economists would acknowledge that no mathematical utility function accurately captures the tastes and preferences of a single individual, and even less does a utility function reflect the characteristics of a group of CEOs. Thus, it might be objected that this approach to ESOs inappropriately diminishes the true value of ESOs. However, we will see in the next chapter that real-world CEOs act in ways that demonstrate that they very often do not value their ESOs at anything approximating the value of the options would have if they were tradable.

Executive Stock Option Programs
THE BEHAVIOR OF CEOS, FIRMS, AND INVESTORS

CEO Wealth, Pay, and Performance

Perhaps the attack made by the managerial power hypothesis that resonates most forcefully with the public is the claim that CEO pay bears little relation to performance. After all, Bebchuk and Fried titled their book *Pay Without Performance: The Unfulfilled Promise of Executive Compensation.*[1] If we think of the various elements of a typical CEO's pay package—salary, annual bonus, pension holdings, restricted stock, ESOs, and long-term incentive plans—some of these elements vary directly with the fortunes of the firm's stock, while others do not. CEO salaries do not tend to fluctuate greatly year to year; this is similar to most salaries throughout the economy. Firms often link the CEO's annual bonus to accounting results, and it is quite possible for a firm to have good accounting results in a year of poor stock market performance. As a consequence, what the CEO realizes from a long-term incentive plan may not be well-aligned with the stock market results of her firm in a given year. In addition, the value of the CEO's pension promise is also relatively invariant with the firm's results. Sometimes total annual payments to the CEO may not be linked to the firm's current stock market performance—sometimes payments come due according to the terms of the plan even if the firm's shares are performing poorly.

Thus, it would seem that the major elements of the CEO pay package that are most likely to vary with the current year's stock market results are the value of the CEO's restricted stock and ESO holdings. The link between pay and stock market performance for these elements is somewhat difficult to measure. Obviously, the value of ESOs and restricted stock strongly vary with even day-to-day stock price movements. However, cash receipts by the CEO may not be so directly linked to contemporaneous stock price movements. If a CEO sells formerly restricted stock or exercises vested ESOs when the stock market is down, her receipts from these two sources may be high exactly when the stock market is performing poorly.[2]

On some occasions, the link between pay and performance tends to work according to the incentive alignment theory, and this seems to have been the case in 2010. The Hay Group-*Wall Street Journal* survey of pay for CEOs of 350 large firms in 2010 shows such a relationship. Figure 5.1 graphs the relationship between cash realized from CEOs' long-term incentive plans and the total percentage return to shareholders for the calendar years 2008–2010, with the firms categorized into three groups. The worst-performing third of firms netted shareholders a loss of 15 percent, while the CEOs of those firms realized \$2.055 million in cash on average. By contrast, the best-performing third of firms netted shareholders 9.4 percent over the three years, and the CEOs realized an average of \$6.259 million from their incentive plans. Thus, during this particular sample period, there was a strong relationship between this aspect of pay and the firm's stock market performance.

However, this is perhaps small comfort. First, even those firms that, on average, lost 15 percent over the three-year period, the CEOs still walked away with an average payout of more than \$2 million from their long-term incentive plans. Even the best-performing third of firms had nothing brilliant to report. These firms netted only 9.4 percent for shareholders over three years; although the years covered include the most dismal days of the financial crisis. For this ultimately poor performance, CEOs netted long-term bonuses of \$6.259 million in 2010. Thus, two contrary facts seem to be true: (1) CEOs have an incentive to boost returns for shareholders because they personally do better when shareholders prosper; and (2) CEOs seem to make out pretty well even when their shareholders incur large losses. Yet, the observation that CEOs appear to prosper under most circumstances does not speak to the incentives CEOs face. It can well be true that CEOs make plenty of money in almost all years, but it can also be true that they have

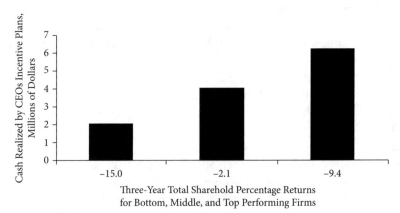

FIGURE 5.1 *Cash Realized by CEOs from Incentive Plans versus Three-Year Shareholder Returns, 2008–2010.*

Source: Hay Group-*Wall Street Journal* Study of CEO Compensation in 2010.

strong financial incentives to make their firms prosper. And that, indeed, seems to be the case.

The CEOs' incentives to do a good job and increase the value of the firm stem mainly from their holding of equity-related incentives rather than from the pay they receive in a particular year. Thus the pay-for-performance link really turns mainly on the connection between firm performance and the level of the CEO's longer-term wealth. This link between CEO financial health and firm performance has been well recognized at least since 1998, when Brian Hall and Jeffrey Liebman found "a strong link between the fortunes of CEOs and the fortunes of the companies they manage. We find that virtually all of the pay to performance sensitivity is attributable to changes in the value of CEO holdings of stock and stock options. Our main empirical finding is that CEO wealth often changes by millions of dollars for typical changes in firm value."[3] They go on to say that "there is a difference of about $4 million dollars in compensation for achieving a moderately above average performance relative to a moderately below average performance."[4]

Table 5.1 substantiates this view, focusing on the equity exposure of the three highest-paid executives at the 50 largest firms measured across various decades. The first column shows the effect on the executive's wealth for a 1 percent increase in the value of the firm. Because all of the amounts in table 5.1 are expressed in 2000 dollars, they are easily comparable. The figures show that the responsiveness of executive wealth has increased over the years, and by the 2000–2005 period increasing the value of the firm by 1 percent increased the executive's wealth by $227,881. Given that, even taking the financial crisis of 2007–2009 into account, the typical share price has averaged a 9 percent increase over these decades; an average performance

TABLE 5.1 Executive's Wealth Changes and Wealth Levels Tied to Their Firm (in 2000 dollars)

Period	Dollar Effect of a 1 Percent Increase in Firm Value on Executive's Holdings	Dollar Value of Executive's Holdings	
	Stock + Options	Stock	Options
1936–1940	18,670	1,566,287	0
1941–1949	6,814	679,429	0
1950–1959	13,975	1,169,857	0
1960–1969	38,978	2,333,663	212,150
1970–1979	21,743	1,281,266	244,082
1980–1989	34,679	1,604,861	926,869
1990–1999	120,342	4,068,013	3,622,806
2000–2005	227,881	4,966,035	7,160,898

Source: Adapted from Carola Frydman and Dirk Jenter, "CEO Compensation," *Annual Review of Financial Economics*, 2010, 2, 75–102, table 2, p. 85.

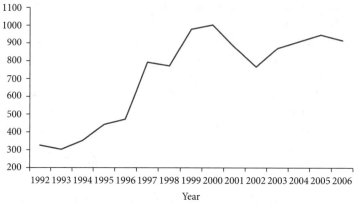

FIGURE 5.2 *Mean Sensitivity of CEO Wealth to Firm Performance for S&P 500 Firms (thousands of dollars).*

Source: Michael Faulkender, Dalida Kadyrzhanova, N. Prabhala, and Lemma Senbet, "Executive Compensation: An Overview of Research on Corporate Practices and Proposed Reforms," *Journal of Applied Corporate Finance*, winter 2010, 22:1, 107–118, figure 1, p. 109.

would net the executive about $2 million, while an inferior or superior performance would have significantly different outcomes. The last two columns of table 5.1 show the equity exposure of these same executives. By the 2000–2005 period, the executives had over $12 million of personal wealth exposed to the equity of the firm, with the significant majority of this exposure being concentrated in ESOs. Certainly this exposure both ties the wealth of the CEO to the fortunes of the firm and provides a strong incentive to increase the value of the firm.

While table 5.1 focuses on the highest-paid executives from the very largest firms, figure 5.2 pertains to the average CEO at a firm in the S&P 500 for the period from 1992 to 2006. It shows that the CEO's wealth has always been sensitive to firm performance and that this sensitivity has been rising. Currently CEOs have considerable exposure to the equity of their own firms, providing every reason to try to increase share values.

Among all the spectacular debacles associated with the financial crisis of 2007–2009, none was more dramatic than the implosion of the investment bank Lehman Brothers, as well as the accompanying fall of Lehman's CEO Richard Fuld from his pinnacle of power and prestige.[5] Fuld was called to testify before Congress in October 2008, a month after Lehman declared bankruptcy, and was subjected to a humiliating congressional inquiry in which Congressman John Mica informed him: "If you haven't discovered your role, you're the villain today. You've got to act like a villain."[6] Fuld testified:

I'm not proud that I lost all that money…but my point is, that the [compensation] system worked…I received 85 percent of my compensation in stock. All the stock that I got, for the last five years, I lost that.

Compensation that I received back to '97, '98 and '99, I could have gotten it seven years ago. But I went to the compensation committee and extended it to a 10-year [vesting period]. I lost *all of that*. I got no severance, no golden parachute. I got no contract. I never *asked* for a contract. I never sold my shares, and that's why I had 10 million [shares] left. *I believed in this company*. I could have sold that stock. But *I did not*, because I believed we would return to profitability.[7]

Much of Fuld's grilling focused on his compensation, with one congressman referring to his compensation as "unimaginable," pointing out that he got to keep almost $500 million after the demise of Lehman. Fuld attempted to diminish the size of his compensation, putting the figure closer to $300 million, but still admitted that it was a "large number."[8]

Well, how large a number? Bebchuk, Cohen, and Spamann (hereafter BCS) analyzed the realized compensation and incentives that faced executives at Bear Stearns and Lehman Brothers over the years of the twenty-first century leading up to the demise of these firms.[9] The situation of Dick Fuld is particularly instructive in illustrating general points about incentives, stock holdings, and risk.[10] BCS reported that from 2000 to 2008 Fuld received a total of $70,594,415 in bonuses and nonequity-based compensation. He also sold 12,422,277 shares of Lehman for a total of $470,695,782. At the collapse of Lehman, Fuld still held 10,851,540 Lehman shares, which BCS estimate as having zero post-bankruptcy value. Thus, Fuld received $541,290,697 in bonuses and as proceeds from the sale of Lehman stock from 2000 to 2008, all measured in 2009 dollars. At the end of 2007, a Lehman share was worth $65.44. Assuming for convenience that Fuld held the same number of shares at the beginning of 2008 that BCS reported he held at the collapse—10,851,540 shares—the bankruptcy cost him more than $710 million.[11]

There can be little doubt that CEOs of financial firms in the run-up to the financial crisis had strong personal incentives to increase the risks at their firms. As we have seen, however, the great ascendancy of agency theory that began in 1990 and rocked executive compensation in U.S. companies from then to the present explicitly developed pay plans designed to induce CEOs to boost their firms' risk in the belief that such policies would benefit shareholders. If CEO incentives were properly aligned with those of shareholders, then the increases in risk that promised personal enrichment for CEOs would serendipitously benefit shareholders as well. In assessing a disaster like the financial crisis, the question arises whether CEO incentives were poorly aligned with those of shareholders and whether CEOs selfishly took positions for personal benefit, knowing that the likely consequences for shareholders could be very poor indeed.

As an anecdotal account, we have seen that Lehman's CEO, Dick Fuld, made out quite well personally in a purely financial sense; although, he lost a tremendous amount of wealth in 2008 and suffered dramatic career and personal reversals. Other CEOs in the early twenty-first century also reaped huge rewards, as shown in a study by Fahlenbrach and Stulz. For example, in the financial industry at least 20 CEOs held equity stakes in their companies that were valued at more than $100 million at the end of 2006, and on average CEOs at financial firms owned 1.6 percent of their own firms' shares. Further, some stakes held by CEOs at the end of 2006 were extremely large, the five-largest being: Fuld at Lehman, $1,003 million; Cayne at Bear Stearns, $953 million; O'Neal at Merrill Lynch, $359 million; Mack at Morgan Stanley, $320 million; and Mozilo at Countrywide Financial, $285 million.[12]

The picture that we have seen for Lehman and Fuld is fairly representative and was widely repeated, although often on a much-smaller scale, as reported by Fahlenbrach and Stulz. Examining the fates of CEOs at 98 large banks, they found a number of interesting results. Like Fuld, other bank CEOs tended to be quite wealthy and to be heavily invested in their own firms. On average, the CEOs lost $31.5 million in their equity stakes over 2007–2008. Few CEOs cashed out a large portion of their holdings, and more than 75 percent of CEOs did not sell any shares during 2007–2008. This leads Fahlenbrach and Stulz to conclude that "CEOs made large losses on their wealth during the crisis and that most of these losses came from holding on to their shares. Had CEOs seen the crisis coming, they could have avoided most of these losses by selling their shares. They clearly did not do so."[13]

Thus the picture that emerges is not one of CEOs ruthlessly taking risks with their firms merely for their personal enrichment. Instead, the following broadly seems to be the case:

- Well before and through the crisis, CEOs operated with pay plans that were designed to give them personal incentives to take risks, in the belief that such a design would benefit shareholders.
- CEOs actively guided their firms to take large risks in general, and they increased those risk levels as the crisis approached.
- CEOs failed to anticipate the crisis, and they suffered large wealth losses as a result of the crisis.
- Nonetheless, CEOs made out extremely well financially as a result of their stewardship of their respective firms, holding many millions of dollars of personal wealth even in the aftermath of the crisis.
- CEOs generally did much better financially than rank-and-file employees and shareholders in their firms.

As the case of Richard Fuld dramatizes, CEO incentives very often work largely, or even mainly, through the equity positions they hold in their firms. If Fuld's almost 11 million shares of Lehman did not provide him with incentives to be a good steward for Lehman shareholders, it is hard to imagine what would be a sufficiently powerful incentive.

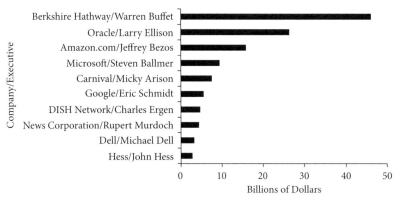

FIGURE 5.3 *Executives with Largest Value of Executive Stock Option Holdings.*
Source: Pradnya Joshi, "We Knew They Got Raises. But This?" *New York Times*, July 2, 2011.

The incentive power of executive holdings of their firm's shares and ESOs can be emphasized by considering some well-known executives with extremely large holdings of their wealth in the form of ESOs. Figure 5.3 shows the 10 CEOs with the highest value of ESOs as of the end of 2010, with values ranging from just under $3 billion to more than $46 billion. It is interesting to note the long and intimate association with their firms that characterize almost all of these individuals. Some are founders, such as Hess, Dell, Ergen, Schmidt, Bezos, and Ellison. Others have been long-time employees at their firms: Ballmer is employee number 30 at Microsoft, while Micky Arison is the son of the founder, Ted Arison. Rupert Murdoch and Warren Buffet built up their firms over decades from much more humble beginnings.

Exercise of ESOs

For a plain vanilla stock option, for example one with no vesting period or restrictions on sale or transfer, the owner is generally better off if he does not exercise the option. (There can be an exception to this if the underlying stock has a sufficiently high dividend.) If the option owner wants to dispose of his position, he is much better off selling the option. Exercising the option captures only the option's intrinsic value, which is either zero, if the stock price is below the exercise price, or equals the stock price minus the exercise price, if the stock price exceeds the exercise price. Options are typically worth more than their intrinsic value, and exercise discards that additional value inherent in the option.

Sometimes this additional value, over and above the intrinsic value can be considerable. In chapter 3 we considered our base-case option, which had a 10-year period until expiration, a four-year vesting period, and a $16.85 value at the time of issue, based on the prevailing $50 stock price and exercise price. We considered a case of normal performance in which the stock price grew at a rate of 11 percent, the long-term typical rate of return on stocks, for a five-year period. At the end of that five-year period, the stock price would stand at $84.25. For the CEO who owns such an option, the option is exercisable when the option vests. Exercising the option captures the intrinsic value of $34.25 (the $84.25 current stock price, less the $50 exercise price). However, the unexercised option would be worth $42.63. So exercising the option discards almost exactly 20 percent of the option's value.

Note that the only way the executive can garner immediate cash from the option is by exercising it and selling the stock she receives upon exercise. Even though the option is vested after the four-year wait, it is still not transferable. So the situation the executive faces is to hold the option until it expires in six more years, or be forced to exercise if she departs the firm during those six years, or exercise the option early and discard the option's value that is over and above the intrinsic value of the option.

At the end of chapter 4, we discussed the role of utility in executive preferences and in their incentives. Based on that discussion and the considerable research on utility functions in executive compensation, we saw that stock option compensation is inefficient compensation in a particular sense— awarding the option costs the company more than the value the executive attaches to it. The reason for this is that executives generally hold portfolios that are poorly diversified, with exceedingly large proportional commitments to the equity of their firm. Richard Fuld could serve as the poster child for a poorly diversified executive considering his 11 million shares in Lehman Brothers. Most executives would prefer not to have so much of their wealth tied to their firm. Therefore, the behavior of executives in exercising their ESOs presents a natural experiment to see the extent to which executives are willing to discard economic value by avoiding their firm's shares.

We can classify the various motivations for early exercise under four umbrellas. First, an executive may exercise in order to adjust her investment portfolio and avoid excessive commitment to her firm's shares. In short, she may choose to exercise just to diversify. Second, she may be pessimistic about the future of the firm and believe that the present is the best time to exercise before the stock price falls and the options drop in value. A third broad motivation might be a desire for liquidity. A fourth motivation for exercise may be a desire to exploit inside, or private, information about the firm's condition or prospects. We have seen that ESOs are extremely illiquid and the paper wealth that they represent may be massive, but none of this wealth is available for consumption or other uses. When executives exercise the ESOs, they sometimes announce their motivations, but, generally, they do not. In fact, the main reason executives might make a statement about their exercises is to reassure shareholders that they are not exercising out of concern for the firm's future, but that they desire the cash for consumption or to achieve better diversification.

On the whole, there is strong evidence that executives exercise their ESOs long before the options expire, discarding a substantial part of the value of those options in the process. Anderson and Muslu find that CEOs realize less than half the total value of the options due to their early exercise.[14] Similarly, Bettis, Bizjak, and Lemmon similarly find that, on average, exercises occur less than two years after vesting and more than four years prior to expiration. These early exercises appear to be somewhat concentrated in firms with high dividend rates—an economically efficient decision in some situations. However, exercises are more frequent immediately following a jump in stock price.[15] For their part, Boyd, Brown and Szimayer find behavior in Australia to be somewhat similar and somewhat different than the studies just summarized. They discovered that dividends play a key role in determining early exercise, but they also found that many exercises occur well before maturity, but that these exercises nonetheless sacrifice little option value.[16]

Huddart and Lang examined the exercise behavior of more than 50,000 employees, not all of whom were top executives. They found that exercise typically occurred years before expiration and that this early exercise resulted in a loss of half the option's value (had the option been a tradable option).[17] Sautner and Weber find that early exercises are often quite extreme, discarding as much as 90 percent of the option's value and that the exercises are concentrated in a few sizable transactions.[18]

In some cases, it is surprising just how early some exercises occur. Fu and Ligon found that slightly more than 12 percent of exercises occurred immediately (within two days) of vesting. They concluded that these immediate exercises were predominately motivated by portfolio considerations.[19] But apparently not all exercises are driven by economic considerations. Heath, Huddart, and Lang find that exercise decisions are driven to a significant degree by what they term "psychological factors." For example, exercises are concentrated, almost doubling, when the stock price exceeds a 52-week high. Heath, Huddart, and Lang also find that exercises tend to follow a run-up in stock prices and to occur before a period of falling stock price. However, as we will see, this exercise decision may not be due merely to an effort to capture the run-up in prices but may also reflect the extent to which the executives anticipate falling stock prices due to their privileged information.

In the United States, it is generally illegal to exploit private, or nonpublic, information to guide a trading strategy. For example, a board member who participates in merger talks pertaining to his firm is most likely committing a felony if he uses that private information to guide a strategy of trading his shares. While the exact interpretation of insider trading statutes is fraught with difficulty, the underlying concept is clear—it is generally illegal to use privileged access to information to direct a trading strategy, especially if the information is collected by holding a position in a firm. Nonetheless, there appears to be compelling evidence that executive stock option exercises are driven by private information. This may be a situation in which the law is somewhat unclear, but, at least on the surface, such exercises appear to be quite similar to actions that have, in some cases, resulted in criminal prosecution and conviction.

Carpenter and Remmers, in an early study, concluded that private information played little role in option exercises and said that "option exercises in the current regulatory regime take place primarily for non-informational reasons."[20] However, this study is certainly atypical of the general tenor of research in this area. Instead, most studies find a powerful association between exercise behavior and unusual stock price behavior. That is, most studies find that option exercises appear to be motivated by private information. The results of Huddart and Lang are more typical. In essence, they find that exercises are low just before a stock price increase and that exercises tend to be high following a price run-up. Exercise following a stock price increase could be simply a matter of trend following or a desire to capture the recent stock price increase, and this does not necessarily reflect the exploitation of private information. However, how does this picture change if the exercises tend to occur just at the peak of the run-up in prices and if the stock price stagnates or falls immediately thereafter? Exercises following such a pattern would certainly appear to be exploiting inside information. Also, a pattern of exercising just before bad stock results strongly suggests that exercises are occurring because of inside information about the firm's future dismal prospects.[21]

Not all exercises are the same, because they can be driven by different strategies. First, an executive can exercise the ESO and hold the stock. Second, the ESO owner can exercise and sell the stock immediately. Third, many firms allow executives to engage in a "cashless" or "semi-cashless" exercise. Instead of paying the exercise price with their own cash, the exercising executive returns some of the exercised shares to the firm to cover the amount of the exercise price. In this third strategy, the executive can complete the exercise without having all of the exercise price in hand before exercising. The ultimate economic result is the same for the executive and the firm. Aboody, Hughes, Liu, and Su found that about 30 percent of exercises were not followed by an immediate sale. In other words, the shares went into the executive's personal portfolio. When they partitioned the exercises by various strategies, they found that exercise and immediate sale tended to occur just before a stock price decline. However, when there was an early exercise and no sale of stock, the stock price usually did quite well. Finally, they also found that executives who could exercise, but did not, were rewarded by good stock price performance in the near future. All of these patterns suggest that the executives were exploiting their private information about the firm's prospects in guiding their exercise decisions.[22] Sternberg and Witte extended, confirmed, and strengthened the results of Aboody et al. by screening out exercises that appeared to be driven by a desire to capture dividends. They also found evidence in support of the view that executives used private information to guide exercise strategies, and, focusing on their subsample of exercises not driven by dividend capture, their results were three times those found in the Aboody et al.[23]

The benefit of timing exercises based on private information appears to be high. In Huddart and Lang's study of the exercises of more than 50,000 employees, they split time periods into high- and low-exercise activity and concentrated on the six months of stock returns following the option exercises. When exercise activity was low, the six-month stock returns were 10 percent higher than when exercise activity was high. In other words, these employees seemed to know what was coming for the firm's stock. When the future returns were expected to be low, it appears they exercised their options and disposed of the stock before the period of poor stock market performance.[24] In two further studies, Cicero also established that executives use private information to guide their exercises decisions, as did a study by Brooks, Chance, and Cline.[25]

Many studies find strong evidence that executives use their private information to make wise exercise decisions. These effects can be substantial and result in real economic advantages for executives. This is illustrated by considering just one clear result from the study by Brooks, Chance, and Cline. If we focus on the exercise of ESOs that occur at the expiration date of the option, we would expect the stock market performance before and after the exercise to be completely ordinary—that is, we would not expect any positive or abnormal performance. This is the case because an exercise at expiration is forced to occur at that time and is unlikely to be driven by the option owner's special information. By contrast, if we consider a large sample of early exercise decisions and find that, on average, they occur just after a large abnormal stock price run-up and are followed by mediocre or negative abnormal stock market results, it would suggest that the choice of the exercise date was likely driven by special information.

With this background, we can turn to figure 5.4, drawn from a study by Brooks, Chance, and Cline, which shows the average stock market performance following exercise for two different subsamples: one is a subsample of exercises that occur at the option's expiration; the other is a subsample of exercises that occur at a time the executive chooses before expiration. The latter is defined as being more than 30 days before expiration. The exercise occurs on day zero. The graph shows the abnormal returns for a year after exercise, expressed as 252 trading days. (The sample was sizable, encompassing more than 31,000 exercises, 94 percent of which were early exercises.)

Figure 5.4 shows pretty much what we would expect for abnormal returns for options that occur at the option expiration and that are, therefore, unlikely to

BOX 5.1 DETECTING ABNORMAL STOCK MARKET PERFORMANCE

In finance research it is common to look at the abnormal market performance
of a group of stocks, especially in reaction to a news event. For example,
researchers wondered how the shares of acquiring and target firms respond to
the announcement of mergers. Or, how do shares respond to the unexpected
death of a CEO? This box explains the methodology that finance researchers use
to evaluate these abnormal stock price reactions to various kinds of events, and
we will see the importance of this technique for understanding incentives in
executive compensation. This methodology originated in a paper by Fama, Fisher,
Jensen, and Roll (hereafter FFJR) in 1969.[26]

Often the stock price reaction that investigators want to examine occurs in
response to a particular event, but an event of a certain type, such as a merger
announcement that occurs today. FFJR solved this problem by examining stock
returns in "event time" rather than calendar time. That is, they define the day
of various merger announcements as day zero for many merger announcements
that occur on different calendar days, and then they examine how stock returns
behave on days before the event, e.g., day -1, -2, and so on; the day of the event,
day zero; and days after the event, day 1, day 2, etc.

For a single merger announcement, the effect of the announcement on the
returns of a given security might be overwhelmed by other news. While we
know that merger announcements generally lead to favorable results for the
target firm, the target firm's stock price might fall if the general market trend
is downward or if some other factors influence the target's stock price on the
day of the announcement and on subsequent days. However, across many
merger announcements, we would expect other factors unrelated to the merger
announcement to average out, leaving the average response of the many target
stocks to reveal the effect of the merger announcement.

Often researchers use a model of what the expected stock price movement
would have been on a given day without the effect of the event. For example, some
studies use the Capital Asset Pricing Model to estimate the normal movement
in the shares in response to general market movements on a particular day and
then focus on just the abnormal portion. This is not always necessarily the case,
because there are many wrinkles and refinements in this methodology. We will
first consider a study of how stock prices respond to exercises of ESOs, and this
will also serve as an example of how this methodology reveals important general
trends that would otherwise be difficult to observe.

---

be driven by exploiting private information. While abnormal returns deviate
somewhat from the zero level, those deviations are quite modest, with the
stocks acquired by exercising at expiration losing an abnormal 1.06 percent
in the year following exercise. However, for the sample of stocks acquired by
early exercise, the year following exercise gave an average abnormal return
of –3.47 percent. We know that most shares acquired by exercising ESOs are

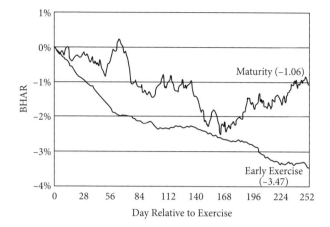

FIGURE 5.4 *Abnormal Returns for ESOs Exercised Before and at Maturity.*

Note: BHAR indicates the buy-and-hold abnormal, or excess, stock returns for the year [252 trading days] following the option exercise.

Source: Robert Brooks, Don M. Chance, and Brandon N. Cline, "Private Information and the Exercise of Executive Stock Options" (April 2012, working paper, figure 2A), forthcoming in *Financial Management.*

sold almost immediately. The idea here is that executives anticipate that the shares of their firm will not do well in the coming year, so they choose to exercise early and then dispose of the shares before the poor share performance occurs. If all of the shares acquired by early exercise were sold immediately, the executives acquiring these shares would avoid the 3.47 percent underperformance over the year following exercise. Thus, these executives seem to time their exercise decisions quite well, and it is difficult to think of any other plausible explanation—except that executives who exercise early possess and use their privileged inside information to exercise at an advantageous time.

It should be stressed that these are results for a large sample of exercises. Surely some of these exercises did not involve inside information, so we cannot conclude that any particular individual exercise was driven by private information. However, it seems extremely clear that, on the whole, executives use their inside information to direct their exercise decisions.

Unwinding Incentives

We saw in chapter 4 that executives avidly seek ESO grants, but that they generally do not desire the concentrated exposure to the risk of their firms that come with them. They would prefer the cash value of the options, and often they are willing to settle for the much lower intrinsic value of the options that they can secure by exercising. Of course, exercises lessen the executive's incentives and often lead to the firm's replenishing the executive's option position by issuing new options. Many executives would greatly like to lessen their risk exposure to the firm without adopting the value-destroying expedient of exercising options before expiration and thereby discarding such a high percentage of the options' value.

One way that executives can reduce their personal risk exposure to the firm is to use financial derivatives to offset their restricted stock or ESO positions while continuing to leave their restricted stock and ESO holdings undisturbed. For firms that are publicly traded, and for which options also trade, the executive could sell options in the market to offset their restricted stock and ESO holdings. Whether options trade on the firm's shares or not, the executive could also go to a derivatives dealer and have a bespoke derivatives position created that would offset the CEO's exposure to her own firm's equity.

There are four problems with this strategy. First, such a strategy involves betting against the CEO's firm. Such behavior is awkward and difficult to explain at best. Second, when top executives trade in the securities of their own firms, they are required to disclose these transactions to the Securities Exchange Commission. This heightens the probability that their betting against their firms will be detected and publicized. Third, top executives face insider trading laws and regulations that restrict trading their firms' securities and implementing risk-reducing strategies might run afoul of those laws and regulations. Fourth, we have seen that firms grant ESOs partly as a form of compensation and partly as a tool for spurring the executive's incentive to perform. Thus, the firm is quite likely to take a dim view of such an unwinding of these incentives, and the board is quite likely to discover the practice due to the required disclosures to the SEC.

Despite these good reasons for not unwinding incentives, it certainly has been done. Bettis, Bizjak, and Lemmon were able to find 89 instances of executives using derivatives to unwind their equity incentives in the three years from 1996 through 1998.[27] During this period, the SEC's reporting requirements were somewhat unclear, but they have been strengthened in subsequent years. Ofek and Yermack studied how executives dispose of their firms' stock and found that they very effectively reduced their risk exposure and their incentives by merely disposing of their shares in accordance with laws and regulations.[28] Others believe that the problem is not severe, pointing to the small sample size of the Bettis, Bizjak, and Lemmon study (which appears to be the only documented evidence of the use of derivatives to unwind these equity incentives), and that top executives hold large equity positions in any event.[29] Other researchers emphasize the weakness of corporate restrictions against such practices,[30] and it must be acknowledged that some of this unwinding almost certainly happens surreptitiously.

We have seen that ESO compensation is costly, and, as we noted, it is inefficient because the cost of awarding an ESO to an executive is greater than the value the executive attaches to the option. This gives firms strong reasons to keep executives from unwinding their equity incentives, whether through exercises, sales of restricted stock, or surreptitious hedging with derivatives. It is obviously quite expensive to create the incentives, see them dissipated, and then restore them.

Reflecting on that state of affairs, several have proposed measures to prohibit the unwinding of incentives. Jensen and Murphy recommend that "remuneration committees should include explicit unwinding constraints (or required permissions) in executive incentive awards. They should monitor the portfolio holdings of top-level executives and related parties to ensure that they are not inappropriately unwinding the incentives that have been put in place by the committee and the board and paid for by the company."[31] For their part, Bebchuk and Fried suggest new restrictions that would affect what executives can do with their restricted stock after it vests. Currently, once a share vests or once a share comes to an executive through exercise, she can dispose of it immediately. Bebchuk and Fried recommend that there be an additional holding period following the vesting period.[32] Executives would surely find such a new restriction onerous and could be expected to resist it fiercely.

{ 6 }

Executive Incentives and Risk Taking

As previous chapters discussed, a revolution in executive pay in the United States began in the early 1990s with a conscious effort to incentivize top executives to undertake risky projects with the aim of increasing firm value. We also noted that these incentives work principally through compensation vehicles linked to equity, most notably restricted stock and ESOs, with ESOs being the far more powerful incentive tool.

When we think of a standard ESO, one that is issued at-the-money, such an option has considerable, even enormous, value. But that value is inaccessible when it is issued because of vesting restrictions and the nontradability of ESOs. While the option may have great value, there are other impediments to the CEO turning the option into cash. Most notably, the option will not have exercise value unless the stock price rises from where it stood on the date of issue. If the stock price never moves, the option will vest, and the executive may hold it until it expires worthless on its expiration date. From this point of view, the option is worthless unless something positive happens to the stock price—or unless the CEO acts to increase the value of the firm's shares.

Let us assume momentarily that the CEO is the chief driver of firm value. If she acts, she can hope to increase firm value and make her options pay off when she eventually exercises them. If she does not act, the options will expire worthless. The executive might well reason that the options are inherently worth zero cash value, but that they can possibly be turned into something valuable by taking risks. From this perspective, there is little or no downside to the option's value. They cannot pay less than zero; the eventual yield in the absence of a stock price increase. Thus, the CEO's holding of a substantial portfolio of ESOs provides a strong personal incentive to try nearly anything to increase the stock price. If the CEO is paid only with ESOs, she has every reason to "swing for the fences"—that is, she has the ultimate incentive to increase risk.

While firms may wish CEOs to be more accepting of risk in pursuit of greater firm value, they certainly do not want the CEO to adopt wildly risky strategies. Shareholders, in particular, want the firm to undertake risky projects that have a commensurate probability of generating high returns.

But shareholders also have a lot to lose from wild and unsuccessful corporate investments that drive share prices down.

Bondholders are in a different position. They have been promised a fixed stream of payments for the loans they made to the firm. There is no chance that the bonds will pay more than the borrower promised; thus, highly risky corporate strategies increase the prospect that the firm will be unable to make the payments it promised. The wise bondholder understands that firms are built to incur risk and that the ability of the firm to generate enough cash flow to make the promised payments on the bonds depends on the success of the firm's risky projects. So the bondholder must accept the idea that the firm is a risk-taking enterprise, and this recognition is implicit in the bond investment. If the bondholder wanted a zero-risk investment with a commensurately low return, he could have invested in U.S. Treasury securities. By choosing to invest in a corporate bond, the bondholder accepts some risk in pursuit of a higher return. But the bondholder certainly does not want to invest in a company with a given risk level, only to see the firm significantly increase the level of risk it pursues. In sum, the stockholder has a lot to lose, but a great deal of upside potential if the stock price rises. The bond investor holds a promise of a future stream of payments with no upside potential but has a lot to lose if the company undertakes risky projects that fail.

If the firm's CEO is compensated only with ESOs, the three parties— CEO, shareholders, and bondholders—have wildly different desires for the level of risk that the firm undertakes. The firm needs to set an executive pay package that incentivizes risk-taking in the right amount and in the right way. In addition to the encouragement that ESOs provide to take risk, the firm also needs to restrain the payoffs from excessive risk-taking. We have seen that salary, bonuses, and the value of pension promises are relatively invariant with respect to firm performance. This leaves the firm with two essential means of restraining the CEO from incurring excessive risk. First, there is monitoring by the board of directors, coupled with the ultimate threat of dismissal. But the board is distant from the daily operations of the firm and cannot monitor firm performance in detail. The CEO and her management team can present very risky projects in a way that is likely to receive board approval, even if the board would not approve the project if it understood its true risk level. If the CEO undertakes a very risky project that fails, the firm can always fire her. But, this is not a satisfactory management technique, because the sanction would be imposed after the CEO has led the firm to a substantial failure. Instead, the firm needs to use a second technique to restrain the CEO's risk-taking impulses, by giving her something to lose. If the CEO holds a substantial commitment to the firm's shares, then a falling stock price has a profound negative impact on the CEO's wealth. Ideally, the right mix of ESOs and restricted stock in a pay package can provide the right incentives to incur risk. The potential upside of the ESOs pushes the CEO to take risk, but the potential downside restrains excessive risk-taking.[1]

These reflections on the incentive effects of stock holdings and ESOs are broadly consistent with the executive pay packages observed across the corporate landscape. They almost all utilize a mix of both restricted stock and ESOs as incentivizing and restraining elements in the CEO's pay package. Different firms use different mixes of compensation elements, and the mix varies over time in a single firm, particularly one with a long-serving CEO. Part of this variance is due to the different environments that firms face. Some firms operate in less risky industries, while others compete in high-risk industries dominated by research and development or fast-paced technological change. Not surprisingly then, such dissimilar firms need pay packages particular to their risk-taking environment. Further, the risk-taking profile of firms in the same industry also depends on corporate cultures: some firms are simply more comfortable with accepting greater risks. There are other important considerations that should determine the right risk incentives for corporate leaders. These factors turn on the personality, character, and personal circumstances of the CEO.

In chapter 4, we considered the standard mathematical utility function that economists use to explore executive compensations and saw that it contained terms for wealth and the executive's level of risk aversion. The wealth component can be decomposed into different elements—the CEO's private wealth not connected to the firm, ownership of restricted shares of the firm, and ESOs. These diverse components of wealth create different incentives that influence the CEO's risk-taking decisions. For example, if we contrast the CEO's holdings of restricted stock with her position in ESOs, the two instruments encourage different responses to bad investment outcomes.

Figure 6.1 graphs a CEO's hypothetical holding of restricted stock and ESOs, with each of the portfolios initially valued at $10 million. The stock price is assumed at an initial value of $50 per share. The option is our base-case option from chapter 4, with a price of $16.85 and the other features specified there (10 years to expiration, four years to vesting, an exercise price of $50, a risk-free rate of 5 percent, a 2 percent dividend rate, with a stock volatility of 40 percent). Thus, these two $10 million portfolios consist of 200,000 shares of stock or 593,472 options. Figure 6.1 shows how two portfolios of initially equal value fluctuate as the stock price changes. Both move directly with changes in stock prices. The value of the stock portfolio is a simple linear function of the stock price. By contrast, the value of the option portfolio is more volatile, reflecting the inherent leverage of options. Thus, the option portfolio gives the executive greater rewards for success and greater penalties for a dropping stock price compared with the restricted stock portfolio. These differential responses to changing stock prices imply that the asset mix of the executive will affect her attitude toward risk taking.

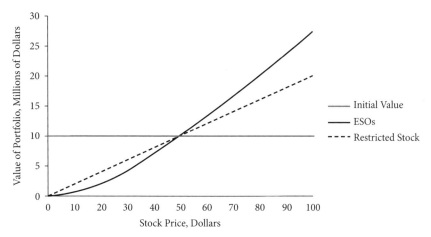

FIGURE 6.1 *Value of Two Portfolios: ESOs and Restricted Stock (initial value of each portfolio = $10 million).*

Thus far, we have focused on a single ESO as part of the executive's portfolio, but the situation is more complex. We noted that firms typically make option grants to the CEO each year. So these various option grants will be issued at various exercise prices and will vary in the number of options granted. Over time, the CEO will come to hold a portfolio of options with different characteristics, which imply various incentives for risk taking. As an illustration, figure 6.2 shows a typical feature of options called "time decay." In general, options with a longer time to expiration are more valuable than options closer to their expiration date. From the date of issue up to the expiration date, the value of a typical option falls in a predictable manner as the value of the option decays over time. Figure 6.2 shows how the value of a plain

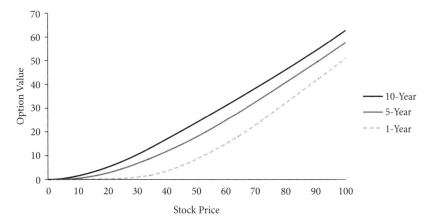

FIGURE 6.2 *Time Decay of a Plain Vanilla Option; 10 Years, 5 Years, and 1 Year to Expiration.*

vanilla option that was originally issued with 10 years until expiration falls after five years and then with only one year remaining until expiration. This option is essentially like our standard ESO, except the values are computed assuming that there is no exit rate, that the option is vested immediately upon issuance, and that it is freely tradable. Thus, this option is a "plain vanilla" option—one with no special complicating features. As the graph of figure 6.2 shows, the value of the option decays over time in a very predictable manner. As an example, for a constant stock price of $50, the 10-year option is worth $23.46, but with only five years until expiration and the same stock price of $50 the option falls to $18.04, and with only one year until expiration the value of the option decays to $8.40.

The well-behaved time decay of the plain vanilla option in figure 6.2 contrasts markedly with the behavior of a typical ESO, such as our base-case ESO. Figure 6.3 shows the time-decay pattern of this standard ESO. At the original time of issue, our base-case option has a value of $16.85 and 10 years until expiration. But after five years, again assuming a stock price of $50, the base-case option value has fallen slightly to $16.22. Then, with the same stock price of $50 and only one year until expiration, the value of the ESO has decayed to $8.20. However, for higher stock prices, both the one-year and five-year options are actually *more* valuable than the ten-year base-case option. For example, at a stock price of $90, the one- five- and ten-year options are worth $41.31, $47.53, and $39.88, respectively.

The "crossing" of the price graphed in figure 6.3 is unusual for most options. It is driven by the vesting provision and the exit rate with the probability these features create that the options will never pay off. One reason the five-year option is more valuable than the otherwise identical 10-year option at a stock price of $90 is that the five-year option is already vested (given the original four-year vesting requirement), so if the executive exits the firm, she can exercise the ESO because it is in-the-money.

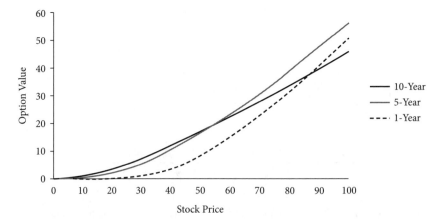

FIGURE 6.3 *Time Decay of ESOs Reflecting Vesting and Exit Rates.*

Figure 6.3 helps illustrate an important point about the portfolio of a CEO and risk-taking incentives. The executive probably holds the three options depicted in figure 6.3 as part of her ESO portfolio, and each has different pay-offs depending on an increase or decrease in firm value. In addition, the CEO will have some wealth invested outside the firm, plus a position in restricted shares of the firm's stock. These investment holdings, as well as her personal attitude toward risk taking and her other individual characteristics such as her age, which might affect her investment and career time-horizons, compli-cate the assessment of the CEO's inclination to increase or decrease the risk of the firm.

In general, these complications of personal psychology, personal circum-stances, and a complicated investment portfolio make ex ante assessment of CEO risk taking nearly impossible. However, there is a rich theoretical and empirical literature that explores how CEOs as a group actually respond to their risk-taking incentives in the real world.

Equity Compensation and the CEO's Risk Appetite

When we observe human behavior in any walk of life, there is almost always a great deal of uncertainty in identifying the actual motivation of that behav-ior. Does a politician advocate a certain position out of calculated self-interest or might she actually believe her favored policy is wise? Even in our own behavior, we often have difficulty in correctly identifying our motivation, and self-deceit is a common fact of human existence. In the context of execu-tive compensation, this uncertainty over motivation is an extremely difficult problem. Largely for that reason, a number of studies explore the effect of incentive compensation in a simplified setting.

Chapter 4 introduced the power utility function presumed to describe the CEO's behavior as a utility-maximizing individual who has a certain degree of risk aversion, some personal wealth that she holds in investments outside the firm, a package of equity-related instruments (restricted stock and ESOs) tied to the value of the firm, and a continuing relationship with the firm and its associated compensation package. Studying the behavior of a hypotheti-cal CEO in this simple context has proven surprisingly fruitful, producing a number of predictions about risk-taking behavior, which, mostly, have been confirmed by empirical studies that examined the behavior of large groups of CEOs.

Jennifer Carpenter conducted a seminal study using this approach.[2] In general, Carpenter showed that managers have a strong personal incentive to seek outcomes that drive the share price away from the exercise price of the option. In some cases, the manager will seek a dramatic increase in the vola-tility of the firm's shares. A CEO can achieve enhanced volatility in the firm's stock price by committing the firm to extremely risky investment projects. This motivation to augment risk and accept risky investment projects is particularly powerful when the CEO's stock option is deeply out-of-the-money. After all, if the firm's stock price is significantly below the exercise price of the ESO, the option will almost certainly expire worthless unless something about the firm alters drastically. On the other hand, if the CEO holds deeply in-the-money stock options that are not yet vested, the risk-taking incentives are transformed. In that case, the CEO will likely want to operate the firm in a conservative manner. With options that are deep in-the-money, the CEO will want to capture that sure value, which she can do by exercising the options once they vest. With deeply in-the-money options, risky projects can turn out badly, making the value of the share prices fall, taking the CEO's options out-of-the-money.

Carpenter strongly emphasizes that understanding the risk-taking behavior of the CEO even in a fairly simple theoretical model is complex: "In general, the effects of option compensation on the manager's appetite for risk are more complex than simple intuition about option pricing might suggest."[3] Carpenter's finding about the complexity of the relationship between the compensation package and the manager's risk-taking appetite provides the best guiding principle for understanding the relationship between executive compensation and the firm's risk posture—that is, matters are much more complicated than they appear. Subsequent studies have consistently reinforced this conclusion and have sought to clarify the relationship between executive pay and corporate risk taking.

Another important feature of incentivizing executives to adopt the right level of risk is the changing effectiveness of equity compensation as the mix of options, restricted stock, and other forms of pay interact. Yisong Tian utilized the familiar utility-maximization framework and asked the following question: For a compensation package with a fixed total cost, how does varying the proportion of options in the package affect the CEO's risk-taking incentives?[4] One might expect that the more options in the mix, the more aggressively the executive would pursue the maximization of the firm's stock price, but Tian found that this was not true. Instead, Tian concluded that there is some critical threshold for the proportion of options in the mix that maximizes the incentive effect and that this proportion could be as low as 40 percent. This is substantially lower than the proportion of options in the pay mix for some recent years.

As mentioned, part of the problem with the incentivizing power of options is that executives value them less than the cost that the firm incurs to provide them. Increasing the portion of options in the pay mix increases the executive's risk, so she naturally reduces the subjective value that she ascribes to the options. Because of this, the CEO with a high proportion of option pay will want to reduce the firm's idiosyncratic risk—the risk unrelated to broad market movements. This idiosyncratic risk is not compensated with additional expected return, because it is diversifiable by investors, but not by the firm. Also, the executive cannot diversify her excess exposure to the firm because her restricted stock and ESOs are not tradable. As noted, one of the key reasons for offering equity compensation in the first place is to expose the CEO to the firm's risk with the aim of giving her the proper incentives.

While the CEO may wish to reduce idiosyncratic risk, a high proportion of options in the compensation mix will incentivize her to increase systematic risk—the risk related to broad market movements and is nondiversifiable—because the market compensates systematic risk with increased expected return. So these two effects—the incentive to decrease idiosyncratic risk and to increase systematic risk—pull the total risk of the firm in contrasting directions, and the ultimate incentive effect for the executive to increase or reduce the risk of the firm depends on which of these two effects predominates. Further, the strength of both of these effects depends on the executive's degree of personal risk aversion, the total proportion of option wealth held by the executive, as well as various firm characteristics.

Tian also finds that the choice of exercise price significantly affects the incentivizing character of ESOs. The more the option is out-of-the-money, the greater the executive's subjective discounting of the value of the ESO. This subjective discounting affects the incentivizing power of the options, such that Tian finds that the incentivizing power of options is maximized if the exercise price is below the current stock price. Although some features of the analytical frameworks of Tian and Carpenter differ, their results regarding the impact of the moneyness of the options appear somewhat contrasting. While Carpenter found that deep out-of-the-money options could lead to excessive risk taking, Tian's results seem to suggest that at least moderately in-the-money options have a more beneficial incentivizing result: "Holding the cost of the option grant constant, the firm may maximize the incentive to increase stock price by setting exercise price moderately below the grant-date stock price. The incentive-maximizing exercise price is typically greater than zero but less than the stock price, and its precise value depends on the executive's risk aversion, proportional option wealth, and characteristics of the firm and the market portfolio."[5]

Also working within the utility-maximizing framework, Nohel and Todd further confirm the importance of complications in the incentive problem—even though the overall conceptual framework, like that of Carpenter and Tian, abstracts from many real-world complications.[6] Nohel and Todd emphasize that the executive's appraisal of her human capital also figures in the analysis and that the value of her human capital varies with the stock price of the firm she leads. So a risk-averse CEO concerned about the value of her human capital will strive to avoid negative outcomes and will be less inclined than the firm's shareholders to undertake risky projects. Nohel and

Todd capture this issue of the CEO's human capital under the rubric of "career concerns," and they stress that the manger's incentives to invest and to take on risky projects depends on the exercise price of the options; how wealthy, diversified, and risk averse the executive is; and on the extent of her career concerns. All of these factors interact to determine the executive's risk-taking propensities.

Within this framework, Nohel and Todd find that increasing the strength of incentives in the compensation mix does not necessarily induce a higher level of firm investment or risk taking and may even lead the executive to reduce the firm's risk. Further, Nohel and Todd find that the exercise price relative to the stock price is crucial in shaping the CEO's incentives. Specifically, at-the-money options maximize the executive's incentive to take risk. Notice this contrasts with Carpenter's finding that being deeply out-of-the-money can induce excessive risk taking and Tian's result that the ideal exercise price is one that places the option in-the-money.

The entire issue of the best exercise price for creating the right incentives proves to be quite difficult, as the contrasting results just summarized indicate. Much of the literature, especially the early work of Lambert, Larcker, and Verechhia, along with that of Carpenter, focused on European options, which contain the critical feature that they can be exercised only at expiration. Brisley, by on the other hand, pursues this issue by considering the effect of early-exercise provisions and modulating the vesting policy to create the right incentives.[7] Brisley argues that traditional ESOs issued at-the-money provide strong risk-taking incentives. But if the firm is successful, those options can move deep in-the-money and still be unvested and therefore unexercisable. In this event, Brisley shows that the executive's holding of these in-the-money options can actually give the CEO counterproductive incentives such that she will actually reject valuable risky projects. This occurs because undertaking even a worthy risky project may work out poorly with a resultant loss in the value of the executive's portfolio of ESOs. Brisley urges that firms let options vest when they become sufficiently deep in-the-money so that the options with counterproductive incentives will be liquidated and those perverse incentives eliminated. In a similar vein, Barron and Waddell conclude that options that are too far out-of-the-money can provide incentives to incur too much risk, while Garvey and Mawani argue that an exercise price near the current stock price maximizes the strength of the risk-taking incentives.[8] (Interestingly, this result suggests that the accounting-driven policy of issuing options with exercises prices that place them at the money is best for stimulating CEO risk taking.)

Yet, other theoretical studies include more complicating factors, such as the extent to which the executive's skills are firm-specific, finding that the optimal incentives are weaker than they would be for an executive whose skills are broadly applicable.[9] In addition, it appears that the CEO's willingness to behave in a truly entrepreneurial fashion is quite sensitive to the design of the pay package.[10]

Because these theoretical conclusions are so sensitive to the exact specification of the compensation model and the characterization of the CEO's personal attributes, an empirical examination of the behavior of executives is necessary to understand the role of risk-taking incentives. Perhaps Core, Guay, and Larcker summarize the conclusion most succinctly: "It is almost always necessary to understand the objectives of shareholders, the characteristics of managers, and other elements of the decision-making setting before drawing any conclusions about the desirability of observed equity-based incentive plans or the level of equity ownership by managers. Sweeping statements about governance and compensation, without a detailed contextual analysis, are almost always misleading."[11]

Executive Compensation and the Risk-Taking Behavior of CEOs

In this section, we turn from the formal examination of risk-taking behavior to empirical examinations of the interaction between incentive compensation and the behavior of executives in accepting risky investment projects and in structuring the risk posture of their firms. As we will see, the results generally conform to the intuitions elaborated by the theoretical studies discussed. The most important features of the empirical examinations are that CEOs with strong risk-taking incentives in their compensation packages do accept riskier projects; and, second, the research shows how boards can modulate the risk-taking preferences of their CEOs by subtly varying the structure of executive compensation.

The first crucial conclusion is that CEOs do respond to risk-taking incentives. These incentives stem almost entirely from equity-based compensation generally and from ESOs in particular. The oil and gas exploration industry faces the inescapable imperative to embark on risky projects, such as drilling new wells. The prospect of dry holes as well as, often vicious, price swings in oil are two major risks firms in the industry face. In a study of the industry, Rajgopal and Shevlin find a clear and strong relationship between CEO equity-based incentives and the willingness to undertake exploration risk.[12] Rajgopal and Shevlin examine how the CEO's stock-based wealth responds to an increase in the volatility of the firm's stock price, not merely how their wealth changes with respect to an increase in the price of the shares; thus, their research approach provides a direct measure of the response to risk.

This can be an important difference. Guay examines this issue from a similar perspective but uses another time period and a completely dissimilar sample.[13] He illustrates his point by relating an anecdote about two CEOs in his sample, one the CEO of Conrail, Inc., the other the CEO of GTE Corp. The

Conrail CEO held 94,400 shares of stock and 102,500 options worth a total of $10.3 million. (This was near the end of 1993.) The GTE CEO held 61,100 shares of stock and 539,000 stock options, worth a total value of about $6.4 million. Table 6.1 presents information on their portfolios and the responses to an increase in the firm's stock price and stock price volatility. If the stock price of each firm grew by 5 percent, the portfolios of both CEOs would have increased by about $600,000; the two portfolios had almost identical dollar responsiveness to an increase in the stock price.

However, the two portfolios would have radically different responses to a rise in the volatility of the firm's stock price. An increase in the volatility of the firm's stock price would not have a direct effect on the value of the firm's stock—although it could have an effect based on the market's perception of the underlying reasons for the volatility. By contrast, an increase in the volatility of the firm's stock price directly increases the value of the options. The Conrail CEO's equity-based holdings would rise in value by $55,000 given an increase in the standard deviation of the firm's stock price. However, the same increase in volatility would increase the wealth of GTE's CEO by $505,000, almost 10 times as much. Part, but only part, of this differential is evident from examining table 6.1. Clearly the GTE CEO holds many more options and a greater percentage of the equity-based portfolios as options, so we might expect greater responsiveness of his portfolio to an increase in stock volatility. However, the equity-based portfolio of the Conrail CEO is 60 percent larger than that of the GTE CEO ($10.2 versus $6.4 million), so a perusal of table 6.1 might suggest that the dollar increase for the Conrail CEO might be greater both in response to a stock price increase or a stock volatility increase. Instead, the actual responsiveness indicates that very much depends on the composition of the equity-based portfolio. The division between restricted stock and ESOs is important, but the actual character of the options that the

TABLE 6.1 Response of Equity Portfolio Values to Stock Price and Stock Price Volatility

	CEO of Conrail	CEO of GTE
Shares Owned	94,400	61,100
Value of Shares	$6.3 million	$2.1 million
Options Owned	102,500	539,900
Value of Options	$3.9 million	$4.3 million
Total Equity Portfolio Value	$10.2 million	$6.4 million
Percentage of Equity Exposure Held as Options	38.2	67.2
Approximate Wealth Change if the Firm's Stock Price Increases by 5%	+$600,000	+$600,000
Wealth Change if Standard Deviation of Firm's Stock Price Increases by 5 Points	+$55,000	+$505,000

Source: Adapted from Wayne R. Guay, "The Sensitivity of CEO Wealth to Equity Risk: An Analysis of the Magnitude and Determinants," *Journal of Financial Economics,* 1999, 53, 43–71.

CEO holds also matters. The responsiveness of the options depends on many factors: time until expiration, the relationship of the exercise price to the current stock price, the level of interest rates, the initial level of the stock's volatility, time remaining until vesting, and the probability that the CEO will exit the firm either before the options vest or before they expire. In addition, most CEOs receive annual options grants, so each type of option will have its own price response to a change in the level or volatility of the firm's stock price.

Guay's overall findings are consistent with his anecdote of the two CEOs. Across his sample, the equity-based holdings of CEOs expose them to strong incentives to increase the value of the firm's shares. In addition, the equity-based holdings also encourage them to increase the risk of the firm, and this incentive to increase risk operates mainly through the holding of ESOs rather than restricted stock. Guay summarizes matters: "I find stock options, but not common stockholdings, significantly increase the sensitivity of CEOs' wealth to equity risk."[14]

Guay's findings illustrate the general tenor of research in this area. Wright, Kroll, Davis and Jackson (WKDJ) reach a similar conclusion.[15] First, they find that small amounts of restricted stock in the CEO's portfolio increase the CEO's willingness to take risk. However, for large holdings of restricted stock, there is actually a tendency for the CEO to constrain or even reduce the risk of the firm. Thus, as the CEO has a larger restricted stock position and a larger portion of her wealth committed to the firm's shares, risk aversion comes to predominate. ESOs in the CEO's portfolio have a different effect, WKDJ find. Increasing the level and portion of ESOs in the CEO's portfolio consistently increases the risk-taking behavior of CEOs, and they point out that the total effect of the equity-based holdings depends on the potentially offsetting tendency of large restricted stock holdings to encourage risk reduction, while large option holdings encourage increasing risk.

Other studies confirm the broad conclusions of Guay and WKDJ, for example, an analysis by Devers, McNamara, Wiseman, and Arrfelt (DMWA). As an overall conclusion, they say: "In general, this study provides evidence that CEO equity-based compensation significantly influences strategic risk, but that this influence is more nuanced and complex than conventional treatments of executive compensation assume."[16] What are these nuances and complications? First, DMWA find a strong relationship between CEO equity-based holdings and changes in firm strategy, with greater equity compensation encouraging the adoption of riskier strategies. Second, distinct elements of equity-based compensation have distinct incentive properties, with those incentives changing around vesting and as stock prices fluctuate around the exercise price of the options. DMWA conclude: "This finding suggests that CEOs are motivated to enhance the value of unexercisable options and that, as the value of these options grows, they invest more in strategic risk actions likely to further increase their value."[17] DMWA also find that sizable holdings of restricted stock encourage CEOs to attenuate risk, consistent with Guay's results. As an additional contribution, DMWA stress that compensation and its risk-incentivizing effect is best understood as a part of social interaction within the firm that includes senior managers and directors. For example, board directives have an effect on strategic risk decisions as well as the CEO's amount and structure of compensation.

The risk level of the firm's shares does not change merely because someone wishes it so, but rather the standard deviation of returns on a stock depends mainly on specific actions and policies of the firm, a point stressed by Coles, Daniel, and Naveen, who study the specific policies by which CEOs affect the risk level of their firms.[18] Coles, Daniel, and Naveen find that CEOs with strong risk-encouraging incentives choose to invest in riskier assets and that they invest more in research and development. These same executives invest less in property, plant, and equipment. In addition, these highly incentivized CEOs tilt the financing policies of their firms toward the greater use of debt, thereby augmenting the firm's leverage and overall risk. Finally, they also find that firms led by CEOs with strong equity-based incentives focus the firm on fewer lines of business, rather than building a diversified structure of divisions.

While these preceding studies are consistent with the weight of the evidence—that CEOs with strong risk-encouraging pay packages actually do increase firm risk—there are notable and interesting studies that reach contrasting or even contradictory conclusions. Chen and Lee conclude that equity incentives do stimulate risk taking, but that this effect is short-lived and decays within three years after the firm sets the incentives. Thus, their ultimate conclusion is that ESOs do not really succeed in aligning the executive's risk-taking preferences with the long-term needs of the firm.[19] Cohen, Hall, and Viceira find that ESOs do encourage risk taking, also consistent with the weight of the literature, but they similarly conclude the effect is minute, which is contrary to most findings. On a brighter note, the weak power of these incentives leads the authors to argue that ESOs do not translate into excessive risk taking.[20]

Sanders and Hambrick identify what they believe is a more destructive role of risk-taking incentives. ESOs, they maintain, encourage a high level of investment, but these investments are concentrated in larger projects (consistent with the greater-focus finding of Coles, Daniel, and Naveen), and the investment outcomes vary widely. Even worse, Sanders and Hambrick find that these large and high-variance investment bets more often result in sizable losses rather than sizable gains: "Finally, we find that option-loaded CEOs deliver more big losses than big gains."[21]

Another fairly consistent result of the literature on the relationship between CEO incentives and firm risk is that highly incentivized CEOs perform less risk-management on behalf of the firm. For example, Tufano found that gold-mining firms led by CEOs with strong equity-based incentives did less to manage their firm's exposure to gold-price risks.[22] This is similar to a finding by Rajgopal and Shevlin that hedging of oil price exposure by oil production firms was lower if the CEO held robust incentives.[23] Finally, Rogers finds that CEOs with strong equity-based incentives make a more limited use of derivatives for hedging the firm's risk.[24]

We noted that Coles, Daniel, and Naveen found that highly incentivized CEOs adopt a higher degree of financial leverage than do less-incentivized CEOs. This result is well-supported in the literature. For example, Dong, Wang, and Xie argue that elevated ESO compensation induces CEOs to adopt capital structures for their firms that rely too heavily on debt.[25] Further, they maintain that the problem is so severe that it constitutes excessive risk taking. For their part, bondholders appear to understand quite well how the CEOs risk-taking incentives are likely to affect them. For example, according to Billett, Mauer, and Zhang, the announcement of ESO grants leads to opposing results for shareholders and bondholders: Stock prices rise, but bond prices fall.[26] This outcome is consistent with the uniform appraisal of the effects of the ESO grants in encouraging the CEO to augment firm risk. However, given their distinct holdings, this common outlook on the future of firm risk has opposite wealth implications for stockholders and bondholders. Ortiz-Molina reaches a similar conclusion, asserting that, "The evidence suggests that rational bondholders price new debt issues using the information about a firm's future risk choices contained in managerial incentive structures, and that lenders anticipate higher risk-taking incentives from managerial stock options than from equity ownership."[27] Benston and Evan find a similar overall relationship in banks. There, incentive contracts encourage CEOs to take unprofitable risks that shift wealth from bondholders to stockholders.[28]

However, it also appears that boards can modify the financial policies of the firm and the compensation mix that they offer to executives to offset this tendency to pillage bondholders. Brockman, Martin, and Unlu explain that including a higher portion of short-term debt in the firm's capital structure restrains the CEO's inclination to take risks because of the necessity of either paying off or rolling over the debt.[29] To repay the debt, the firm must have immediate cash flow; to roll the debt over, the firm must meet a market test. By using short-term debt in this way, the CEO's incentives come more closely into alignment with the desires of bondholders.

Summing up these findings on executive incentives and risk-taking, it seems clear that equity-based compensation, particularly ESOs, can effectively encourage CEOs to adopt riskier strategies for their firms. The empirical evidence on how incentives work in practice is congruent with the theoretical framework of the CEO acting as a maximizer of personal utility, in which her utility depends on her degree of risk aversion; the structure of her compensation from the firm, particularly her equity-based incentives; and her personal wealth held outside the firm, such that wealthier CEOs exhibit lower risk-aversion, a finding confirmed by Becker.[30] However, within this theoretical utility-maximization framework the concept of risk aversion remains somewhat opaque. An emerging body of research attempts to characterize the relationship between the CEO's personal characteristics and her propensity to incur risks.

One of the riskiest corporate strategic actions is to acquire another firm. Malmendier and Tate consider the relationship between the level of the CEO's confidence (or overconfidence) and the tendency both to initiate takeovers and to pay too much for targets.[31] To develop a measure of overconfidence, the authors survey the major financial publications and search for words applied to CEOs of big companies such as: confident, optimistic, frugal, conservative, cautious, and steady. They use the results to develop a measure of how outsiders perceive the personal degree of overconfidence for these CEOs. Malmendier and Tate also examine the behavior of these CEOs in exercising their ESOs. We have seen that there are good reasons for CEOs to exercise their ESOs before expiration, particularly to diminish their exposure to the risk of the firm and to diversify their personal portfolios. Malmendier and Tate argue persuasively that CEOs who hold their options long after vesting are confident in the firm's prospects and their abilities. Thus, they essentially have two measures of overconfidence—one based on the perceptions of the financial press, the other derived from the CEOs' revealed level of confidence as expressed in their option-exercising behavior. Other factors being held constant, Malmendier and Tate find that overconfident CEOs make more frequent and lower-quality acquisitions, especially if the firm has abundant financial resources. Also, these overconfident CEOs destroy shareholder value by their acquisitions.

Delgado-Garcia, Fuente-Sabaté, and Quevedo-Puente consider whether some CEOs are too negative to take risks.[32] They use a standard measure of positive and negative "affective traits" and relate this psychological disposition of bank CEOs to the risk position of their banks. Negatively inclined CEOs take lower risk, operate banks with a lower level of credit risk, and move their banks to hold loan portfolios that are less risky. By contrast, they find that CEOs with predominately positive affective traits do not take particularly aggressive risk positions.

Incentive Compensation, Risk Taking, and the Financial Crisis of 2007–2009

There is a strong consensus that the structure of executive compensation in the financial services industry played a significant role in causing the financial crisis of 2007–2009, a crisis with effects that lingered into 2012.

The Institute of International Finance surveyed its member institutions with significant wholesale-banking business. Even among these industry institutions, 98 percent of respondents agreed that compensation structures in the financial services industry played a role in generating the crisis.[33] The U.S. Treasury Department offered its "Guidance on Sound Incentive Compensation Policies" for the financial services industry in the wake of the crisis, in which it concluded: "Flawed incentive compensation practices in the financial industry were one of many factors contributing to the financial crisis that began in 2007. Banking organizations too often rewarded employees for increasing the organization's revenue or short-term profit without adequate recognition of the risks the employees' activities posed to the organization."[34]

The most dramatic event in the entire financial crisis of 2007–2009 was the sudden collapse and bankruptcy of Lehman Brothers in September 2008. In chapter 5, we saw that Lehman's CEO, Richard Fuld, had an enormous stake in the firm through his holdings of common stock and ESOs. Clearly Fuld had strong equity-based incentives to increase the firm's stock price and to achieve this goal by taking significant risks. The extent of those risks at Lehman, and at similar firms in the industry, was clearly expressed by the elevated degree of financial leverage with which these firms operated. To reiterate, Fuld had an enormous financial stake in the survival of the firm. In addition, there can be little doubt that he operated under a personal imperative to make Lehman as profitable and successful as his competitors at other Wall Street firms. Perhaps Andrew Ross Sorkin provided the best succinct summary of Fuld's position. "It was a telling paradox in the debate about executive compensation: Fuld was a CEO with most of his wealth directly tied to the firm on a long-term basis, and still he took extraordinary risks."[35]

The entire capitalist system is built on firms taking risk, capturing vast riches when successful, and suffering the penalty of bankruptcy when they fail. As we have seen, much of the motivation for providing equity-based incentives to CEOs is to encourage them to move out of their comfort zones and operate the firm at a higher risk level than they might otherwise choose. By contrast, the overwhelming discourse about the financial crisis decries the excessive risk-taking of these financial institutions. Thus, there seems to be a paradox between the general encouragement of firms to augment risk in the pursuit of profit and the loud public outcry about excessive risk taking by financial firms.

If the financial crisis of 2007–2009 proved anything, it showed conclusively that the U.S. government views some firms as too critical to be allowed to face the prospect of bankruptcy. This was proven by the support provided to almost all large private financial institutions during the crisis and the explicit takeovers of Fannie Mae and Freddie Mac. In addition, the bailouts extended to General Motors and Chrysler also bespeaks of the magnitude with which the federal government regarded these firms.

Leaving the automakers aside, the financial crisis also emphasized a fact that most economists and policymakers have long realized: financial institutions are special in two ways. First, because the provision of credit is so vital throughout the economy, financial institutions have a systemic importance that firms in many other industries lack. Thus, a giant financial firm may have greater systemic importance than an industrial firm of the same size. Second, and most critically, for some time, the federal government has provided financial guarantees to financial institutions, both explicitly and implicitly. Explicit guarantees include insurance on bank deposits by the Federal Deposit Insurance Corporation (FDIC). The outcome of the financial crisis proves that, in duress, the federal government's implicit guarantees to financial institutions become explicit.

The clearest example that implicit guarantees will be made explicit comes from the two big governmentally sponsored enterprises (GSEs), Fannie Mae and Freddie Mac. Prior to the crisis it was not uncommon for policymakers to deny that the government would offer such guarantees. For example, Congressman Barney Frank, chair of the House Financial Services Committee made that claim in 2003: "There is no guarantee. There's no explicit guarantee. There's no implicit guarantee. There's no wink-and-nod guarantee. Invest and you're on your own. Nobody who invests in them should come looking to me for a nickel. Nor anyone else in the federal government."[36] As the takeover of Fannie and Freddie proved, when the U.S. government guaranteed all obligations of both firms, this unequivocal statement was utterly false.

Given that the federal government stands as the ultimate guarantor of the financial system and given the systemic importance of the finance industry, it does make sense for the financial industry to operate under distinct risk policies versus other industries. Through regulation, the federal government has sought to control the risk taking of financial firms. The financial crisis of 2007–2009 proved the inadequacy of those efforts, and part of that failure almost certainly was the failure to control the risk-taking incentives of financial executives. This seems to be acknowledged, judging by the new efforts underway to constrain the risk-taking incentives of CEOs of financial firms. The initiative to constrain risk-taking incentives of financial executives is evidenced by several provisions of the Dodd-Frank Financial Reform Act and the active involvement in these issues by the Federal Reserve and Treasury Department.[37]

Incentive Compensation and the Management of the Firm

As explored in chapter 6, the executive's incentive compensation arrangements strongly influence the risk posture that she chooses for the firm. In part, the move to incentive compensation, which took root in the early 1990s and persisted for 20 years, was aimed at increasing the risk level that CEOs choose. However, we saw that induced risk-taking behavior had some undesirable outcomes. For example, an elevated level of equity-based incentive compensation may encourage a manager to unfairly shift risk to bondholders. More striking, many observers assert that incentive compensation in financial institutions induced excessive risk-taking that helped cause the financial crisis of 2007–2009.

Against the general background of risk taking considered in chapter 6, this chapter focuses on the link between incentive compensation and how CEOs manage their firms in several key dimensions. The key wealth-creating decision that the CEO makes is the capital-budgeting decision, or choosing the investment portfolio that the firm will pursue. The CEO can increase the value of the firm by undertaking large-scale projects with a high expected rate of return relative to the riskiness that the investment commitment entails. To secure funds to carry out wealth-generating projects, the firm must issue a mix of debt and equity to constitute the firm's capital structure. Thus the investment and financing decisions lie at the very heart of managing the firm and are the keys to successful corporate management. Setting an incentive compensation plan that encourages CEOs to make the best investment and financing decisions is a key element of overall corporate success, and this chapter explores the interaction between these decisions and the CEO's incentive compensation.

Beyond the capital-budgeting and capital-structure decisions, incentive compensation is interrelated with other specific aspects of firm management: the firm's dividend and share repurchase decisions; the willingness of a firm to be acquired and to take over other firms; whether and how to engage in risk management—a decision that goes beyond choosing the right overall risk level for the firm; and how the firm discloses information about the firm and how accurate those disclosures will be. This chapter considers each of these issues in turn.

Incentive Compensation and the Firm's Investment Program

As discussed, incentive compensation can induce CEOs to increase the general risk level at which the firm operates. But different firms may appropriately operate at different risk levels. Taking the firm's choice of its overall risk level as fixed, the investments the firm makes can be wise or foolish. Because no incentive contract can perfectly align the interests of the principal and agent, we would expect that the intensity and structure of incentive compensation would influence the specific investment choices the CEO makes. Most research supports this conclusion.

One persistent complaint lodged against U.S. corporations maintains that firms focus too much on short-term performance, sacrificing the creation long-term value. If the CEO has a short-term time horizon and directs the firm's investment policy, we would expect firms to emphasize projects with shorter lives that closely match the CEO's preferred time horizon. For CEOs who have a larger portion of their compensation in the form of annual bonuses, incentives suggest an even more extreme focus on the short run. In an early study, Guidry, Leone, and Rock found that managers with relatively more significant bonus compensation in fact emphasized short-term results and were willing to sacrifice longer-term value creation.[1] Valle and Pavlik similarly find that managers with in-the-money ESO holdings emphasize shorter-term and safer corporate-investment decisions, consistent with a desire to protect the value already impounded in their ESO portfolio.[2]

This short-run emphasis follows a number of different routes. For example, Hall and Liedtka concentrate on firms that outsource vital information technology (IT) services. They argue that these firms not only outsource the commodity aspects of IT, but that they also outsource even the vital IT functions on which the execution of the firm's business strategy depends. This outsourcing can augment short-term reported earnings, but Hall and Liedtka contend that it does so at the greater long-term cost of creating greater risk to the firm. This greater long-term risk results because the firm is dependent on the whims of the IT provider. According to Hall and Liedtka, the tendency to engage in large-scale outsourcing maneuvers ties in with the CEO's ESO holdings. As they put the point: "Our research underscores the fact that IT outsourcing can benefit CEOs and often their firms, by generating illusory improvements in reported expenses and profits."[3]

On the other hand, compensation packages can also influence the firm's investment decisions by stimulating risk taking and a focus on the long run.

Oil and gas firms undertake exploration projects that are inherently risky and typically pay off over a long time horizon. The problem with "dry holes" is legendary, and even when an exploration program succeeds, firms typically suffer an extended delay from exploration outlays to receiving cash flows from exploiting the discoveries. Rajgopal and Shevlin focus on oil and gas firms and study the relationship between a willingness to undertake exploration and the CEO's compensation package. If a CEO holds options that have a long term to vesting and a long term to expiration, theory suggests that these options can incentivize greater risk-taking, as we discussed in chapter 6. But a large holding of deeply in-the-money ESOs can also encourage CEOs to focus on the short run and to avoid undertaking expensive and risky investment projects. As we noted in chapter 6, Rajgopal and Shevlin conclude that executive compensation incentives work in a constructive manner by successfully encouraging risky exploration projects: "Overall our results are consistent with ESOs providing managers with incentives to mitigate risk-related incentive problems."[4] Thus, ESOs not only stimulate additional risk taking, but they can also encourage the undertaking of projects with long time horizons.

Another particularly risky project is investing in research and development. Like oil or gas exploration, the outcomes of such investments are difficult to predict and positive cash flows from such investments are likely realized after a lengthy delay. Coles, Daniel, and Laveen explore the relationship between the sensitivity of CEO wealth to stock volatility and the corporate policies that CEOs implement. They find that CEOs, whose wealth positions are sensitive to the riskiness of the firm's stock price, carry out a higher level of investment in research and development and that they also implement riskier policy choices overall.[5]

Free cash flow is cash flow over and above that which the firm requires to fund its investment projects and to service its debt commitments. The *free cash flow problem* is the tendency of corporate managers to retain cash within the firm and invest it in low-return projects or to retain excessive cash to reduce firm and managerial risk. This free cash flow problem is a fundamental difficulty of the principal-agent relationship, because shareholders would prefer that managers return cash to shareholders rather than invest those funds poorly. (One reason given for a move to increased debt financing is to absorb free cash flow and get it out of the hands of management. This often happens in corporate takeovers in which outsiders gain control of a firm and multiply its debt load significantly.)

To address the free cash flow problem, a firm can structure the CEO's compensation package to induce her to make the wisest possible use of the firm's incoming cash. Broussard, Buchenroth, and Pilotte find that pay packages that are better aligned with shareholder interests help to address this free cash flow problem. Specifically, CEOs with compensation arrangements better aligned with shareholder interests do not overinvest as much as CEOs with poorly aligned incentives, and better-aligned compensation structures also reduce the tendency of managers to underinvest as a form of managerial shirking.[6] However, it also seems that firms which create aggressive risk-taking incentives actually need to hold more cash, because bondholders demand that the firm hold more cash to demonstrate their ability to honor their bond obligations if the firm plans to undertake aggressive investments.[7]

As an initial summary, it appears clear that the structure of the CEO's compensation package strongly affects the investment program that the firm chooses. The overall result can either succeed or fail to align the CEO's incentives with the creation of firm value. Thus, Benmelech, Kandel, and Veronesi find that equity-based compensation both "induces managers to exert costly effort," but that it can also encourage them to "conceal bad news about future growth options and to choose suboptimal investment policies."[8] For their part, Valle and Pavlik find perverse outcomes: "We also present the argument that managers can easily disguise their self-interests, or managerial opportunism, by manipulating firm investment decisions to favor alternatives that provide the greatest likelihood of personal gain in the short term."[9]

Perhaps the results of a study by Nohel and Todd sum up the sometimes beneficial sometimes harmful relationship between the CEO's compensation package and the firm's investment policies. They focus mostly on ESOs and gauge the manager's incentive to invest. They conclude that the manager's existing wealth, level of risk aversion, degree of diversification, and willingness to put her human capital at risk by undertaking significant firm investments all play a role. Sometimes pay packages that are poorly aligned with the interests of shareholders can cause underinvestment, but if poor alignment is in an opposite direction, compensation incentives can encourage overinvestment. This can lead to major problems: the acceptance of very poor investment projects and the rejection of projects that are actually very attractive. Nohel and Todd find that "firm value is not a strictly increasing function of a manager's incentive compensation or conventional pay-performance sensitivity metrics. Stronger managerial incentives to invest can benefit or harm a firm."[10]

Equity-related compensation changes incentives in a variety of ways that result in some unanticipated alteration in firm management. For example, firms with high levels of long-term equity-based compensation tend to spend more on advertising, consistent with a view that such firms emphasize the long-term.[11] Firms that depend heavily on research and development, and thus have a necessarily long-term perspective, are inclined to use more long-term incentive compensation, according to Erkens, who finds that these firms use options with longer vesting periods and expiration, apparently "to reduce the leakage of R&D-related information to competitors through employee mobility."[12]

Overall these studies emphasize that the key wealth-creating or wealth-destroying decisions of the firm are highly sensitive to the CEOs pay incentives.

Not only will the CEO's decisions vary with the strength of incentives, but the actual construction of the pay package is critical in that one cannot hope to achieve better alignment between the interests of the CEO and the firm merely by implementing strong incentives. Rather, the detailed construction of the pay package matters a great deal.

CEO Incentives and the Firm's Financing Decisions

In chapter 6, we considered the strong evidence that a high degree of equity compensation can stimulate risk taking by CEOs, and we have seen this confirmed with respect to the relationship between CEO compensation and the firm's investment policies. Every firm secures financing by issuing a mix of equity and debt. In general, a higher degree of financial leverage (a greater portion of debt in the financing mix) implies a higher level of firm risk. Similarly, short-term debt is riskier than long-term debt because the firm with short-term debt must return to the financial markets more frequently to replace maturing debt. (In the financial crisis of 2007–2009, some investment banking firms, notably Lehman Brothers, were brought low by their extreme reliance on very short-term financing.) Thus, other factors being equal, we would expect CEOs with strong equity-based compensation to adopt a riskier capital structure for the firm—the capital structure being the mix of debt and equity financing and the mix of short- and long-term debt financing for the portion of its capital that is secures through borrowing.

Those who lend to firms put their principal at risk in exchange for a promise of a stream of fixed payments; at least this is true for most debt, which typically bears a fixed rate of interest. Thus, the debt holder has no upside from her investment, and the best she can hope is that the borrowing firm will pay as promised. Given this situation, debt holders prefer that the firm not surprise them with large jumps in their risk levels that increase the probability that the firm will be unable to pay as promised. Even if the firm moves to a riskier posture to capture attractive investments, this can still harm the bondholder because lucrative, but risky, investments often fail.

Strong equity-based compensation may tempt executives to select riskier projects and to shift the posture of the firm to a riskier strategy. Lenders to the firm are, of course, aware of these incentives facing the CEO. As a result, the firm's financing decision is a complicated one in which the CEO's incentives interact with lender's willingness to lend. These interactions are resolved and are ultimately expressed in the firm's actual capital structure. Coles, Daniel, and Naveen find that CEOs with their wealth more closely tied to the firm's equity do choose higher leverage, and Dong, Wang, and Xie support this view, even concluding that the CEO's incentives can make managers adopt capital structures so risky that they destroy firm value.[13]

However, not every study finds a positive relationship between the CEO's equity-related incentives and a higher reliance on debt financing. For example, Katharina Lewellen finds that options actually discouraged risk taking and led to lower leverage in the financing mix.[14] In general, one might expect more ESOs to compel riskier choices, but deep in-the-money options can actually incentivize the CEO to prefer a low-risk posture and to rely less on debt financing.

There is, at least, one other important reason that ESOs can actually lead to lower leverage. For firms with a high reliance on ESOs as a form of compensation, especially if stock options are granted to employees below the executive ranks, the exercise of these options can provide an essential source of financing to firms, which reduces firm reliance on capital markets. This appears to have been especially true of high-tech firms in the dotcom boom. Issuing stock options in lieu of paying wages substitutes for the issuance of additional firm equity, thus shifting the firm's capital structure away from debt and toward equity.

Consider a firm with steadily rising stock prices, such as high-tech firms during the dotcom boom. When option holders exercise their options, the corporation receives a tax deduction that equals the difference between the exercise price of the options and the firm's current stock price. In this situation, numerous option exercises provide a large tax shelter to firms. Thus, these option exercises act as a substitute for debt by providing a tax shield— the exercise-driven tax shield functions much like the deductibility of interest on debt payments. In this situation, firms may not need the tax shield provided by debt, and they will be inclined to have lower leverage than otherwise. This is exactly what two studies find, one by Graham, Lang, and Shackleford; and a second by Kahle and Shastri, who say: "Theory suggests that firms with tax benefits from the exercise of stock options should carry less debt since tax benefits are a non-debt tax shield. We find that both long- and short-term debt ratios are negatively related to the size of tax benefits from option exercise."[15] Kahle and Shastri also note that U.S. companies cut their tax bills by as much as $56.4 billion in 2000 at the height of the dotcom boom. For their part, Graham, Lang, and Shackleford similarly note that in 2000 stock option deductions reduced marginal tax rates for high-tech firms from 31 to 5 percent.[16] In summation, Kahle and Shastri assert: "Overall, these results are consistent with the notion that firms view the tax benefits from option exercise as a substitute for the tax benefit from debt, and that these tax benefits can explain why some firms appear to be underleveraged."[17]

By the same token, ESOs and more widely distributed options provide a kind of equity financing for corporations as well. A firm issues an employee stock option at least partially in lieu of immediate compensation and issuing the option requires no immediate cash flow and no sequence of cash flows to repay a debt obligation. Thus, unlike direct borrowing, issuing an option provides a kind of employee financing that is more akin to equity financing than debt financing. As Babenko, Lemmon, and Tserlukevich put the point in their study: "Firms increasingly issue equity *indirectly* by granting stock options to their employees...Our results suggest that indirect equity issues to employees as part of compensation plans are an important source of financing, particularly for firms with limited internal liquidity and those facing high costs of accessing external capital markets."[18]

A central problem of corporate governance is managing the conflict of interests between equity holders and bondholders. Other things being equal, equity holders prefer that the firm operate at a higher risk level than the firm's bondholders would select. The problem is exacerbated when the CEO holds a sizable endowment of ESOs. Simply increasing the riskiness of the firm will raise the price of options but reduce the value of bonds. So the CEO can make investment and financing decisions that disadvantage bondholders relative to stockholders and relative to her own holdings of stock and options in the firm.[19]

If the potential risk shifting is of significant concern to bondholders, we would expect bondholders to be displeased at news of increased equity-based compensation for CEOs. This seems to be the case. When a firm announces a new grant of equity-based compensation, stock prices tend to rise, and bond prices tend to fall.[20] This is consistent with the view that bondholders regard such incentive compensation as making their holdings riskier and therefore worth less. This increased risk to bondholders leads to higher borrowing costs for firms. Ortiz-Molina finds that the yield on newly issued corporate bonds tends to be higher if the manager's interests are more highly aligned with those of shareholders: "The evidence suggests that rational bondholders price new debt issues using the information about a firm's future risk choices contained in managerial incentive structures, and that lenders anticipate higher risk-taking incentives from managerial stock options than from equity ownership."[21] Further, this yield effect is higher if the equity-based compensation is focused on ESOs rather than restricted stock. As Ortiz-Molina says: "This result is consistent with stock options providing better risk-taking incentives than stock, and with prospective bondholders anticipating higher risk-shifting incentives from managerial stock options than from equity ownership."[22] In sum, high executive ESO holdings encourage greater risk-taking in general and greater risk-shifting to bondholders in particular.

However, the overall effect of executive compensation and capital structure is complex, and these complexities help to explain why executive compensation plans have so many elements. One role of the board of directors is to mitigate conflicts among the firm's various stakeholders. A board that provides the CEO with risk-taking and risk-shifting incentives that are too powerful is in danger of not only having an investment policy that is too radical, but those incentives can also impair the ability of the firm to issue debt. To illustrate, a firm determines the mix between equity financing and debt financing, but this still leaves open the question of whether to issue short-term or long-term debt. If the firm issues long-term debt, locking in the debt financing for a long time horizon, the bondholders as a group are stuck with whatever policies the firm then initiates. Having issued long-term debt, a CEO that has strong equity incentives has strong incentives and an opportunity to shift risk to the class of captive bondholders. (Of course, any particular bondholder can sell the bonds, but the bonds cannot be cashed out with the firm. So the risk policies of the firm will affect the value of the bonds and the fortunes of the bondholders conceived as a group, no matter which individuals hold the bonds at a given time.) By contrast, the firm that issues short-term debt has two choices when the debt comes due: it can either repay the debt or it can refinance. If the CEO has adopted policies that are too risky, she is in danger of being unable to refinance, and the firm will go bankrupt. Alternatively if the firm plans to refinance, but if it also initiates policies that abuse its current short-term lenders, then it will struggle recruiting new lenders to refinance its expiring short-term debt. Thus, issuing short-term debt rather than long-term debt helps to constrain the risk-taking incentives of CEOs and also helps to minimize the incentive to abuse debt holders. In their study, Brockman, Martin, and Unlu find exactly those incentive effects.[23]

Prospective lenders to the firm are aware of these incentives and respond accordingly in at least two ways. First, we saw that borrowing rates will be higher if the firm's CEO is highly incentivized. Second, bondholders can refuse to lend unless the firm offers assurances about their behavior over the life of the bonds. In this situation, firms find themselves compelled to offer various restrictive covenants on the firm's behavior over the life of the debt obligation. In their study of the relationship between managerial incentives and bond covenants, Chava, Kumar, and Warga find that borrowing firms tend to offer covenants that variously restrict dividend payments, types of investment, further financing during the life of the debt being issued, and firm behavior in times of financial distress or takeovers. As Chava, Kumar, and Warga make the point: "Bond covenants play a prominent role in the agency theory of the firm...namely that firms voluntarily proscribe their operational flexibility to lower agency risk for bondholders and reduce the cost of debt financing."[24]

Within the firm, conflicts may erupt among the parties. As we just discussed, corporate boards sometimes act to reduce potential conflicts between managers and bondholders, presumably aiming at the overall well-being of the firm. But divergent preferences can arise among managers as well, and these are expressed in the policies of the firm. Chava and Purnanandam found that the CEO's incentives for higher or lower risk help to determine the firm's degree of leverage and its holding of cash balances. By contrast, the CFO's risk incentives appear to influence the mix of short- and long-term debt and the extent to which the firm tries to smooth its reported earnings.[25] Given that the CFO reports to the CEO, it is not clear why the CFO's risk incentives find any expression at all in the policies of the firm. This unexplained phenomenon emphasizes the complexity of the relationship among incentives, incentive conflicts, and the policies that firms ultimately adopt, especially in the area of capital structure.

Compensation Incentives, Dividends, and Share Repurchases

Firms can distribute funds to their shareholders in two basic ways: by paying cash dividends or by buying the firm's shares in the open market. When a firm pays a cash dividend, the value of the outstanding shares typically falls by the amount of the dividend payment. After all, paying a dividend changes nothing about the firm's operations, and it reduces the cash that the firm holds by the amount of the dividend. (Dividend payments in general and changing dividend policy in particular, may also carry a signal to the marketplace about the firm's ability to sustain payments.) Rather than pay a dividend, a firm may use cash to buy shares in the open market. This also does nothing to change the future cash flows of the firm, but it does change the number of shares outstanding. Thus, in general, paying a dividend of a given total amount will reduce the value of outstanding shares, while using the same total amount to repurchase shares will leave the value of the remaining shares unchanged.

A simple example illustrates this general principle. Assume an all-equity firm has 1,000,000 outstanding shares that currently trade for $100 per share: a total market value of $100 million for the firm's shares. Let us assume that the firm pays a dividend totaling $5 per share or $5,000,000. A holder of one share receives a cash payment of $5 and the share now represents a claim on $5 less of assets held by the firm, so the share price after the dividend should be $95. By contrast, if a firm devotes $5 million to purchasing shares, it buys 50,000 shares. Having just spent $5 million, the total value of the firm's shares should fall from $100 million to $95 million. However, after the share repurchase, there are only 950,000 shares outstanding, so each remaining share should still be worth $100. In most contexts, the choice between dividends and share repurchases is not a particularly important decision, but the choice of how to relay money to investors has significant interactions with the structure of incentives in executive compensation.

Whether a firm issues a dividend or engages in a share repurchase, the exercise price of a standard ESO remains static. This means that ESOs are not dividend-protected. Therefore, when the firm pays a dividend and the share price falls by the amount of the dividend, the ESO moves away from the money by the amount of the dividend. However, when the firm returns funds to shareholders via a stock repurchase, the share price remains unchanged, and the value of an ESO is unaffected. In an early study, Lambert, Lanen, and Larcker hypothesized that this differential gave executives who hold ESOs a strong incentive to prefer share repurchases over dividend payments.[26] Subsequent research strongly supports the conjecture of Lambert, Lanen, and Larcker. That is, executives holding ESOs respond to their personal wealth incentives and tilt away from dividend payments toward share repurchases as the preferred method of distributing cash to shareholders.

Beyond the personal interests of executives there is another reason that firms might prefer to repurchase shares rather than pay dividends. For firms with hefty employee stock-ownership programs (that is, firms that distribute shares to many employees beyond top executives), firms may want to repurchase shares to avoid diluting the ownership rights of existing shares when employees exercise their options. As a result, research in this area has had to disentangle these two motivations—avoiding diluting the value of shares and maintaining the value of ESOs held by top management.[27] We focus on the evidence pertaining to ESOs and executive compensation.

When executives hold significant ESO positions, research has demonstrated a very strong predilection of firms to favor repurchases over dividends. In the absence of large ESO holdings, there is a reduced tendency to replace dividends with share repurchases. Fenn and Liang find "a strong negative relationship between dividends and management stock options...and a positive relationship between repurchases and management stock options. Our results suggest that the growth in stock options may help to explain the rise in repurchases at the expense of dividends."[28] Examining firm behavior during the 1990s, Kathleen Kahle found a similar result, with firms preferring repurchases both to fund option programs and to sustain the value of ESOs. Ghosh, Harding, Sezer, and Sirmans examine a sample of share repurchases among REITs (Real Estate Investment Trusts) and find the same strong preference for repurchases by firms in which executives hold strong ESO positions.[29] As we have seen, paying dividends reduces the value of ESOs. But if an executive holds restricted stock, she generally receives the dividend, so the restricted stock, but not an ESO, is dividend-protected. Therefore, executives that hold the equity of their own firm more in the form of restricted stock rather than ESOs should be more willing to pay dividends. Aboody and Kasznik find exactly that result.[30]

Aside from the merely self-interested preference of executives for repurchases over dividends, there are other effects. Babenko finds that "share repurchases increase pay-performance sensitivity of employee compensation and lead to greater employee effort and higher stock prices." In addition, she notes that "the market reacts favorably to repurchase announcements when employees have many unvested stock options. Managers are more likely to initiate share repurchases when employees hold a large stake in the firm.

Moreover, since employees are forced to bear more risk in firms that repurchase shares, they exercise their stock options earlier and receive higher compensation."[31]

On the whole, then, firms with employee and executive option holdings prefer repurchases rather than dividends, both to protect the fractional ownership interests of shareholders that continue to hold the firm's stock and to protect ESOs against a loss of value incurred by issuing dividends. According to Cuny, Martin, and Puthenpurackal, the desire to protect ESOs against a loss of value from dividends is a dominating factor, and firms with high ESO ownership have lower payout levels overall.[32] Thus, perhaps it comes as no surprise that the personal financial interests of top executives strongly affect the dividend and share-repurchase behavior of corporations.

Corporate Mergers, Acquisitions, and Liquidations

Corporate mergers and acquisitions involve two CEOs with their own incentives that diverge in some respects but are congruent in others. Most ESOs grants specify a *change-in-control* provision that allows the CEO's ESOs to vest if the firm is acquired. This gives a target CEO an incentive to "get the deal done" so that her options will vest, allowing her to exercise her ESOs and effectively cash out of the firm. In short, an unvested option bears a certain "illiquidity discount," but if the merger goes through and the options vest at that point, they are suddenly liquid and become more valuable. On the other hand, the CEO of a target firm that is acquired will probably leave the firm, or will at least lose primacy of position in the merged firm. Almost all mergers involve a *merger premium*—the excess of the price paid for shares in the merger over and above the share price prevailing before the merger news reached the public. However, the target CEO also faces certain costs in allowing the merger to occur. A CEO approaching retirement who holds a portfolio of deep in-the-money vested options may find the opportunity to retire and cash out her ESOs very attractive, while a young CEO with unvested out-of-the-money options might have strong personal reasons to resist the merger because it will mean relinquishing control of the firm and seeking new employment.

For the CEO of the acquiring firm, a range of possible incentives comes into play, but two are particularly notable. First, the CEO may wish to command a larger and more prominent firm simply to inflate her sense of self-importance. Also, CEOs of larger firms tend to receive higher pay, as we have seen, so building an empire may ultimately lead to greater compensation as well as ego gratification. Second, and probably more important, the CEO of a potential acquirer typically holds a significant portfolio of equity-based compensation. If this is the case, the acquiring CEO may be anxious to undertake value-increasing mergers, the completion of which will raise the value of her restricted stock or ESOs. If the CEO of the prospective acquirer holds little equity-based compensation, then she may be more motivated simply to build her empire by enlarging the size of the firm she directs, and she may be less concerned with building firm value through the merger.

Most of the research in this area supports the overall conclusions which the preceding reflections suggest: The CEO of a target firm will be more willing to agree to being acquired the larger the illiquidity discount that the merger will remove; the CEO of a target with little equity-based compensation will be more likely to resist the merger, having little to gain and her position to lose. When they examined 250 completed mergers, Cai and Vijh found that "target CEOs with a higher illiquidity discount accept a lower [merger] premium, offer less resistance, and more often leave after acquisition."[33]

Corporate boards appear to be well-aware of the incentives that CEOs face in prospective mergers, and this awareness is reflected quite strongly in firms that are ultimately acquired. By allowing her firm to be acquired, we have noted that CEOs typically lose their prominence in the firm and even their jobs. It appears that firms grant additional incentive compensation in the run-up to mergers. Such equity-based compensation could be regarded as rent extraction by the CEO—a bribe for the CEO not to resist a beneficial merger. Alternatively, the increased incentive compensation might be interpreted according to the incentive alignment framework—by granting additional equity-based compensation the firm's board may actually be working to align the incentives of the CEO with the interests of the firm by removing the CEO's incentive to resist a beneficial acquisition. Whichever of these two interpretations is correct, firms do tend to sweeten the CEO's incentive compensation shortly before a firm is acquired.

Heitzman studied this issue and found that equity grants to the CEOs of target firms tended to be larger in the year before the firm is acquired. He suggests that part of the reason for these grants is to compensate the CEO for the loss she will suffer when the merger happens. However, he also notes that firms that make these grants just before mergers receive larger merger premiums, consistent with an incentive-alignment interpretation of the grants' purpose. He concludes: "Overall, the evidence suggests that equity awards to the target CEO reflect the CEO's and board's information and incentives relating to the upcoming acquisition consistent with shareholder wealth maximization within the market for corporate control."[34] Thus, Heitzmann finds that the CEO receives a windfall from the incremental equity-based compensation, but the firm also prospers because the merger premium expands when the firm grants that compensation.

However, not all studies find this happy conclusion for both the CEO and the target firm she leads. For example, Fich, Cai, and Tran find that managerial rent extraction is a common feature of mergers. They examined 364 mergers over the 1999–2005 period and found that in more than 25 percent of those cases the target CEO received an increase in ESO-based compensation just before the merger, but that the target shareholders suffered losses because the merger premiums the firms received were smaller than they otherwise would have been. The benefits to the highest quartile of rent-extraction CEOs averaged $19 million, with the shareholders of the target firms collectively losing many millions of dollars.[35]

If we consider acquisitions from the point of view of the acquiring firms' CEOs, the findings are generally much more supportive of the incentive-alignment view. Datta, Iskandar-Datta, and Raman find that managers with a high level of equity-based compensation pay lower merger premiums and acquire firms with better growth prospects. When mergers are undertaken by CEOs with high equity-based compensation, the stock price of the acquiring firm actually tends to rise upon the announcement of the prospective merger. This is striking, because on the whole, merger announcements are usually accompanied by a fall in the acquirer's stock price and a rise in the target's stock price. Following the merger, the merged firms that resulted from acquiring CEOs with a high level of equity-based compensation outperformed those merged firms that resulted from CEOs with low levels of equity-based compensation.[36] Minnick, Unal, and Yang find broadly confirming results in their study of the banking industry, in which they conclude that banks led by CEOs with greater pay-for-performance sensitivity (i.e., more equity-based compensation) were less likely to engage in value-reducing mergers, and that the mergers these CEOs undertook generally had better subsequent operating performance.[37]

The incentive-alignment goals of inducing managers to increase risk also seems to be borne out in the merger arena. Datta, Iskandar-Datta, and Raman find that mergers led by CEOs with higher equity-based compensation lead to the creation of riskier postmerger firms, which is consistent with the goal of using equity-based compensation to encourage managerial risk taking.[38] Williams, Michael, and Rao find broadly confirming results, concluding that "the risk-incentive effect of CEO stock options is positively related to the post-merger level of equity risk."[39] Also supporting the general efficacy of equity-based pay in encouraging risk-taking behavior by acquiring firm CEOs, Sanders found that CEOs with more ESOs rather than restricted stock were more willing to engage in risky strategies.[40]

Not all of the research on managerial incentives and merger behavior is univocal. Consider a firm led by a CEO who knows that the shares of her company are temporarily overvalued. This excess valuation provides an incentive for the CEO to acquire other firms and to pay for the acquired firms with the overvalued shares of her company. For example, during the dotcom boom many mergers were undertaken; the target firms' shareholders received the overvalued shares of the acquiring firm, and then they suffered large losses when the market restored to a more sober valuation for the acquiring firms shares.

Fung, Jo, and Tsai find that firms with overvalued stock undertake more value-destroying mergers, but consistent with the incentive-alignment account of executive compensation, this tendency is mitigated if CEOs have more performance-based compensation. They conclude: "The main finding suggests that market-driven acquisitions could be value destroying when managers engage in opportunistic acquisitions for reasons of self-interest." This is especially true when these managers are not constrained by their own holdings that are related to the success of the firm.[41] Cai and Vijh find contrasting results. In situations in which CEOs lead firms that are overvalued, they conclude that "acquirer CEOs with higher [equity-based] holdings pay a higher premium, expedite the process, and make diversifying acquisitions using stock payment."[42]

Sometimes firms should be liquidated and doing so can benefit shareholders, but the CEO of such a firm will lose her position in the liquidation. Further, the CEO might be in a position to frustrate a beneficial liquidation and could have a strong incentive to keep the firm going merely to maintain her employment. Mehran, Nogler, and Schwartz found that CEOs with strong equity-related incentives more willingly acquiesced in the dissolution of their firms.[43]

This consideration of mergers, acquisitions, and liquidations emphasizes the nuances of the incentives that compensation packages create. Incentives for acquiring CEOs that are too weak can lead to value-destroying behavior in mergers. For CEOs of target firms, incentives that are too weak can lead them to too aggressively resist merger overtures, while incentives that are too strong can encourage them to too readily agree to poor terms of acquisition. The complexity of so many dimensions of firm management, the variety of human circumstances and psychology, and the almost always unexpected turn of events conspire to make even the most upright compensation committee's task difficult, if not impossible, to furnish the right level and mix of compensation that secures the CEO's best behavior in the widest array of circumstances.

Compensation Incentives and Corporate Risk Management

As we have seen in a variety of contexts throughout this book, a central feature of executive compensation programs seeks to align the interests of CEOs and the firms they lead and that firms attempt to achieve this alignment by using equity-based compensation. Awards of restricted stock tie the wealth of a CEO to changes in the firm's stock price, as do grants of ESOs. However, an ESO grant provides the CEO with heightened exposure not only to the firm's stock price but also to the risk level of the firm. We have also seen that a compensation tilt toward restricted stock reduces the risk-taking incentives of CEOs. By contrast, a heavy reliance on ESOs in the pay package can stimulate risk taking, an outcome that many firms have long regarded as desirable.

Merely increasing the riskiness of the firm's stock increases the value of ESOs, but such an increase in risk does not raise the value of the firm or its shares. To augment the value of the firm and its shares, a company must undertake projects that are sufficiently profitable to earn a higher rate of return than investors demand for providing capital for projects of a given risk class. So the risk-incentivizing purpose of ESO compensation is to induce the CEO to adopt projects that are riskier than she would otherwise choose but that are *also* profitable considering the level of risk the projects entail.

So the typical firm wants the CEO to amplify firm risk, but only by seeking profitable risky projects that increase firm value. However, the CEO with an ESO-laden compensation portfolio can benefit merely by boosting the riskiness of the firm, even if she does not undertake any new and worthwhile risky projects. Other things being equal, the firm would like the CEO to avoid risks that do not promise increased profits. For a given set of investment projects, the firm's investors would like the CEO to operate the firm in a manner that reduces risk if those risk reductions can be achieved at a low cost.

Hedging provides a key means of reducing risk for many firms. While there are many definitions of hedging, we can think of hedging as using financial markets to reduce a risk that a firm normally faces in carrying out its business plan. Two examples illustrate the idea of hedging and the methods by which it can be implemented. In the early 2000s, Southwest Airlines received considerable praise for clever hedging of its fuel costs. Knowing that it would face a continuing demand for jet fuel as an input to its core business operations, Southwest used a variety of energy derivatives contracts to lock in certain prices for the future delivery of fuel. As time passed, fuel prices rose substantially and Southwest took delivery of fuel through its derivative contracts at a substantially lower price than had they purchased fuel in the open market. The important point is that Southwest contracted at one time to establish a fixed price for the future delivery of its fuel. Fuel prices rose, so Southwest essentially secured its fuel at lower prices than it would otherwise, so this hedging contributed significantly to the firm's profits. However, if Southwest had established a set price for the future delivery of fuel and prices had fallen, Southwest would have suffered by effectively paying a higher price than it would have obtained by buying fuel to meet immediate demand. While Southwest benefited by hedging in the early 2000s, it wound up losing because of its hedging activities in 2011. The purpose of this kind of hedging is to establish future prices for key inputs to reduce risk—the purpose of hedging is not to make profits.

As a similar example, consider a gold-mining firm that knows it will produce and sell gold bullion on a continuing basis. If gold prices rise, the mining firm will become more profitable because its production costs are relatively fixed in the short run. Conversely, if gold prices fall, the firm's profits will be lower. To reduce the riskiness of the firm's profitability, the firm could hedge the price of gold by using derivatives contracts to establish today the price it will receive for the gold it produces in the future. For example, at the end of 2011, the gold market was flying; gold had enjoyed an extended and steep run-up in prices. The price of gold stood at about $1750 per ounce for immediate delivery. At the end of 2011, the futures price for delivery of gold in December 2016 was about $1900 per ounce. In December 2011 the gold-mining firm could contract to deliver gold in December 2016 for $1900 per ounce, simply by selling December 2016 gold futures at $1900 per ounce. In December 2016, the gold miner must deliver the gold and receive $1900 per ounce. If the cash market price of gold in December 2016 turns out to be below $1900, the gold miner profits on the hedge. However, if the December 2016 cash price is greater than $1900, the hedge will lose money because the miner must still deliver gold for $1900. Thus, hedging the output of the mine will reduce risk by establishing a predictable price for the mine's output, but it does not ensure greater profits. In fact, placing the hedge transaction may ultimately have the effect of reducing future profitability. Thus, again, hedging aims at reducing risk, not making profits.

As a last general point about reducing risk, it is important to note that some risk reduction is nearly costless, while other forms are quite expensive. Mitigating risk against natural hazards, for instance, can involve very substantial real costs, such as building breakwaters against flooding, thinning forests to reduce fire hazard, and so on. By contrast, hedging with derivatives is very low cost, even nearly costless, because hedging with derivatives merely requires conducting a financial transaction.

We now return to considering the equity-based incentives inherent in CEO pay packages. A CEO with a high level of restricted stock might be expected to behave like a shareholder and be anxious to reduce the assortment of risks the firm faces. By contrast, if ESOs dominate the pay mix, the CEO will actually benefit from greater volatility in the firm's stock price and therefore have a significant incentive to keep the firm's risk up. This could be expressed by not undertaking costly risk-reducing projects like building breakwaters or thinning forests. But not undertaking those expensive projects could also be explained by arguing that their risk-reducing benefits do not justify their costs. The CEO with the intensive ESO pay package might also want to forego inexpensive risk-reduction opportunities, such as hedging, merely because she has financial incentives through her ESOs to keep the firm's risk at a higher level.

A number of studies examined the potential relationship between the equity-based compensation incentives of CEOs and the risk-management behavior of their firms. Almost without exception they reach the same con-clusion. CEOs with option-intensive pay packages engage in weaker hedging and risk-management efforts than do CEOs with pay packages that empha-size other forms of compensation. In a seminal study, Peter Tufano exam-ined the practices of risk management in the gold-mining industry. He found that "firms whose managers hold more options manage less gold price risk" and that "not only the level of management's equity ownership, but also the form by which that equity stake is held is related to firms' risk management choices."[44] Further, Tufano raises the essential question of the potential incen-tive conflict that firms may create by the way they construct the CEO's pay package: "By inducing greater pay-for-performance through stock and option grants, are firms encouraging managers to move closer to, or farther away from, the 'optimal' level of risk management that well-diversified outside shareholders would prefer?"[45]

Subsequent research has borne out Tufano's findings. Knopf, Nam, and Thornton examined a wide range of industrial firms and found that "as the sensitivity of managers' stock and stock option portfolios to stock price increases, firms tend to hedge more. However, as the sensitivity of manag-ers' stock option portfolios to stock return volatility increases, firms tend to hedge less."[46] Thus, the mix between restricted stock and ESOs is the key in determining the CEO's incentives, and those incentives are expressed in the behavior of the firm. Subsequent studies find similar results: The more ESOs in the compensation mix, the lower the level of risk-management activity; the more restricted stock in the compensation mix, the greater the level of risk-management activity.[47]

Compensation Incentives and Corporate Disclosures

One duty of publicly traded corporations is to provide timely and accurate information about their activities, revenues, costs, assets, and liabilities. The financial scandals of the early 2000s featuring firms such as Enron, Tyco, and HealthSouth, emphasized the importance of providing honest information to the firm's stakeholders. The regulations in Sarbanes-Oxley legislation were aimed mainly at strengthening the requirements that firms make honest and timely disclosures, and as a stipulation of that law, CEOs must personally attest under penalty of perjury to the accuracy of the firm's financial disclosures. This requirement provides a clear signal that the CEO is ultimately responsible for making those disclosures. The CEO's compensation package can be struc-tured in a way that encourages or discourages honest disclosure, and incen-tives influence how well CEOs abide by the requirements of honest reporting.

Under both *FAS 123* and the newer *FAS 123R* firms must reveal information about the details of the executive compensation that they provide to their top management team. As we have seen in our discussion of the determinants of option values, some parameters are immediately observable or at least nearly so, such as the stock price, the exercise price, and the current interest rate. The key parameter that is not immediately obvious is the volatility of the shares that underlie the option, to which option values are extremely sensitive.

Reporting a volatility estimate that is lower than its actual value allows a firm to report a lower than actual value for the ESOs it awards to its executives. If firms engage in such conduct, it would provide further support for the managerial power hypothesis, particularly the view espoused by Bebchuk and others that firms use stealth compensation to enrich their executives. Key research shows that some firms do bend the estimates of volatility to reduce the reported value of the ESOs that they award.

Aboody, Barth, and Kasznik find that firms use volatility estimates that are lower than actual, helping them to increase the apparent profitability of the firm.[48] This result finds broad support in a study by Bartov, Mohanram, and Nissim; an analysis by Hodder, Mayhew, McAnally, and Weaver; and a paper by Lam and Mensah.[49] While the key variable is the stock volatility, Aboody, Barth, and Kasznik find that some firms adjust the expected life of the option and the dividend yield to reduce the reported value of the ESOs they grant.

These studies do not assert that the manipulation of reported ESO values occurs at all firms, and several of these studies attempt to analyze the relationship between underreporting ESO valuations and other firm characteristics. For example, Aboody, Barth, and Kasznik find that underreporting ESO expense occurs more often in firms that they judge to have poor corporate governance. They also develop a measure of "pay-excessiveness" and find that underreporting is associated with firms exhibiting excessive pay. As Hodder, Mayhew, McAnally, and Weaver put the point: "On average, firms that underestimate ESO fair values have incentives to manage earnings and to disguise the size and value of compensation packages."[50] Lam and Mensah provide a useful summary of the factors that lead firms to manipulate their reported ESO expense: "We show that firms with executives who are excessively paid, poorly-performing firms, and firms which are substantially owned by insiders, are more likely to choose the less informative disclosure method. On the other hand, larger firms, firms which are widely covered by analysts, firms with high financial leverage, and those which voluntarily expense their executive options, are more likely to choose the more informative disclosure."[51] Thus, this evidence that some firms intentionally underreport their ESO expense, and that this tendency to underreport is associated with measures of poor corporate governance and apparently excessive pay, fits perfectly with the managerial power hypothesis. However, this conclusion applies only to some firms detected by statistical analyses, leaving the issue of showing exactly which firms are intentionally manipulating their reported values as a completely unresolved issue.

Beyond reporting ESO expense, firms make many other disclosures on a regular basis, and some aspects of executive compensation can encourage more accurate and open disclosure of corporate information. For example, Johnson and Natarajan studied the willingness of CEOs to disclose information at meetings with security analysts. They found that CEOs with larger shareholdings and those CEOs whose contracts included *golden parachutes* (generous promised payments contracted to occur at the CEO's departure from the firm) were more willing to disclose information about the firm.[52] In partial contrast, Donoher, Reed, and Storrud-Barnes examined the factors that propel firms to restate their previous accounting results. They found that managerial stock ownership and incentive compensation were associated with a higher frequency of restatements. However, they also found that strong and experienced boards of directors helped to reduce the occurrence of restatements, once again emphasizing the necessity of good corporate governance.[53] Not all studies reach similar conclusions, however. Nagar, Nanda, and Wysocki found that incentive compensation had an overall beneficial effect in stimulating corporate disclosure: "We find that firms' disclosures, measured both by management earnings forecast frequency and analysts' subjective ratings of disclosure practice, are positively related to the proportion of CEO compensation affected by stock price and the value of shares held by the CEO."[54]

The varied findings regarding disclosure make drawing conclusions difficult. However, tentatively we might summarize the determinants of disclosure as follows: Firms with incentives to understate their ESO compensation, such as those with embarrassingly high compensation, and the opportunity to manipulate the reported compensation downward tend to do so. A strong board of directors tends to improve disclosure. Dishonest disclosure is more likely to occur in firms with poor corporate governance and high executive compensation relative to executive performance. Further, CEOs with a solid standing in their firm and compensation that is also secure, by being more cash based or more tied to restricted stock rather than ESOs, and additionally secured by a generous severance agreement, tend to disclose more information.

Perverse Incentive Effects

EXECUTIVES BEHAVING BADLY

In previous chapters, we saw that incentive structures built into executive compensation often achieve the goal of encouraging, or even inducing, executives to act in a manner that benefits their firms, even if such behavior contrasts with the policies the executives would choose in the absence of those incentives. For example, in chapter 6 we explored the risk-taking behavior of CEOs and found that CEO incentives were often structured to encourage a higher level of risk than that at which the firms had previously operated. (Of course, this increase in risk that firms desire and achieve may not be beneficial from a social point of view, but that is a challenge to corporate governance and firm management that goes beyond gauging the effectiveness of incentives in achieving their intended effects.) While incentives certainly work in general, we documented that they can have less desirable consequences as well.

By contrast with the somewhat mixed story of incentives in previous chapters, this chapter focuses on incentives associated with deceit, crimes, and the destruction of firm value. The two main categories of bad behavior that form the topic of this chapter are what we call "option games" and "earnings management." Both monikers are intended as ironic understatements.

In brief, option games occur when executives fabricate corporate records concerning the date when options were issued. As we will see, simply changing the date of record for an option grant can bring a CEO a huge windfall. In most instances, this misrepresentation involves criminal, fraudulent reporting to the key stakeholders of the firm, to the public, and to the federal government.

Earnings management occurs when firms adjust their earnings reports from a consistent and straightforward basis to achieve some benefit, or more typically to avoid a stock price downturn that would result from announcing unfavorable news. Earnings management has been an endemic problem in accounting for as long as there have been public companies, and the motivation has often been the general one of simply not wanting to deliver bad news. In addition, companies sometimes report less than they actually earn to "hoard" earnings for a subsequent period with the aim of not disappointing the market in a later reporting period. Incentive compensation appears to play a special role in the manipulation of earnings reports. While many firms might be tempted to manage their earnings, we will see that there is strong evidence that firms tend to engage more strongly and more frequently in earnings management if their CEOs and other top executives hold strong equity-based incentives to keep the firm's stock price high.

Earnings Management

I believe that almost everyone in the financial community shares responsibility for fostering a climate in which earnings management is on the rise and the quality of financial reporting is on the decline. Corporate management isn't operating in a vacuum. In fact, the different pressures and expectations placed by, and on, various participants in the financial community appear to be almost self-perpetuating. This is the pattern earnings management creates: companies try to meet or beat Wall Street earnings projections in order to grow market capitalization and increase the value of stock options. Their ability to do this depends on achieving the earnings expectations of analysts. And analysts seek constant guidance from companies to frame those expectations. Auditors, who want to retain their clients, are under pressure not to stand in the way.

—*ARTHUR LEVITT*
CHAIRMAN, SECURITIES AND EXCHANGE COMMISSION, 1998

Consistency of methods and criteria is a foundational principle of good accounting. The firm should use reasonable rules and apply them in the same manner over time. If the supposedly rigid and stable yardstick of accounting is transformed into one made of rubber, then accounting reports become much less useful or even meaningless. At first it might seem surprising that firms would bother to lie about their earnings for a particular quarter. After all, reality eventually catches up and overwhelms a sequence of fabricated earnings reports. So, in the long run, managing earnings is counterproductive because the dishonest firms eventually get caught. While the truth about earnings may eventually be revealed, managers have a much shorter time horizon it seems, because earnings management has proven endemic. So the longstanding life of earnings management and its frequent practice offer sufficient proof that incentives to manage earnings are quite strong. Key portions of the Sarbanes-Oxley Act of 2002 aimed at putting an end to the practice of earnings management, and one of the key provisions of that act was to require the CEO to personally attest to the truthfulness of the firm's accounting statements under penalty of perjury.

When circumstances eventually force out the truth about earnings, the market generally punishes the firm severely, and sometimes the top executives face legal proceedings that may ultimately lead to prison. Earnings management was a primary ingredient in some of the most famous scandals of the early 2000s. Enron, Tyco, WorldCom, and Fannie Mae all engaged in earnings management as part of their illegitimate, unethical, and illegal activities. In addition, the inflation of earnings frequently coincides with hefty exercises of ESOs, as was the case at Enron, Waste Management, Tyco, and Xerox.[1]

As an example of how strong the incentive to manage earnings can be, consider the fate of Research in Motion (RIM), best known as the maker of Blackberry smartphones, which once ruled the market but have recently suffered at the hands of Apple's iPhone. In April 2011, RIM cut its earnings forecast, which led Wall Street analysts to predict an average earnings forecast of $5.5 billion for the first quarter of the 2012 fiscal year. RIM reported their actual first-quarter earnings of $4.9 billion—an "earnings miss" of $600 million, or 11 percent. The market reaction was swift and brutal: in after hours trading, RIM's stock price fell 15 percent. This plunge occurred on the announcement day. RIM had already talked down the market's expectations about earnings by cutting estimates two months previously. So the 15 percent drop that occurred on the announcement was only part of the effect of RIM's poor earnings on the firm's stock price.[2]

Compared with the average effect, RIM suffered especially harsh treatment, perhaps because the earnings miss was so large and perhaps due to the general perception of the iPhone's market ascendancy. Nonetheless, the typical treatment of firms that miss the Street's earnings estimates is severe. On average, a firm with a negative earnings surprise (an earnings miss) suffers a 3–5 percent negative stock price reaction on the announcement, and firms that provide a positive earnings surprise experience a positive earnings reaction in the same range.[3]

There are three prime channels through which an unfavorable earnings announcement can cause an immediate loss to an executive: an effect on the CEO's meeting her target annual bonus, a drop in the value of her holdings of restricted stock, and a price drop in the value of her ESOs. (In addition, of course, a record of poor earnings might convince the board of directors that the firm should replace the CEO.) In chapter 3, we considered the typical bonus-award structure of figure 3.1 that shows a discontinuity in the level of the annual bonus at the performance threshold and at the budget cap. For a firm that uses earnings as a performance measure, a poor earnings report can threaten to take the CEO below the performance threshold and wipe out her chance of receiving the annual bonus.[4] For her restricted stock, she might reasonably expect the typical drop in the stock price of about 5 percent, which translates into a direct loss in the value of her holdings.

As we have seen, options have inherent leverage, and the value of an option will change by a larger percentage than a stock for a given percentage change in the stock price. Taking our base-case option as an example emphasizes the point. With our typical initial condition of a stock price of $50 per share, the option is worth $16.85. A 5 percent drop in the stock price to $47.50 makes the price of the base-case option fall to $15.56, for a 7.7 percent loss. For a firm with this kind of option that is punished with a loss like RIM's 15 percent loss of stock value, the share price would fall to $42.50 and the option price would crater to $13.04, for a loss of 22.6 percent. When we consider that the CEO might hold tens of thousands of shares and hundreds of thousands of options, these price drops imply very significant dollar losses.

Perhaps no single firm makes a better case study for the linkage from incentive compensation, to earnings mismanagement, to a disastrous societal income than Fannie Mae. Before turning to the facts surrounding Fannie Mae, it should be emphasized that the author does not really know why the firm's executives behaved as they did. Understanding the motivations of another person is always difficult, especially when the attempt at understanding is conducted at a distance. However, the Fannie Mae case does illustrate the incentives that executives face and the results from earnings management.[5]

In December of 2004, crisis overtook Fannie Mae, and its board of directors demanded the departure of the firm's CFO, Timothy Howard, and its CEO, Franklin Raines, who had been director of the Office of Management and Budget from 1996–1998 under President Clinton. Fannie Mae classified these two departures as "retirements." Shortly before their dismissal, the SEC had determined that Fannie Mae had misstated its earnings for several previous years, at least from 1998 to 2004, and that the firm's earnings had been inflated by more than $11 billion in those years. The SEC penalized Fannie Mae $400 million for its failings. In Senate testimony, the chairman of the SEC called this debacle "one of the largest restatements in American corporate history" and added: "The significance of the corporate failings at Fannie Mae cannot be overstated."[6]

Table 8.1 shows the compensation of CEO Franklin Raines during his key years at the helm of Fannie Mae. Less than 6 percent of his compensation came from salary, due in part to Fannie Mae's practice of keeping salary below $1 million in accordance with the incentives provided by section 162(m) of the federal tax code, as discussed in chapter 1. As a result, more than 94 percent of Raines's pay was performance based.

Not only was the pay of the two top executives heavily grounded on the firm's performance, but the board instituted an additional incentive scheme that laid on even stronger incentives. As Bebchuk and Fried explain in their case study of the Fannie Mae/Franklin Raines debacle:

> Seeking to turbo-charge executives' incentives to increase reported earnings, in 2000 Fannie Mae's board adopted a special option grant

TABLE 8.1 Compensation of CEO Franklin Raines at Fannie Mae, 2000–2003

Year	Salary	Bonus	Long-Term Incentive Plan	Options and Stock	Total Pay
2000	$992,000	$2,481,000	$4,589,000	$5,829,000	$13,891,000
2001	$992,000	$3,125,000	$6,803,000	$7,946,000	$18,866,000
2002	$992,000	$3,300,000	$7,234,000	$6,680,000	$18,206,000
2003	$992,000	$4,180,000	$11,621,000	$3,007,000	$19,800,000
Total	$3,968,000	$13,086,000	$30,247,000	$23,462,000	$70,763,000
% of 4-Year Total	5.61	18.49	42.74	33.16	100.00

Source: Reproduced with slight modification from Lucian A. Bebchuk and Jesse M. Fried, "Executive Compensation at Fannie Mae: A Case Study of Perverse Incentives, Nonperformance Pay, and Camouflage," *Journal of Corporation Law*, 2005, 30, 807–822. See p. 810.

program, "Earnings Per Share Challenge Option Grants." Under its terms, these options would become vested and exercisable in January 2004 if reported earnings per share (EPS) equaled or exceeded $6.46 by December 31, 2003. Raines and Howard were awarded 213,000 and 57,000 such options, respectively. Rising to the challenge, Fannie Mae's executives delivered this result—EPS reached $7.91 by the end of 2003—and enjoyed immediate vesting of the options.[7]

Less than one year later, the SEC was forcing Fannie Mae to restate these fraudulent earnings that had ensured that Raines and Howard "hit their numbers." Sent packing in December 2004, a special clause in Raines's employment contract came into play. His contract stipulated that his existing unvested options would immediately vest upon his departure. Contrary to the usual form of ESO grants, Raines was not compelled to exercise the options on departure. Had he exercised immediately when he departed, he would have received the intrinsic value of the options of about $215,000. Instead, he was allowed to hold the options, with a value that Bebchuk and Fried estimated at $7 million. Thus, the departing executives received a double windfall—their options did not expire worthless upon their departure because Fannie Mae granted them immediate vesting, and they were not forced to exercise the options.[8] Given the nature of their exit from the firm, it may seem that Fannie Mae should have sought to recover some of the compensation that was being lavished upon these two officers, but the firm never sought any restitution.

The outcome at Fannie Mae obviously had a sizable social cost—losses not only to the firm and its stakeholders but also to the public. Fannie Mae stood, and still stands, at the heart of the financial crisis of 2007–2009. As a federal government sponsored enterprise, it played a major role in pumping up housing prices through its policies.[9] Fannie Mae and its twin GSE Freddie Mac have received bailouts from the federal government of $103.8 billion and $65.2 billion, respectively. By year-end 2011, neither firm had repaid a cent, they both have little prospect of repaying the federal government fully, and they may never repay anything at all. At the end of 2011, Fannie Mae was petitioning the federal government for yet more support.

These reflections are not intended to assert that the documented incentives that confronted Raines and Howard led them to fabricate Fannie Mae's earnings reports or to assert that their actions led to the financial crisis. But their incentives were apparent, and the costs imposed on society by Fannie Mae were evident. The proximity of the incentives and the disastrous outcome emphasize how incentives can easily turn perverse and lead to devastating results. While this account of Fannie Mae illustrates the potential problem, it is ultimately an anecdote about a single firm. However, the general connection between strong equity incentives and earnings management has been documented in a wide range of detailed academic studies.

In terms of the incentives to manage earnings, the three key types of performance-based compensation—bonuses, restricted stock, and ESOs—provide somewhat different incentives to manage earnings. First, consider an executive who may receive a bonus by meeting an earnings target and who holds a fixed portfolio of restricted stock and ESOs. In this situation, missing an earnings target will typically affect the executive adversely through all three channels, bonus, restricted stock and ESOs. If the CEO in this position manages earnings, she surely will want to manage earnings to at least meet the market's expectation. If the executive manages earnings to exceed the market's expectation, this will maximize the price effect on her restricted stock and ESOs. However, managing earnings in the current quarter to beat the market's expectation may not lead to a bigger bonus, because the bonus may be at the cap, simply by meeting or slightly exceeding the market's expectation. If the manager's bonus is a large component relative to her stock and option holdings, she will want to inflate earnings just enough to capture her bonus. Wildly beating the bonus threshold might lead to greater expectations for the next period and the board may set a higher earnings threshold if they did not know that the earnings reported were fabricated in the first place. Also, if a CEO manipulates earnings upward in one period, it makes it harder to fabricate higher earnings in the next period. That is, there is some limit, even for an Enron, on how much earnings fabrication is possible.

If a manager is willing to manage earnings and holds a different portfolio than the one just described, the earnings-management incentives can change substantially. Consider a manager with a small potential bonus and a limited portfolio of restricted stock and ESOs, but who anticipates that the firm will award her a large ESO grant a few weeks after the earnings report. Other things being equal, the lower the stock price at the time the ESOs are granted the better, because ESOs are almost always issued with an exercise price equal to the current stock price. In this situation, the CEO has a strong incentive to manipulate earnings downward in anticipation of the ESO grant. Then, with the newly issued ESOs in hand, the next earnings report can be quite rosy since some of the genuine earnings in the earlier period were suppressed and may be reported in a quarter after the executive has received the ESOs with a low exercise price. These musings about CEO's grants, stock holdings, and their ESO portfolio interacting with the amount and direction of earnings manipulation may seem highly theoretical and unlikely to have an influence in the real world. However, considering some of the research in this area quickly shows how strongly these incentives lead to real-world outcomes.

Several studies have found a definitive linkage between CEO bonus-related incentives and earnings manipulation. For example, Healy found that executives managed earnings when the firms' earnings were close to affecting their bonuses, even manipulating earnings downward in some cases.[10] Holthausen, Larcker, and Sloan confirmed Healy's key result and stated: "Like Healy, we find evidence consistent with the hypothesis that managers manipulate earnings downwards when their bonuses are at their maximum."[11] In a confirming study, McVay, Nagar, and Tang find an association between equity incentives and just meeting or just beating earnings estimates.[12]

While bonus plans do induce manipulation in some instances, the really strong link between earnings manipulation and incentive compensation is due to equity compensation. Bergstresser and Philippon find a higher degree of earnings manipulation at firms where the CEO's total compensation depends more heavily on her stock and option compensation. Zhang, Bartol, Smith, Pfarrer, and Khanin similarly state that "we found that CEOs were more likely to manipulate firm earnings when they had more out-of-the-money options and lower stock ownership."[13] Similarly, Peng and Röell, summarize their results by saying: "Our evidence supports the prediction that a high sensitivity of executive compensation to the short term share price encourages price manipulation."[14] Like Zhang et al., Peng and Röell find that much of the incentive runs through stock options. A strong association between ESOs and earnings fraud is a constant refrain through much of this research literature.[15]

Thus, these findings point to the key incentive-manipulation link. Bonuses and stock may stimulate earnings manipulation, but ESOs are the compensation feature with the power to really induce earnings fraud. Burns and Kedia examine the various forms of compensation and find that stock options compensation is the key: "Relative to other components of compensation, stock options are associated with stronger incentives to misreport because convexity in CEO wealth introduced by stock options limits the downside risk on detection of the misreporting."[16] In harmony with Burns and Kedia, Efendi, Srivastava, and Swanson find that "the likelihood of a misstated financial statement increases greatly when the CEO has very sizable holdings of in-the-money stock options."[17] A number of other studies confirm the powerful effect of ESOs in stimulating earnings manipulation.[18]

While the weight of evidence clearly supports a powerful connection between ESO-driven incentives and earnings management, it should be noted that not every study agrees. For example, Johnson, Ryan, and Tian find that CEO holdings of unrestricted stock, but not restricted stock, and not ESOs are associated with earnings manipulation: "Controlling for firm, governance, and CEO characteristics, the likelihood of corporate fraud is positively related to incentives from unrestricted stockholdings and is unrelated to incentives from restricted stock and unvested and vested options."[19] Nonetheless, it is apparent that compensation arrangements provide CEOs with strong incentives to manage earnings and that some CEOs act on these incentives to commit earnings fraud. In doing so, they respond most strongly to the incentives embedded in their equity compensation in general, and ESOs carry the real power to incentivize them to lie about the firm's performance.

Option Games and Exploitation

As early as 1997, David Yermack noted a very interesting and peculiar association between good stock performance and grants of ESOs to CEOs.[20] He found that almost immediately after the day of an ESO grant, the firm's stock price started performing very well. Figure 8.1 shows this effect for 620 grants that occurred at S&P 500 firms from 1992 to1994. In the 20 trading days before

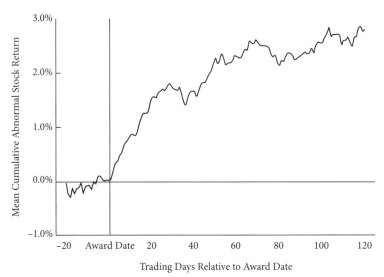

FIGURE 8.1 *Abnormal Stock Returns Following Receipt of Stock Options by CEOs.*

Source: David Yermack, "Good Timing: CEO Stock Option Awards and Company News Announcements," *Journal of Finance*, 1997, 52:2, 449–476, figure 1, p. 450.

the option-award date, the firms that were just about to make an award had a stock market performance just about the same as the market as a whole. But, in the 120 trading days following the award, the shares of these firms increased by an *extra* amount of almost 3 percent compared with the market as a whole. This is 3 percent over and above what one would have expected these firms to earn if there was no response to the option award.

Yermack considered two explanations for this striking result: "Incentive compensation might motivate managers to make superior decisions. Alternatively, managers might have influence over the terms of their own compensation and use this power to obtain more performance-based pay in advance of anticipated stock price increases."[21] The first explanation is that the option award makes the CEO so incentivized that she immediately improves the management of the firm and that this is rewarded virtually immediately by the market, even though the award only becomes known to the public a few months later when the firm makes its proxy statement disclosures. Yermack does not say so, but this possible explanation is presumably presented with tongue in cheek.

Yermack also considers, but ultimately dismisses, a third possible explanation for the very good stock market performance: CEOs may manipulate the timing of good news so that it comes right after they receive their ESO awards. Part of the reason Yermack discounts this third explanation is because it might well violate the law, and he closes his study with his ultimate conclusion: "Managers who become aware of impending improvements in corporate performance may influence their compensation committees to award more performance-based pay, as a low-risk method of capitalizing on investors' expected reactions to news of the operating improvements."[22] The practice of making an ESO grant just before the release of good corporate news is called *springloading*. Other studies have confirmed that the practice results in a windfall for the CEO who has just received an option grant and that the practice is associated with poor corporate governance, particularly when CEOs have greater managerial power and more influence over their boards.[23]

While Yermack was reluctant to suggest that firms manipulate the timing of corporate news announcements, we review very strong evidence that such disclosure timing is widespread. However, the ultimate behavior behind the phenomenon that Yermack was first to notice is even more nefarious, and it took several years before the mystery was fully solved. The giant step toward a solution to the puzzle of amazing stock performance just after an ESO grant was provided by Erik Lie in 2005, when he said: "Unless executives possess an extraordinary ability to forecast the future market-wide movements that drive these predicted returns, the results suggest that at least some of the awards are timed retroactively."[24] Lie surmises that the grant is actually made on a day some time after a run-up in stock prices, but it is reported as having occurred on an earlier day when stock prices were lower—this is the practice of option *backdating*.

To see how this works, consider figure 8.2 which shows a constructed series of stock prices for a company dubbed "Imaginative Backdating Corporation." These stock prices are arranged relative to the announced option-award date, day zero, when the stock price is $50. Let us assume that the actual award date is day 24, when the stock price is $60.80—in other words, that is the day that the board actually grants the options and $60.80 should be the reported exercise price of the options, assuming they are granted at the current stock price. At some time after day 24, the firm announces in its proxy statement that the grant was made on day zero, with an exercise price of $50, which equals the stock price on that day. (Under rules in force until August 29, 2002, firms had 45 days to report a grant; since the imposition of the Sarbanes-Oxley law on that date, firms have only two days after the grant to report.)[25]

Thus, Imaginative Backdating has really issued an ESO with an exercise price of $50 when the actual stock price was, and the exercise price should have been, $60.80. It has also lied to the Securities Exchange Commission, which is a felony in this situation. Further, it has exploited the safe harbor of APB 25 and *FAS 123* to take advantage of the rule that an ESO awarded with an exercise price equal to the current stock price need not affect the firm's reported earnings or the taxes due on those earnings. So by this lie, the firm has also defrauded the IRS of corporate income tax that would be due if they had reported truthfully. In addition, it has granted the CEO a large windfall and misled its investors.

How much is this lie worth to the executive in our example? Surely, such a blatantly dishonest and illegal act must be rare, is it not? And beyond our example, how much difference did this practice of backdating actually make in the real world? The lie can be worth quite a bit. As a point of comparison,

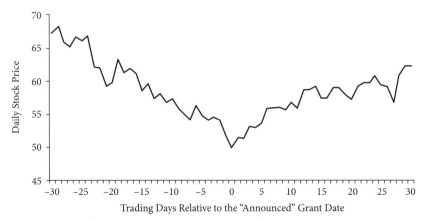

FIGURE 8.2 *Daily Stock Prices for Imaginative Backdating Corporation.*
Source: Graph by author.

consider again the base-case option (exercise price of $50, issued when the stock price really was $50, 10 years to expiration, four years to vesting, 7 percent annual chance of departure). This option is worth $16.85 as discussed in chapter 4. In our example, Imaginative Backdating issues an option with essentially the same terms—especially important is an exercise price of $50—when the current share price was actually $60.80. The executive in the example receives an option worth $22.71, a difference of $5.86 or one-third more than the $16.85. As the backdating is surreptitious, the firm represents to all outside parties that the option issued had terms that made it worth only $16.85. With a $5.86 per option difference, and an option grant of a representative 300,000 options, the lie in our example is worth $1.76 million dollars to the executive receiving the option.

The practice of backdating was fairly widespread. In his pioneering study, Erik Lie noted that some option grants follow an annual schedule, falling in roughly the same calendar week each year, while some are unscheduled, occurring at various times of the calendar year, but following the typical practice of making option grants each year. He found that the evidence of backdating was strong for both types of option grants, but that it was much stronger for unscheduled options. Being unscheduled, they could be announced at any time when the payoff was best. Further, when he divided the analysis into different time periods, 1993–1994, 1995–1998, and 1999–2002, he found that the pattern characteristic of backdating got stronger and stronger. Either firms and executives were getting better at predicting the future of stock returns, or the practice of backdating was becoming more widespread. Figure 8.3 shows

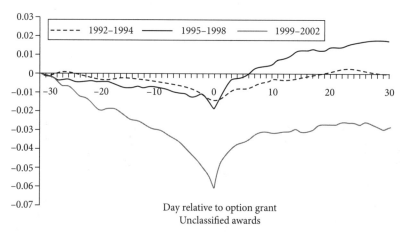

FIGURE 8.3 *Abnormally Low Stock Returns Before Option Grants and Abnormally High Stock Returns After Option Grants for Firms that Issued Unscheduled Option Awards.*

Source: Erik Lie, "On the Timing of CEO Stock Option Awards," *Management Science*, May 2005, 51:5, 802–812. See figure 2.b, p. 808.

a graph of the abnormal returns from Lie's paper for unscheduled awards for each of these three time periods. It shows that, on average, option grants occurred when stock prices hit a 30-day low, having lost about 6 percent in the preceding 30 days. In the 30 days following the grant, the shares of the option-issuing firms gained about 3 percent (bouncing back from -6 percent in the graph up to -3 percent). These figures, the 6 percent loss and the 3 percent gain, are abnormal returns. That is, they filter out the effect of general market movements.

To demonstrate even more conclusively that the remarkable price effect of figure 8.3 was due to backdating, rather than brilliant stock-price predicting, Randy Heron and Erik Lie used the tightening of the reporting requirements of the Sarbanes-Oxley Act that came into effect on August 29, 2002. This act limited the reporting lag (the time from option issuance to the required reporting date) to two days, instead of the 45-day lag that was permitted previously. They found that 80 percent of the backdating effect of figure 8.3 disappeared.[26] But what about the remaining 20 percent? Heron and Lie found that firms exploited the two-day lag to backdate and that some firms reported late, providing an excess over two days to choose the best date to pretend to have issued the options. In a further study, Heron and Lie tried to determine the extent of the practice of backdating. Expanding their period to cover 1996–2005, they estimated that 13.6 percent of all options issued over that decade were backdated, and that 23 percent were backdated before Sarbanes-Oxley took effect, but that 10 percent were still backdated even after Sarbanes-Oxley tighter reporting requirements came into effect.[27]

Table 8.2 lists nearly 150 firms that were implicated in the backdating scandal up to September 4, 2007. Many of these firms are household names, and many CEOs resigned in the wake of the scandal. For some, matters became even worse. As an example, consider the outcome for Brocade Communications. Brocade's CEO, Gregory Reyes, was convicted on 10 criminal counts associated with the firm's backdating, from which he benefited. The charges included conspiracy and fraud.[28] He was sentenced to 21 months in prison, but appealed and won on grounds that the prosecutor lied during the trial. He never served a day in prison on that conviction. Also charged and convicted was Stephanie Jensen, the human resources director at Brocade. She also appealed, but her conviction was upheld, and she served a four-month sentence.[29] Note that she did not receive the options, but merely conspired with the fraudulent record-keeping. It must be a bitter irony for her that her boss who got the options never served a day, but that she did not profit from the plan *and* she got the actual prison term. (At least that was the initial outcome.) For its part, Brocade eventually settled civil suits coming out of the scandal, agreeing to pay more than $160 million.[30] Reyes was eventually retried, convicted on nine counts, and sentenced to 18 months on June 25, 2010.[31] In October 2011, his sentence was upheld by the Ninth U.S. Circuit Court of Appeals.[32]

TABLE 8.2   Firms Scrutinized in Options-Backdating Scandal According to the *Wall Street Journal*, through September 2007

Activision	Corinthian Colleges
Affiliated Computer Services	Costco Wholesale
Affymetrix	Crown Castle International
Agile Software	Cyberonics
Alkermes	Dean Foods
Altera	Delta Petroleum
American Tower	Dot Hill Systems
Amkor Technology	Electronic Arts
Analog Devices	Emcore
Apollo Group	Endocare
Apple Inc.	Engineered Support Systems
Applied Micro Circuits	EPlus
Applied Signal Technology	Equinix
ArthroCare	Extreme Networks
Aspen Technology	First American
Asyst Technologies	Foundry Networks
Atmel	Forrester Research
Autodesk	F5 Networks
Barnes & Noble	Gap
Bed, Bath & Beyond	Getty Images
BEA Systems	Hansen Natural
Biomet	HCC Insurance Holdings
Black Box	HealthSouth
Blue Coat Systems	Home Depot
Boston Communications Group	IBasis
Broadcom	Insight Enterprises
Brocade Communications Systems	Integrated Silicon Solution
Brooks Automation	Intuit
CA	J2 Global
Cablevision	Jabil Circuit
Caremark Rx.	Juniper Networks
CEC Entertainment	Company
Ceradyne	KB Home
The Cheesecake Factory	King Pharmaceuticals
Children's Place	Keithley
Chordiant Software	KLA-Tencor
Cirrus Logic	KOS Pharmaceuticals
Clorox	Linear Technology
CNET Networks	L-3 Communications Holdings
Computer Sciences	Macrovision
Comverse Technology	Marvell Technology Group

(Continued)

TABLE 8.2 (Continued)

Maxim Integrated Products	Restoration Hardware
McAfee Inc.	Research In Motion
Meade Instruments	RSA Security
Medarex	SafeNet
Mercury Interactive	Sapient
Michaels Stores	Sanmina-SCI
Company	Semtech
Microsoft	Sepracor
Microtune	Sharper Image
Mips Technologies	Sigma Designs
Molex	Silicon Image
Monster Worldwide	Silicon Storage Technology
msystems	Sonus Networks
Nabors Industries	Stolt-Nielsen
Newpark Resources	Sunrise Telecom
Novell	Sun-Times Media
Novellus Systems	Sycamore Networks
Nvidia	Take-Two Interactive Software
Nyfix	THQ
Openwave Systems	Trident Microsystems
Pediatrix	Ulticom
Pixar	UnitedHealth
PMC-Sierra	Valeant Pharmaceuticals
Power Integrations	Verint
Progress Software	VeriSign
Quest Software	Vitesse Semiconductor
QuickLogic	Western Digital
Rambus	Wind River
Redback Networks	Witness Systems
Renal Care	Xilinx
	Zoran

Note: This list contains companies that disclosed government probes, misdated options, restatements and/or executive departures as of September 2007.

Source: Wall Street Journal, September 4, 2007. Available at http://online.wsj.com/public/resources/documents/info-optionsscore06-full.html.

The website also has a list of executives from these firms that appear to have been implicated.

Option Games: A Warning About Incentives in Executive Compensation

The radical misbehavior that encompassed the backdating scandal is a glaring warning about the incentive power of certain elements of executive compensation, most notably executive stock options. The deceit, fraud, and illegality that characterized the behavior of many executives in the affair were blatant in numerous instances, and the practice has been thoroughly criticized on grounds of both poor corporate governance and unethical behavior.[33]

From the point of view of incentives and their management, the backdating scandal conveys three critical messages. First, it is transparently clear that some CEOs have managerial power over their own compensation. In some instances of backdating, the CEO acted without the board's knowledge to increase their own pay through backdating. This was the case with Reyes at Brocade Communications.[34] In other instances, the backdating was accomplished with the connivance of the board. Second, "stealth compensation," *pace* Bebchuk and Fried, does exist, as the essence of the backdating schemes was to lie about and fraudulently conceal the true nature of the option grant. Third, and most important for our purposes, the backdating scandal demonstrates how incentives in executive compensation can misfire. Even the best efforts to provide incentives to achieve a desirable result, such as maximizing the value of the firm and thereby increasing social welfare generally, can result in providing perverse incentives. While no incentive system can be expected to perform perfectly—there will always be some residual incentive misalignment—the real question about incentives is whether they provide a net benefit that leads to value-increasing behavior that would be unattainable otherwise.

Incentives in Executive Compensation:
A Final Assessment

Incentive Compensation and the Level of Executive Pay

From 2000 to 2009, average CEO compensation at S&P 500 firms fell by 36 percent from a peak of $15 million to $9.6 million. But pay rose from 2009 to 2010 by almost 19 percent, to an average of $11.4 million. Whether compensation will continue to rise is unclear, but it is certain to maintain quite high levels, especially when measured against the incomes of ordinary workers. In recent years, equity-related pay has stayed relatively constant, constituting about 52–54 percent of total compensation. However, 2010 saw a significant drop in the proportion of pay delivered in the form of ESOs, dropping from 29.83 to 18.93 percent of total pay in just one year. This shift from ESOs to restricted stock represents an important change, one that some will regard as extremely beneficial, but one with disturbing implications as well.

Firms set incentives for their top management teams mainly by granting them equity-related compensation. Between ESOs and restricted stock, ESOs far and away are the more highly incentivizing form of compensation, while large holdings of restricted stock encourage conservatism and may well frustrate the risk-taking entrepreneurialism necessary to create corporate profits and societal wealth. Thus, the shift away from ESOs and toward restricted stock, while holding equity-based compensation as a constant proportion of total pay, implies a substantial weakening of CEO incentives. If we consider the financial sector alone with its critical systemic role and explicit and implicit governmental guarantees, this reduction in incentives may well be socially beneficial. However, for firms in other industries, reducing incentives to take risks and create new products will likely stymie innovation and retard economic growth and employment. At a time when the United States faces intensifying challenges from abroad, this is a disturbing development, particularly if it is the leading edge of a persistent trend.

As we have also seen, compensation through ESOs is an inefficient form of pay, costing the firm more than the value the CEO actually receives. If we were to hold the total pay package of a CEO constant, and shift the mix away from ESOs to restricted stock, the resulting pay package provides more value to most CEOs. As a result, the jump in total compensation of 19 percent from 2009 to 2010 almost certainly understates the increase in value that the average CEO receives—not only is the dollar amount higher, but the form in which it is being delivered has greater personal value to the CEO. Ironically, those who are most outraged about the level of CEO compensation tend to attack ESOs most vehemently. These harsh critics probably do not realize the shift in the form of pay actually increases the value of the pay that firms deliver to their CEOs.

New Legislation and the Shaping of Incentives

In the wake of the financial crisis of 2007–2009, Congress enacted new laws designed to reduce the level of executive compensation and to shape the incentives that compensation carries. The Dodd-Frank Wall Street Reform and Consumer Protect Act became law in July 2010, with sweeping implications for the regulation of the financial sector, including corporate governance and executive compensation. The ultimate consequences of the act will not be apparent for some time because the law requires rule-making by several agencies and an additional period before those rules come into force. Nonetheless, some features pertaining to executive compensation are fairly clear in the intentions they express and the incentives they lay down for firms.

Some provisions aim at reducing the level of pay. The law requires disclosure of executive compensation and the relationship between executive pay and other employees of the firm, including the ratio of the CEO's pay to the pay of all other employees of the firm. This information was already fully accessible from the documents that the firm was required to file with the SEC, but this new requirement may perhaps make the magnitude of pay more salient. This provision clearly relates to the idea that pay can be limited by potential investor "outrage."

Other provisions of Dodd-Frank aim at refining corporate governance. For example, the law requires that firms hold a "say-on-pay" vote on executive compensation at least once during every three-year period. This is a nonbinding vote that expresses shareholder sentiment. Similarly, firms must allow a nonbinding shareholder vote on compensation related to acquisition and mergers, as well as consolidations. This is a mild change, given the nonbinding nature of the vote. Further, early say-on-pay outcomes suggest that the requirement may be trivial. Equilar analyzed the say-on-pay votes held at 2,252 companies in the Russell 3000 that were conducted in the first half of 2011. Of these firms, only 38 companies, or 1.69 percent, received a failing vote. In these same referenda, 1,654 firms approved their say-on-pay vote by 90 percent or more, a rate of 73.45 percent. In over 2,000 firms, 686 voluntarily allowed a binding shareholder vote on the equity-incentive plan, with only six rejections and with more than half of executive pay packages receiving approval at a rate of 86 percent or more.[1] These results clearly show that shareholders who vote their shares are not too distressed regarding executive pay in corporate America. Nonetheless, the say-on-pay requirement may be an opening move in an effort to institute modest reforms in the corporate governance of compensation.

The Dodd-Frank Act also requires that all members of the compensation committee of the board of directors shall be independent directors, that is, not officers or other employees of the firm. This provision aims squarely at the perceived cronyism in the pay-setting process in which the firm's executives succeed in influencing the board to grant them the pay they desire. Whether this requirement will have a material effect on either the level or structure of pay remains to be seen, but it certainly has the salutary effect of at least diminishing the CEO's apparent control over her pay. While these changes— the say-on-pay provision and the compensation committee independence requirement—are quite modest, they point toward reforms in corporate governance, which may have the best chance of improving the pay-performance relationship in executive compensation.

The law also aims at making compensation incentives more effective. It requires firms to disclose whether they allow employees and directors to hedge or offset their exposure to the firm's share price that derives from incentive compensation. This clearly intends to discourage executives from unwinding the incentives that their equity compensation puts into place. As we have seen, beyond the anecdotal, there is little evidence of serious offsetting of incentives, so the practical effect of this provision is unclear. Nonetheless, it demands that firms explicitly address the issue and that can only be beneficial.

Finally, the Dodd-Frank Act directs the Securities and Exchange Commission to adopt rules regarding "clawbacks" of executive compensation that the firm judges to have been awarded inappropriately, and the law expressly includes compensation deriving from ESOs. Clawback provisions allow firms to recoup executive compensation that it judges—after the fact— was undeserved. The Dodd-Frank law mandates a three-year window for firms to demand restitution, but requires them to develop plans under which the clawback provision would be triggered. While the act did not require rules to be developed until 2011, in 2010 about 80 percent of Fortune 100 firms disclosed the conditions that would trigger clawback actions. As table 9.1 shows, the leading three triggers for clawbacks were a financial restatement coupled with ethical misconduct; a financial restatement alone; and the trifecta of a financial restatement, ethical misconduct, plus a noncompete violation. As we saw in discussing the dismissal of Franklin Raines, firms have been reluctant to diminish the pay of departing directors, even when there was every reason to think that pay was undeserved. In addition, the tendency of firms

TABLE 9.1 Required Triggers for Clawback Provisions at Fortune 100 Firms

Trigger	Percentage of Firms Using Trigger
Financial Restatement and Ethical Misconduct	40.7
Financial Restatement Only	17.6
Financial Restatement, Ethical Misconduct, and Noncompete Violation	16.5
Ethical Misconduct Only	9.9
Financial Restatement, Ethical Misconduct, Noncompete Violation and/or Other	9.9
Ethical Misconduct and Noncompete Violation	3.3
Noncompete Violation Only	2.2

Source: Equilar, *Dodd-Frank Financial Reform Act—SEC Alert* (Redwood City, CA: Equilar, Inc., February 2011). See p. 20.

to provide apparently gratuitous departure compensation has become legendary. So once again, while the practical consequences of this innovation are likely to be modest, the clawback provision, at least, forces firms confront the issue directly.[2]

How Dysfunctional Is Executive Pay?

In any reckoning, the changes to the regulation of executive pay in the Dodd-Frank law are cautiously modest and are unlikely to produce a dramatic effect on the level or structure of executive pay. If that is the case, it leaves open the question of the efficacy of the executive-compensation system. As we explored at some length, the agency-theoretic understanding of executive pay generally emphasizes how well the system works, while the managerial power hypothesis decries what it sees as the endemic failures pervading the system. The former views the problem as that of a few rotten apples, while the latter judges that the entire barrel is largely spoiled. Yet both approaches emphasize the validity and importance of providing executives with incentives to create value. Thus, both main theoretical approaches to executive compensation view attempts to incentivize executives as coherent, valid, and critically important. These two apparently diametrically opposed outlooks ultimately, and merely, disagree about how well the one system that they both support actually functions.

Based on the extensive research results reviewed in earlier chapters, we can draw further conclusions about the efficacy of executive pay as it is presently structured. There can be no doubt that incentive compensation frequently succeeds in encouraging executives to take greater risks, thereby creating significant value over and above what would have been achieved in the absence of those incentives. When it works "according to theory," there can be little doubt that the operation of incentives creates more value than a nonincentiv-izing approach to compensation.

While the system may work well when it functions as designed, it is also apparent that malfunctions are pervasive. In particular, the research, docu-mented in previous chapters, shows two important types of deficiencies. First, the system presents executives with incentives that often lead them to direct their firms in ways that benefit them personally but that fail to benefit, or actually harm, the firms they head. For example, the predilection for share repurchases over dividends induced by the nondividend-protected character of ESOs tends to change the firm's behavior, largely or merely, for the personal aggrandizement of the ESO holders. In more serious cases, incentives can induce the CEO to undertake too much or too little risk—to forgo attrac-tive and profitable enterprises or to embark on unworthy projects, to resist a beneficial merger or to make an unprofitable acquisition, and so on. These are matters of the utmost seriousness because they destroy firm value, hurt the overall economy, and make our society poorer for the satisfaction of the personal desires of already richly compensated managerial elites.

But there is worse yet. We have seen that the strength of incentives embod-ied in equity compensation, particularly in ESOs, can induce CEOs to com-mit felonies in pursuit of personal aggrandizement. This emerged most clearly in the backdating of ESO grants, where documentation made it possible to establish the criminal behavior of individuals—at least in a portion of the actual infractions.

Unfortunately, when CEOs sacrifice the interests of the firm for personal desires, detection of the bad behavior of individuals is difficult or impossible. Almost all of the evidence we examined shows that bad behavior is reflected statistically in the aggregate behavior of large samples. For example, an exam-ination of a set of mergers may convince us that a significant portion are not pursued to benefit the firm, but to benefit a significant portion of the indi-vidual CEOs in the sample. But not every merger in a sample is defective in this way, and it is virtually impossible to identify the malefactors individually. After all, strategic decisions such as mergers are inherently risky and even well-intentioned mergers may misfire. Nonetheless, the numerous instances of statistically detected misbehavior across many aspects of firm behavior should convince the disinterested observer that bad behavior is fairly wide-spread, albeit not universal.

On Balance, Is Incentive Compensation Beneficial?

The system of incentive executive compensation described in this book has dominated the U.S. corporate landscape for more than 20 years now. But to tell whether it has been beneficial on balance, it would be very helpful to know how the system would have performed without such a compensation scheme. That information is, of course, not available. There are no controlled experiments in which a researcher arranges for some giant firms to use incentive compensation while other relevantly similar firms operate under a compensation system devoid of incentives.

Nonetheless, there is one key litmus test that is available to shed light on this important issue. We can approach the overall validity of incentive compensation by asking the question: "Do Stockholders Like Incentive Pay?" If that question receives an affirmative answer, then at least one key, perhaps *the* key, stakeholder group finds the system of incentive compensation preferable to other alternatives.

Without question, research shows that shareholders do, in fact, approve of incentive-compensation plans. In briefest terms, when the stock market learns of the implementation of incentive-compensation plans, stock prices surge. The evidence on this issue is almost perfectly univocal. Virtually every study of this issue strongly confirms a general shareholder approval of incentive pay, particularly pay including ESOs. Studies by Brickley, Bhagat, and Lease; by DeFusco, Johnson, and Zorn; by Gerety, Hoi, and Robin; by Martin and Thomas; and by Billett, Mauer, and Zhang all confirm that shareholders respond to ESO plans and ESO grants by bidding up share prices significantly higher than they were immediate prior to the ESO news reaching the market.[3] For example, Billett, Mauer, and Zhang find that, in the two months following an ESO announcement, stock prices rise 2.5 percent more than they would have otherwise. Beyond these studies that focused principally on U.S. markets, other studies have found similar results in markets as diverse as Finland and Japan.[4]

While this evidence is compelling, it is not fully conclusive. For example, Billett, Mauer, and Zhang found that while share prices surged on the ESO announcement, bond prices sagged by about 1 percent. So ESOs may benefit some stakeholders and harm others. Thus, it may not be possible to assess the ultimate societal benefit or detriment by solely examining the reaction of security prices. Nonetheless, these findings provide a compelling touchstone in a debate in which hard evidence is difficult to obtain.

To Improve Executive Compensation, Improve Corporate Governance

While compensation systems with incentives may be better than those without, that conclusion does not imply that the present system cannot be improved. The defects of incentive compensation documented in this book present a compelling case for the necessity of improving the system. There is good reason to believe that there is a way to improve the performance of the incentive system without abandoning the overall structure of business organization and corporate governance that served the United States quite well during its ascendency to the premier economic power in the world—even if its halcyon days now appear to be receding.

A substantial body of evidence documents the beneficial effects of strong and effective corporate governance in harnessing the power of incentive compensation to pull the wagon of value creation. Specifying the exact characteristics of a good board has proven difficult, and there is no generally accepted metric of the overall quality of corporate governance.[5] Nonetheless, it is clear that the composition of the board of directors matters a great deal to the level of executive compensation and to tying executive pay to firm performance. In briefest summary, boards that are more independent of the CEO, boards that do a better job of monitoring the performance of the firm and the CEO, and boards whose members have a personal stake in the fortunes of the firm lead to lower levels of compensation and better corporate performance for each dollar of executive pay.

In support of these general conclusions, Petra and Dorata find that separating the roles of CEO and chairman of the board disperses power and influence and leads to lower levels of executive compensation.[6] Hartzell and Starks find that boards with high levels of stock ownership by financial institutions also exhibit lower pay levels and a stronger pay-for-performance relationship.[7] These outcomes apparently result from financial institutions with large stockholdings possessing a sufficient incentive to monitor executive behavior and firm performance. Similarly Bertrand and Mullainathan find that firms with a large stockholder on the board exhibit a tighter relationship between CEO pay and firm performance, or, as they put the point, there is less "pay for luck."[8] In the same vein, Chhaochharia and Grinstein find that greater board independence and better board monitoring reduce compensation.[9] Emphasizing the importance of board members having a stake in the firm, Cyert, Kang, and Kumar find that a board with a single, large share owner and with greater overall share ownership by the board imply a lower level of pay for executives.[10] Bringing other factors into consideration, Sun, Cahan, and Emanuel find that the following features of the board's compensation committee all lead to a strengthening of the relationship between executive pay and firm performance: Fewer committee members appointed by the current CEO; longer length of service on the board; fewer board members who are themselves CEOs; directors with more stock ownership; board members with fewer other directorships; and boards with more members.[11]

Thus, it seems that strengthening corporate governance—more board independence, stronger monitoring, and an equity stake in the firm by board members—are at least three keys to both reducing executive pay levels and tightening the relationship between pay and performance. In addition, some stress the greater need for more direct shareholder power in corporate governance.[12]

Executive Pay, Continuing Inequality, and the
Question of Justice

Compared with almost all other countries, the United States tends to have a greater tolerance and appreciation of great wealth, if it appears to be acquired through merit and the creation of value for others. Those who rage against executive pay may well communicate their thoughts on their Apple computers, yet feel admiration and even fealty to this largest of firms. Many appear to hold great affection for the extremely wealthy Steve Jobs, whose wealth Forbes reckoned at $7 billion shortly before his death. Similarly, top entertainers and sports figures regularly receive annual compensation equal to the income captured by CEOs at the pinnacle of corporate America; yet, they avoid becoming targets of the special vitriol reserved for CEOs.

A key part of the explanation for this differential is the perception, too often correct, that CEOs get paid even for a poor performance. Thus, strengthening the link between pay and performance, and making this link visible to the public should help ameliorate the social conflict that CEO pay arouses. Of course, CEO pay will certainly remain high even with the strongest corporate governance and the strongest pay-for-performance linkages. Ironically, we have seen that a system of executive compensation that utilizes equity compensation as an incentive vehicle almost certainly makes the total level of pay higher than it otherwise would be.

This continuing high compensation of CEOs (and presumably those in other walks of life, such as sports and entertainment stars) raises once again the perennial question of the justness of a system that permits such inequality. For those committed to egalitarianism, there can be no satisfaction in such a system. Others, who focus on the justice of the system of rules that leads to differential outcomes, can certainly take comfort from a system with an improved linkage between strong corporate performance and high pay. In our society, there is a growing awareness of the potential for rising inequality to seriously corrode social cohesion. High levels of CEO pay certainly have been a part of this problem, and executive pay levels will certainly continue to play this undesirable role.

A stronger corporate economic performance for each dollar of executive pay as the result of better corporate governance provides benefits for the entire society. And a tighter actual and perceived linkage between hefty executive paychecks and corporate performance will at least ameliorate some of the social stress occasioned by the present operation of the executive-pay system. Whether or not that desirable outcome can be achieved, executive pay will still be based in large part on incentive compensation, which will continue to be desirable, important, and imperfect. Finally, no matter how refined and improved corporate governance and governmental regulation becomes, the system of executive compensation will still occasionally suffer from the depredations of some unscrupulous CEOs for whom "too much is not enough."

{Appendix}

Binomial Valuation Method for Executive Stock Options

Variable definitions:

IOW = the initial outside wealth of the CEO
S = the stock price at the time the option is issued
X = the exercise price of the ESO
T = the time from the grant date of the option to its expiration
R_f = the continuous risk-free rate of interest
D = the continuous dividend rate on the stock
V = the vesting period
f = the continuous annualized departure rate of the CEO from the firm
ER = the CEO's subjective expectation of the return on the stock
RA = the CEO's level of risk aversion
σ = the standard deviation of the firm's shares, which the CEO will choose
u = the up factor for the stock price movement in each period
d = the down factor for the stock price movement in each period
p = the risk-neutral probability of a stock price increase
Δt = the length of a single period, such that $\Delta t = T/N$
π = the CEO's subjective probability assessment that the stock price will rise

Following the standard treatment for binomial models of Cox, Ross, and Rubinstein (1979), and drawing on the excellent discussion by Amman and Seiz (2004) we have:

$$u = e^{\sigma\sqrt{\Delta t}}$$

$$d = 1/u$$

$$p = \frac{e^{(r-D)\Delta t} - d}{u - d}$$

At the expiration of the option, T, and for any terminal stock price at any node, j, the value of the stock will be $S_{i,j}$, and the value of the option will be $C_T = \max(0, S_{i,j} - X)$. Prior to expiration, the valuation of the option will depend on the vesting condition and the probability that the CEO leaves the firm in that period.

If the option is vested, that is for all $i\Delta t \geq V$, the value at time i for node j, where j indicates the number of steps in which the stock value has increased, and conditional on the current stock price, $S_{i,j}$ is:

$$C_{i,j} = \left(1 - e^{-f\Delta t}\right)\max\left(0, S_{i,j} - X\right) + e^{-f\Delta t}e^{-r\Delta t}\left[pC_{i+1,j+1} + \left(1 - p\right)C_{i+1,j}\right]$$

In other words, if the CEO exits the firm and the option is vested, he captures the exercise value, but if he continues with the firm for the next period with probability $e^{-f\Delta t}$, the value of the option is the same as it would be in the normal binomial model.

Prior to vesting, that is for all $i\Delta t < V$, the exiting CEO receives nothing, so the value of the option is a function of the normal option price and the probability that the executive continues with the firm:

$$C_{i,j} = e^{-f\Delta t}e^{-r\Delta t}\left[pC_{i+1,j+1} + \left(1 - p\right)C_{i+1,j}\right]$$

Because the CEO seeks to maximize his utility, he may choose to exercise the option before exiting and even when doing so discards value. At expiration, time T, the CEO's utility will be a function of his realized wealth at that point and his risk aversion. His wealth at the option's expiration is $IOWe^{rT} + \max(0, S_T - X)$, and his utility at that point is:

$$U(W) = \frac{W^{1-RA}}{1-RA} = \frac{\{IOW\,e^{rT} + \max(0, S_T - X)\}^{1-RA}}{1-RA}$$

Prior to expiration, but after vesting, the CEO must decide at each node whether exercising or allowing the option to continue contributes more to his utility. At each node for each period prior to the option's expiration, the CEO's expected utility from continuing with the firm and holding the option is:

$$U_{i,j}^n = \pi\,U_{i+1,j+1} + \left(1 - \pi\right)U_{i+1,j}$$

Note here that the expected utility is computed using the CEO's subjective probability of a stock price increase, π, rather than the risk-free rate r.

Alternatively, if he is vested and exercises the option, his utility is:

$$U_{i,j}^{E} = U\left\{IOW\, e^{rT} + \left[\max(0, S_{i,j} - X)\right]e^{r\Delta t(N-i)}\right\}$$

So after vesting at each node, the CEO's utility still depends on whether he leaves the firm. If he stays, his utility is the maximum from exercising or holding, whereas, if he leaves, he secures the utility from exercising:

$$U_{i,j} = e^{-f\Delta t}\,\max(U_{i,j}^{H}, U_{i,j}^{E}) + (1 - e^{-f\Delta t})U_{i,j}^{E}$$

Prior to vesting, his utility is given as:

$$U_{i,j} = e^{-f\Delta t}\,U_{i,j}^{H} + (1 - e^{-f\Delta t})U(IOWe^{rT})$$

{ NOTES }

Chapter 1

1. Adolph Berle and Gardiner Means, *The Modern Corporation and Private Property* (New York: Macmillan, 1933).

2. Starting with data for 1992, Standard & Poor's produced a product called ExecuComp, a database of detailed information about the compensation of CEOs and other top executives. To compile the database, ExecuComp draws on reports that public companies are required to file with the Securities Exchange Commission, the firms' 10-k's. In most instances, the firms report detailed compensation on the CEO and the other four most highly paid executives in a given year, specifying the name of the executive along with details on the amount paid through each avenue by which the executive might receive compensation: salary, bonus, grants of restricted stock, grants of stock options, payments from long-term incentive plans, and so on. ExecuComp focuses on the 1,500 largest firms and breaks those down into the S&P 500, the next 400 Mid-Cap firms that S&P follows, along with an additional 600 yet smaller firms. The entire data file encompasses detailed compensation data on more than 33,000 executives and 3,000 different firms.

ExecuComp has become the standard data source for analyzing executive compensation, and it is widely used in both academic and industry studies. This book and the studies it reports draw heavily on the ExecuComp database for the period 1992 forward. The Sarbanes-Oxley Act of 2002 specified some changes in the reporting requirements for firms, and these came into effect in 2006. This change in reporting induces a slight discontinuity in the ExecuComp data, separating it into the 1992–2005 period and the 2006–forward period, but the levels are largely consistent for the two periods. At any rate, data for post–2005 are no longer available in the form in which they were reported prior to Sarbanes-Oxley.

3. Note that amounts reported for individuals can differ markedly depending on the assumptions under which they are computed. For Jamie Dimon of JPMorgan Chase, for example, table 1.1 shows his 2009 compensation as $1.322 million. However, Reuters reports that he also received about $16 million in stock and bonds as compensation for 2009, although this sum was paid in 2010. Other sources are inclined to count this $16 million as part of his 2010 compensation, leading to the potential double-counting of the $16 million in both 2009 and 2010. It might also lead to that amount never being counted. By contrast, the ExecuComp data provide a consistent approach to the compensation issue. See Jonathan Spicer, "JPMorgan CEO Dimon's 2009 Salary $1.32 million," Reuters.com, March 19, 2010. See also NYDailyNews.com, "JPMorgan Chase CEO Jamie Dimon Gets Massive $16M Pay Package," February 5, 2010.

4. Susanne Craig, "Goldman Sachs Gives Blankfein a Big Raise," *New York Times*, January 28, 2011.

5. See, for examples, Michael Faulkender, Dalida Kadyrzhanova, N. Prabhala, and Lemma Senbet, "Executive Compensation: An Overview of Research on Corporate Practices and Proposed Reforms," *Journal of Applied Corporate Finance*, winter 2010, 22:1, 107–118, especially figure 3, p. 112; Arantxa Jarque, "CEO Compensation: Trends, Market Changes, and Regulation," *Federal Reserve Bank of Richmond Economic Quarterly*, summer 2008, 94:3, 265–300., especially figure 2, p. 270; and Xavier Gabaix and Augustin Landier, "Why Has CEO Pay Increased So Much?" *Quarterly Journal of Economics*, February 2008, 123, 49–100, figure 1, p. 73. Gabaix and Landier suggest that the explanation for the rise in CEO pay may be that as firms increase in size and complexity, CEO compensation merely moves commensurately. While they advance an economic model that rationalizes this relationship, such a model could hardly satisfy anyone concerned with the moral dimension of CEO pay.

6. See Brian J. Hall and Kevin J. Murphy, "The Trouble with Stock Options," *Journal of Economic Perspectives*, 2003, 17:3, 49–70. The relevant information is in figure 2 on p. 63. For their graph, Hall and Murphy use different measures of both executive compensation and production workers' wages.

7. See Emily Dugan, "Exclusive: Salaries for Top Executives are Rocketing 'Out of Control,'" *The Independent*, May 15, 2011.

8. See Nancy L. Rose and Catherine Wolfram, "Regulating Executive Pay: Using the Tax Code to Influence Chief Executive Officer Compensation," *Journal of Labor Economics*, 2002, 20, S138–S175, especially p. S140.

9. The study specifically referred to is Tod Perry and Marc Zenner, "Pay for Performance? Government Regulation and the Structure of Compensation Contracts," *Journal of Financial Economics*, 2001, 62, 453–488. For additional insights see also Lucian A. Bebchuk and Jesse M. Fried, "Executive Compensation at Fannie Mae: A Case Study of Perverse Incentives, Nonperformance Pay, and Camouflage," *Journal of Corporation Law*, 2005, 30, 807–822; Hall and Murphy, "The Trouble with Stock Options"; Knut Peder Heen, "The Billion Dollar Gaps: Revisiting Section 162(m)" (February 2010, working paper); William Hughes, "Stock Option "Springloading": An Examination of Loaded Justifications and New SEC Disclosure Rules," *Journal of Corporation Law*, 2008, 33:3, 777–796; and Nancy L. Rose and Catherine Wolfram, "Regulating Executive Pay: Using the Tax Code to Influence Chief Executive Officer Compensation," *Journal of Labor Economics*, 2002, 20, S138–S175.

10. Steven Balsam, *Executive Compensation: An Introduction to Practice and Theory* (Washington, DC: WorldatWork Press, 2007), 124.

11. Rose and Wolfram, "Regulating Executive Pay," quoted on p. S142.

12. Ibid., see p. S147.

13. Heen, "The Billion Dollar Gaps: Revisiting Section 162(m)," see p. 5.

14. See Steven Balsam and Qin Jennifer Yin, "Explaining Firm Willingness to Forfeit Tax Deductions Under Internal Revenue Code Section 162(m): The Million-Dollar Cap," *Journal of Accounting and Public Policy*, 2005, 24, 300–324.

15. To illustrate the difference between a warrant and an option, imagine a firm with a total stock market value of $100 and 100 outstanding shares: each share is worth $1. The exercise of an option requires the transfer of a share from one party to another. This transfer changes nothing about the value of the firm, so the share price remains $1 per-share. Now assume that an executive exercises an ESO, and the firm creates one

new share to give to the executive. This also changes nothing about the real economics of the firm, so the stock market value of the firm stays at the same total of $100. However, with the creation of the new share, there are now 101 shares of the firm. Therefore, the value of all of the shares must fall to reflect the dilution of ownership that occurred. The new value of each of the 101 shares should be $100/101 = $.99001. For an explicit treatment of ESOs as warrants, see Allan C. Eberhart, "Employee Stock Options as Warrants," *Journal of Banking & Finance*, 2005, 29, 2409–2433.

16. Another less important special feature of ESOs is that even after they are fully vested, there are certain "blackout" periods when they cannot be exercised. The executive is likely to be privy to private information about the firm, so around earnings-announcement dates or when the firm is raising money in the capital markets, exercise of ESOs may be prohibited.

17. As mentioned previously, the SEC changed the way it requires firms to report compensation effective in 2006, and that change explains the sharp increase in this other compensation as shown.

18. Bebchuk and Fried, "Executive Compensation at Fannie Mae," see especially p. 818.

19. Lucian A. Bebchuk and Robert J. Jackson, Jr., "Executive Pensions," *Journal of Corporation Law*, 2005, 30, 823–855. See p. 825.

20. The term "stealth compensation" is primarily connected with the name of Lucian Bebchuk. See, for example, Lucian A. Bebchuk and Jesse M. Fried, "Executive Compensation as an Agency Problem," *Journal of Economic Perspectives*, 2003, 17:3, 71–92; and Lucian A. Bebchuk and Jesse M. Fried, "Pay Without Performance: Overview of the Issues," *Journal of Corporation Law*, summer 2005, 647–673. As Bebchuk duly notes, the term "stealth compensation" originated with Robert Monks, who used it to refer to payments that were not expensed on the firm's income statement. See Robert G. Monks, *The Emperor's Nightingale: Restoring the Integrity of the Corporation in the Age of Shareholder Activism* (New York: Basic Books, 1999), 59–62.

Chapter 2

1. As a collective, the following books and articles offer a diversity of views on corporate governance: Renee Adams, Benjamin E. Hermalin, and Michael S. Weisbach, "The Role of Boards of Directors in Corporate Governance: A Conceptual Framework and Survey," *Journal of Economic Literature*, 2010, 48:1, 58–107; H. Kent Baker and Ronald Anderson, eds., *Corporate Governance: A Synthesis of Theory, Research, and Practice* (Hoboken, NJ: John Wiley & Sons, 2011); Lucian A. Bebchuk, "The Myth of the Shareholder Franchise" (March 2007, working paper); Lucian A. Bebchuk and Michael S. Weisbach, "The State of Corporate Governance Research," *Review of Financial Studies*, 2010, 23:3, 939–961; M. Becht, P. Bolton, and A. Röell, "Corporate Governance and Control," in *Handbook of the Economics of Finance*, ed. George M. Constantinides, Milton Harris, and René M. Stulz (Amsterdam: North Holland, 2003); John R. Boatright, "From Hired Hands to Co-Owners: Compensation, Team Production, and the Role of the CEO," *Business Ethics Quarterly*, October 2009, 19:4, 471–496; and Michael C. Jensen and William H. Meckling, "Theory of the Firm: Managerial Behavior, Agency Costs and Ownership Structure," *Journal of Financial Economics*, 1976, 3, 310.

2. The foundational articulation of agency theory is Michael C. Jensen and William H. Meckling, "Theory of the Firm: Managerial Behavior, Agency Costs and Ownership Structure," *Journal of Financial Economics*, October 1976, 3:4, 305–360.

3. Milton Friedman offers the classic justification of this treatment of assumptions in his "The Methodology of Positive Economics," in Milton Friedman, *Essays in Positive Economics* (Chicago: University of Chicago Press, 1966), 3–16, 30–43. Regarding assumptions he says: "The relevant question to ask about the 'assumptions' of a theory is not whether they are descriptively 'realistic,' for they never are, but whether they are sufficiently good approximations for the purpose in hand. And this question can be answered only by seeing whether the theory works, which means whether it yields sufficiently accurate predictions," p. 15. Put in terms of the philosophy of science, Friedman and those in the economics profession who follow this approach choose instrumentalism rather than scientific realism.

4. As we will see in later chapters, shareholders owning a large stake in the firm can often perform an important role as monitors of boards and managers.

5. Adam Smith, *An Inquiry into the Nature and Causes of the Wealth of Nations* (London: Methuen & Co., Ltd., 1904). See book V, chapter I, part III, article I.

6. Michael C. Jensen and Kevin J. Murphy, "Remuneration: Where We've Been, How We Got to Here, What Are the Problems, and How to Fix Them" (2004, working paper), see p. 50.

7. For a good discussion of this point, see John E. Core, Wayne R. Guay, and Randall S. Thomas, "Is U.S. CEO Compensation Inefficient Pay Without Performance?" *Michigan Law Review*, 2005, 103, 1142–1185. See especially section A, "What is an Optimal Contract?" pp. 1160 ff.

8. Chapters 3 and 4 explore the structure of executive stock options in detail.

9. See Lucian A. Bebchuk and Jesse M. Fried, *Pay Without Performance: The Unfulfilled Promise of Executive Compensation* (Cambridge, MA: Harvard University Press, 2006).

10. Lucian A. Bebchuk and Jesse M. Fried, "Pay Without Performance: Overview of the Issues," *Journal of Corporation Law*, summer 2005, 647–673. See p. 648.

11. Ibid., see especially section IV, pp. 654–657, upon which the treatment in these pages relies.

12. Ibid., 656.

13. Ibid.

14. Ibid., see p. 659ff. See also Lucian A. Bebchuk and Jesse M. Fried, "Executive Compensation as an Agency Problem," *Journal of Economic Perspectives*, 2003, 17:3, 71–92. See p. 77ff.

15. Bebchuk and Fried, "Pay Without Performance: Overview of the Issues"; Bebchuk and Fried, "Executive Compensation as an Agency Problem"; and Lucian A. Bebchuk and Jesse M. Fried, "Stealth Compensation via Retirement Benefits" (2004, working paper).

16. Lucian A. Bebchuk and Jesse M. Fried, "Executive Compensation at Fannie Mae: A Case Study of Perverse Incentives, Nonperformance Pay, and Camouflage," *Journal of Corporation Law*, 2005, 30, 807–822. See esp. p. 818.

17. Bebchuk and Fried, "Executive Compensation as an Agency Problem," see pp. 72–73.

18. Bebchuk and Fried, "Pay Without Performance: Overview of the Issues," see p. 650.

19. Core, Guay, and Thomas, "Is U.S. CEO Compensation Inefficient Pay Without Performance?" see p. 1159.

20. Ibid., see p. 1143, note 4.

21. Ibid., see p. 1161.

22. Bebchuk and Fried, "Pay Without Performance: Overview of the Issues," see p. 665.

23. Bebchuk and Fried, "Executive Compensation as an Agency Problem," see p. 82.

24. Bebchuk and Fried, "Pay Without Performance: Overview of the Issues," see p. 650.

25. For discussions of the fiduciary duties of CEOs and boards see John R. Boatright, "Fiduciary Duties and the Shareholder-Management Relation: Or, What's So Special About Shareholders?" *Business Ethics Quarterly*, 1994, 4, 393–407; Alexei M. Marcoux, "A Fiduciary Argument Against Stakeholder Theory," *Business Ethics Quarterly*, 2003, 13:1, 1–24; and Jeffrey Moriarty, "How Much Compensation Can CEOs Permissibly Accept?" *Business Ethics Quarterly*, April 2009, 19, 235–250.

26. For a brief primer on distributive justice see Robert W. Kolb, "Distributive Justice," in *Encyclopedia of Business, Ethics, and Society*, vol. 3, ed. Robert W. Kolb (Thousand Oaks, CA: Sage Publications, 2008), 1216–1225.

27. The idea of decreasing marginal utility is that additional increments of a good bring progressively less satisfaction or utility than the one that preceded it. To take a petty example, the first ice cream cone is good, and the second is pretty good too. But the third is less valuable than the second, and the ninth hardly has any utility.

28. John Rawls, *A Theory of Justice* (Cambridge, MA: Harvard University Press, 1971).

Chapter 3

1. Adam Smith, *An Inquiry into the Nature and Causes of the Wealth of Nations*, par. IV.2.9.

2. Robert K. Merton, "The Unanticipated Consequences of Purposive Social Action," *American Sociological Review*, Dec 1936, 1:6, 894–904.

3. On the Cal State LA website, Museum of Unintended Consequences, http://cs.calstatela.edu/wiki/index.php/Courses/CS_461/Museum_of_unintended_consequences.

4. See Ruth W. Grant, "The Ethics of Incentives: Historical Origins and Contemporary Understandings," *Economics and Philosophy*, 2002, 18, 111–139, esp. p. 114. In this article and her "Ethics and Incentives: A Political Approach," *American Political Science Review*, February 2006, 100: 1, 29–39, Grant provides a very useful understanding of the broader issues surrounding incentives in economics. Her claim for the first use of "incentive" is based on the *Oxford English Dictionary*'s first reported use of the word. However, a very similar use of "incentive" occurred in a most prominent publication as early as 1911. Frederick W. Taylor, in *The Principles of Scientific Management* writes: "The writer repeats, therefore, that in order to have any hope of obtaining the initiative of his workmen the manager must give some special *incentive* to his men

beyond that which is given to the average of the trade. This incentive can be given in several different ways, as, for example, the hope of rapid promotion or advancement; higher wages," p. 18. In fact, "incentive" appears at least 25 times in Taylor's book, often in the phrase "initiative and incentive" which Taylor describes as the best kind of management practice before the advent of his own "scientific management." "Broadly speaking, then, the best type of management in ordinary use may be defined as management in which the workmen give their best initiative and in return receive some special incentive from their employers. This type of management will be referred to as the management of 'initiative and incentive' in contradistinction to scientific management, or task management, with which it is to be compared," 19. Grant is aware of the role of incentives in the advent of scientific management, but she apparently takes this as a somewhat different meaning of the term.

Another instance, drawn from the advent of World War II, appears in Chester Bernard's, *The Functions of the Executive*. Writing in 1938 Bernard says: "An organization can secure the efforts necessary to its existence, then, either by the objective inducements it provides or by changing states of mind... We shall call the process of offering objective incentives "the method of incentives"; and the process of changing subjective attitudes "the method of persuasion." See Chester I. Barnard, *The Functions of the Executive: 30th Anniversary Edition* (Cambridge, MA: Harvard University Press, 1971), 141.

5. Michael C. Jensen, Kevin J. Murphy, and Eric G. Wruck, "CEO Incentives: It's Not How Much You Pay, But How," *Harvard Business Review*, May–June 1990, 138–149. See pp. 139 and 140 for the passages cited.

6. Ibid., see p. 139.

7. Ibid., see p. 138.

8. See Marianne Bertrand and Sendhil Mullainathan, "Enjoying the Quiet Life? Corporate Governance and Managerial Preferences," *Journal of Political Economy*, 2003, 111, 1043–1075. In contrast to Jensen and Murphy's view that CEOs were paid like bureaucrats, other studies of the same time suggest a result that is otherwise. See for example, Brian J. Hall and Jeffrey B. Liebman, "Are CEOs Really Paid Like Bureaucrats?" *Quarterly Journal of Economics*, 1998, 112, 653–691, p. 654: "Our main empirical finding is that CEO wealth often changes by millions of dollars for typical changes in firm value." As we will see, the extent to which CEO compensation from the firm changes with the firm's fortunes and how the CEO's wealth changes when the firm's performance change are two conceptually distinct questions.

9. The reality is, of course, much more complicated. For a detailed exploration of the various causes of the financial crisis, see Robert W. Kolb, *The Financial Crisis of Our Time* (Oxford: Oxford University Press, 2011). For a discussion of CEO incentives at financial firms in the light of the financial crisis of 2007–2009, see also John McCormack and Judy Weiker, "Rethinking 'Strength of Incentives' for Executives of Financial Institutions," *Journal of Applied Corporate Finance*, summer 2010, 22:3, 65–72.

10. Board of Governors of the Federal Reserve System, *Incentive Compensation Practices: A Report on the Horizontal Review of Practices at Large Banking Organizations*, (Washington, DC, October 2011).

11. Equilar, Inc. *TSR Performance and CEO Pay Study* (Redwood City, CA, 2011), 3.

12. Ibid., see p. 14.

13. Kevin J. Murphy, "Performance Standards in Incentive Contracts," *Journal of Accounting and Economics*, 30, 2001, 245–278. See p. 251.

14. See Cynthia J. Campbell and Charles E. Wasley, "Stock-Based Incentive Contracts and Managerial Performance: The Case of Ralston Purina Company," *Journal of Financial Economics*, 1999, 51, 195–217. The present discussion of Ralston Purina draws solely on the Campbell and Wasley account.

15. Ibid., see p. 197.

16. Ibid.

17. Equilar, Inc., *2011 Equity Trends Report* (Redwood City, CA, 2011), 12.

18. See Fischer Black and Myron Scholes, "The Pricing of Options and Corporate Liabilities," *Journal of Political Economy*, 1973, 81:3, 637–654; and Robert C. Merton, "Theory of Rational Option Pricing," *Bell Journal of Economics and Management Science*, 1973, 4:1, 141–183. For an accessible treatment of these option pricing models and other solution methods, see Robert W. Kolb and James A. Overdahl, *Futures, Options, and Swaps,* 5th ed. (Hoboken, NJ: John Wiley & Sons, 2006).

19. For statistics on recent volatility and expected life assumptions, see Equilar, Inc., *Equity Trends Report*.

20. Steven Balsam and Setiyono Miharjo, "The Effect of Equity Compensation on Voluntary Executive Turnover," *Journal of Accounting & Economics*, 2007, 43:1, 95–119, find that restricted stock holdings discourage departure, as do Paul Oyer and Scott Schaefer, "A Comparison of Options, Restricted Stock, and Cash for Employee Compensation" (September 2003, working paper). Brian J. Hall and Kevin J. Murphy, "The Trouble With Stock Options," *Journal of Economic Perspectives*, 2003, 17:3, 49–70, find it rather obvious that executive compensation can encourage retention, but question whether these vehicles do so in the most economically efficient manner. However, C. Edward Fee and Charles J. Hadlock, "Raids, Rewards, and Reputations in the Market for Managerial Talent," *Review of Financial Studies*, winter 2003, 16:4, 1315–1357 conclude that neither stock options nor restricted stock impede executives from jumping ship.

21. The following studies find that underwater options lose their power to retain employees and generally conclude that repricing those options can help restore that power: Balsam and Miharjo, "The Effect of Equity Compensation on Voluntary Executive Turnover"; Swaminathan Kalpathy, "Stock Option Repricing and Its Alternatives: An Empirical Examination," *Journal of Financial and Quantitative Analysis*, December 2009, 1459–1487; Benjamin Dunford, John Boudreau, and Wendy Boswell, "Out-of-the-Money: The Impact of Underwater Stock Options on Executive Job Search," *Personnel Psychology*, 2005, 58:1, 67–101; Mary Ellen Carter and Luann J. Lynch, "The Effect of Stock Option Repricing on Employee Turnover," *Journal of Accounting & Economics*, 2004, 37:1, 91–112; and Narayanan Subramanian, Atreya Chakraborty, and Shahbaz Sheikh, "Repricing and Executive Turnover," *The Financial Review*, 2007, 42, 121–141. However, the results are not unanimous: Catherine. S. Daily, S. Trevis Certo, and Dan R. Dalton, "Executive Stock Option Repricing: Retention and Performance Reconsidered," *California Management Review*, 2002, 44:4, 8–23.

22. Robert X. Cringely, "The Triumph of the Nerds: The Rise of Accident Empires," 1996.

23. Anil Arya and Brian Mittendorf, "Offering Stock Options to Gauge Managerial Talent," *Journal of Accounting & Economics*, 2005, 40:1–3, 189–210. See p. 189.

Chapter 4

1. Brian J. Hall and Kevin J. Murphy, "The Trouble With Stock Options," *Journal of Economic Perspectives*, 2003, 17:3, 49–70. See p. 54. See also Mary Ellen Carter, Luann J. Lynch, and Irem Tuna, "The Role of Accounting in the Design of CEO Equity Compensation," *The Accounting Review*, 2007, 82:2, 327–357, especially p. 328.

2. Financial Accounting Standards Board, *Statement of Financial Accounting Standards No. 123, Accounting for Stock-Based Compensation* (Financial Accounting Standards Board of the Financial Accounting Foundation, October 1995), appendix B, paragraph 273.

3. For a good description of the controversy and the issues involved, see Don M. Chance, "Expensing Executive Stock Options: Sorting Out the Issues" (September 2004, working paper). See also Bradford Cornell and Wayne R. Landsman, "Accounting and Valuation: How Helpful Are Recent Accounting Rule Changes?" *Journal of Applied Corporate Finance*, 2006, 18:4, 44–52.

4. Analytical models, such as the BSM model assume that securities are traded continuously and use stochastic calculus to derive a formula that gives the value of the option. Lattice models operate in a discrete time framework and assume that options can be traded or exercised only periodically. They are called lattice models because a graphical depiction of the valuation process resembles a lattice or tree with many branches. Lattice models consider all the possible payoffs from the option at expiration and work backward period by period to compute the value of the option in each circumstance that can arise in each period before expiration. The end result of the process gives the value of the option. For the same option, analytical and lattice models will generate the same resulting option value if the lattice model uses many time steps. By making the length of each discrete period very short, a lattice model computes an option price that is indistinguishable from the result of an analytical model. While lattice models are much more computationally intensive, they can be used to value options for which no analytical model exists—such as ESOs. For a comprehensive introduction to options and both kinds of pricing models, see Robert W. Kolb and James A. Overdahl, *Futures, Options, and Swaps*, 5th ed. (Hoboken, NJ: John Wiley & Sons, 2006).

5. Equilar, Inc., *2011 Equity Trends Report* (Redwood City, CA: Equilar, Inc., 2011), see p. 22. For each year from 2006 to 2010, this has been remarkably steady with 90 percent, plus or minus 1 percent, choosing a model based on the Black-Scholes-Merton approach.

6. Dividends also have a signaling function for investors. So raising or lowering a dividend communicates information that is particularly believable to the firm's investors. So this discussion of eliminating or raising the dividends assumes that there is no signaling effect.

7. There is considerable evidence that a number of firms accelerated the vesting of option in anticipation of *FAS 123R* coming into effect. See Fayez A. Elayan, Thomas O. Meyer, and Jingyu Li, "Accelerating Vesting of Employee Stock Options to Avoid Expense Recognition" (December 2006, working paper); and Preeti Choudhary, Sivaram Rajgopal, and Mohan Venkatachalam, "Accelerated Vesting of Employee Stock Options in Anticipation of FAS 123-R" (July 2007, working paper).

8. The following studies explore the features of indexed ESOs, and almost all are supportive of their virtues. James J. Angel and Douglas M. McCabe, "The Ethics of Managerial Compensation: The Case of Executive Stock Options," *Journal of Business Ethics*, 2008, 78, 225–235. Lucian A. Bebchuk and Jesse M. Fried, "Pay Without Performance: Overview of the Issues," *Journal of Corporation Law*, summer 2005, 647–673; Don M. Chance and Tung-Hsiao Yang, "At-the-Money Stock Options, Incentives, and Shareholder Wealth" (April 2008, working paper); Joe Cheung, Charles Corrado, J. B. Chay, and Do-Sub Jung, "Hurdle Rate: Executive Stock Options," *Australian Journal of Management*, June 2006, 31:1, 29–40; Michael C. Jensen and Kevin J. Murphy, "Remuneration: Where We've Been, How We Got to Here, What Are the Problems, and How to Fix Them" (2004, working paper); Peter Løchte Jørgensen, "American-Style Indexed Executive Stock Options," *European Finance Review*, 2002, 6, 321–358; Shane A. Johnson and Yisong S. Tian, "The Value and Incentive Effects of Nontraditional Executive Stock Option Plans," *Journal of Financial Economics*, 2000, 57, 3–34; Shane A. Johnson and Yisong S. Tian, "Indexed Executive Stock Options," *Journal of Financial Economics*, 2000, 57, 35–64; Yu Flora Kuang and Bo Qin, "Performance-Vested Stock Options and Interest Alignment," *British Accounting Review*, 2009, 41, 46–61; Kevin J. Murphy, "Executive Compensation" (June 1999, working paper); Paul Oyer, "Why Do Firms Use Incentives That Have No Incentive Effects?" *Journal of Finance*, 2004, 59:4, 1619–1649; and Ming-Cheng Wu, "Selecting Suitable Compensation Plans of Executive Stock Options," *Applied Economics*, 2007, 39, 1185–1193.

9. Johnson and Tian, "Indexed Executive Stock Options," see p. 51.

10. Studies and discussion of these more exotic ESOs, including shouts, lookbacks, performance-vesting and reloads, include Min Dai and Yue Kuen Kwok, "A Tale of Three Options: Reload, Shout and Lookback Features" (n.d., working paper); Dan R. Dalton and Catherine M. Daily, "Director Stock Compensation: An Invitation to a Conspicuous Conflict of Interests?" *Business Ethics Quarterly*, 2001, 11:1, 89–108; Philip H. Dybvig and Mark Loewenstein, "Employee Reload Options: Pricing, Hedging, and Optimal Exercise," *Review of Financial Studies*, 2003, 16:1, 145–171; Jonathan E. Ingersoll, Jr., "Valuing Reload Options," *Review of Derivatives Research*, 2006, 9:1, 67–105; Johnson and Tian, "The Value and Incentive Effects of Nontraditional Executive Stock Option Plans"; and Ronnie Sircar and Wei Xiong, "A General Framework for Evaluating Executive Stock Options," *Journal of Economic Dynamics & Control*, 2007, 31, 2317–2349.

11. There is a very slight difference in the three grant values due to rounding.

12. A number of studies considered the question of the optimal exercise price for options with a single exercise price (e.g., not indexed), reaching somewhat differing conclusions, due perhaps to their using different background conditions. See Chongwoo Choe, "Maturity and Exercise Price of Executive Stock Options," *Review of Financial Economics*, 2001, 10, 227–250; Brian J. Hall and Kevin J. Murphy, "Optimal Exercise Prices for Executive Stock Options," *American Economic Review*, 2000, 90, 209–214; Richard A. Lambert and David F. Larcker, "Stock Options, Restricted Stock and Incentives" (April 2004, working paper); and Oded Palmon, Sasson Bar-Yosef, Ren-Raw Chen, and Itzhak Venezia, "Optimal Strike Prices of Stock Options for Effort-Averse Executives," *Journal of Banking & Finance*, 2008, 32, 229–239.

13. Quoted in Don M. Chance, Raman Kumar, and Rebecca B. Todd, "The 'Repricing' of Executive Stock Options," *Journal of Financial Economics*, 2000, 57, 129–154.

See p. 129. An ironic aspect of this quotation is that Richard Scrushy, founder of HealthSouth and the beneficiary of the repricing was later caught in a scandal involving his activities at HealthSouth. He was charged and tried on 36 counts of criminal activity. Originally acquitted, he was retried on 30 other counts including money laundering, racketeering, and extortion. He was convicted and sent to prison. As of mid-2011, he was pursuing a reversal of his conviction in the U.S. Supreme Court.

14. This account of Alexander's options relies entirely on Graef Crystal, "Alexander is Prime Example of CEO Americanus," Bloomberg.com, December 17, 2003.

15. Quoted in Chance, Kumar, and Todd, "The 'Repricing' of Executive Stock Options," see p. 153.

16. Kevin J. Murphy, "Stock-Based Pay in New Economy Firms," *Journal of Accounting & Economics*, 2003, 34:1–3, 129–147. See p. 137.

17. See Liu Zheng, "Six-Month-and-One-Day Option Exchange: The Impact of the Accounting Rule on Stock Option Repricing" (unpublished manuscript, University of Southern California, 2002).

18. The following papers and articles focus on option repricing. This is by no means a complete list. David Aboody, Nicole Bastian Johnson, and Ron Kasznik, "Employee Stock Options and Future Firm Performance: Evidence from Option Repricings," *Journal of Accounting & Economics*, May 2010, 50:1, 74–92; Viral V. Acharya, Kose John, Rangarajan K. Dundaram, "On the Optimality of Resetting Executive Stock Options," *Journal of Financial Economics*, 2000, 57, 65–101; Avinash Arya and Huey-Lian Su, "Stock Option Repricing: Heads I Win, Tails You Lose," *Journal of Business Ethics*, 2004, 50:4, 297–312; Menachem Brenner, Rangarajan K. Sundaram, and David Yermack, "Altering the Terms of Executive Stock Options," *Journal of Financial Economics*, 2000, 57, 103–128; Neil Brisley, "Executive Stock Options: Early Exercise Provisions and Risk-Taking Incentives," *Journal of Finance*, 2006, 61:5, 2487–2509; Sandra Renfro Callaghan, P. Jane Saly, and Chandra Subramaniam, "The Timing of Option Repricing," *Journal of Finance*, 2004, 59:4, 1651–1676; Jennifer Carpenter, "Does Option Compensation Increase Managerial Risk Appetite?" *Journal of Finance*, 2000, 55, 2311–2331; Mary Ellen Carter and Luann J. Lynch, "An Examination of Executive Stock Option Repricing," *Journal of Financial Economics*, 2001, 61:2, 207–225; Mary Ellen Carter and Luann J. Lynch, "The Consequences of the FASB's 1998 Proposal on Accounting for Stock Option Repricing," *Journal of Accounting & Economics*, 2003, 35:1, 51–72; Mary Ellen Carter and Luann J. Lynch, "The Effect of Stock Option Repricing on Employee Turnover," *Journal of Accounting & Economics*, 2004, 37:1, 91–112; Don M. Chance, Raman Kumar, and Rebecca B. Todd, "The 'Repricing' of Executive Stock Options," *Journal of Financial Economics*, 2000, 57, 129–154; Mark A. Chen, "Executive Option Repricing, Incentives, and Retention," *Journal of Finance*, 2004, 59:3, 1167–1199; N. K. Chidambaran and Nagpurnanand R. Prabhala, "Executive Stock Option Repricing, Internal Governance Mechanisms, and Management Turnover," *Journal of Financial Economics*, 2003, 69:1, 153–189; Jeffrey L. Coles, Michael Hertzel, and Swaminathan Kalpathy, "Earnings Management Around Employee Stock Option Reissues," *Journal of Accounting & Economics*, 2006, 41:1–2, 173–200; John E. Core, Wayne R. Guay, and David F. Larcker, "Executive Equity Compensation and Incentives: A Survey," *Federal Reserve Bank of New York Economic Policy Review*, 2003, 9, 27–50; John E. Core, Wayne R. Guay, and Randall S. Thomas, "Is U.S. CEO Compensation Inefficient Pay Without

Performance?" *Michigan Law Review*, 2005, 103 1142–1185; Catherine S. Daily, S. Trevis Certo, and Dan R. Dalton, "Executive Stock Option Repricing: Retention and Performance Reconsidered," *California Management Review*, 2002, 44:4, 8–23; Cynthia E. Devers, Albert A. Cannella, Jr., Gregory P. Reilly, and Michelle E. Yoder, "Executive Compensation: A Multidisciplinary Review of Recent Developments," *Journal of Management*, 2007, 33:6, 1016–1072; Fabrizio Ferri, "Structure of Option Repricings: Determinants and Consequences" (n.d., working paper); Barbara M. Grein, John R. M. Hand, and Kenneth Klassen, "The Stock Price Reaction to Repricing Employee Stock Options" (November 2001, working paper); Hall and Murphy, "The Trouble With Stock Options"; Brian J. Hall and Thomas A Knox, "Underwater Options and the Dynamics of Executive Pay-for-Performance Sensitivities," *Journal of Accounting Research*, 2004, 42:2, 365–412; Brian J. Hall and Kevin J. Murphy, "Stock Options for Undiversified Executives," *Journal of Accounting & Economics*, 2002, 33:1, 3–42; Jensen and Murphy, "Remuneration: Where We've Been, How We Got to Here, What are the Problems, and How to Fix Them"; Nengjiu Ju, Hayne Leland, and Lemma W. Senbet, "Options, Option Repricing and Severance Packages in Managerial Compensation: Their Effects on Corporate Risk" (December 2002, working paper); Swaminathan Kalpathy, "Stock Option Repricing and Its Alternatives: An Empirical Examination," *Journal of Financial and Quantitative Analysis*, December 2009, 1459–1487; Kwai Sun Leung and Yue Kuen Kwok, "Employee Stock Option Valuation with Repricing Features" (n.d., working paper); Murphy, "Stock-Based Pay in New Economy Firms"; Kevin J. Murphy, "Explaining Executive Compensation: Managerial Power Versus the Perceived Cost of Stock Options," *University of Chicago Law Review*, summer 2002, 69:3, 847–869; Daniel A. Rogers, "Managerial Risk-Taking Incentives and Executive Stock Option Repricing: A Study of U.S. Casino Executives," *Financial Management*, Spring 2005, 34:1, 95–121; Narayanan Subramanian, Atreya Chakraborty, and Shahbaz Sheikh, "Repricing and Executive Turnover," *Financial Review*, 2007, 42, 121–141; Yan Wendy Wu, "The Incentive Effects of Repricing in Employee Stock Options," *Review of Accounting and Finance*, 2009, 8:1, 38–53; Jerry T. Yang and Willard T. Carleton, "Repricing of Executive Stock Options," *Review of Quantitative Financial Accounting*, 2011, 36, 459–490; Valentina Zamora, "Characteristics of Firms Responding to Underwater Employee Stock Options: Evidence from Traditional Repricings, 6&1 Exchanges, and Makeup Grants," *Journal of Management Accounting Research*, 2008, 20, 107–132; and Zheng, "Six-Month-and-One-Day Option Exchange."

19. For example, Kevin Murphy studied "new-economy" firms before, during, and after the dotcom bubble and examined how firms react to underwater ESOs. He found that only 3 percent repriced options, but that 92 percent made a new grant. Eight percent of firms issued new stock; other responses were negligible. (The percentages exceed 100 percent because some firms engaged in multiple responses.) See Murphy, "Stock-Based Pay in New Economy Firms," p. 139.

20. Chen, "Executive Option Repricing, Incentives, and Retention," see p. 1197.

21. This discussion of Apple's option grant to Steve Jobs and the repricing of those options is based entirely on Graef Crystal, "Steve Jobs Takes a 5 Million-Share Bite of Apple," Bloomberg.com, April 8, 2003. All quotations are from this article.

22. For fairly accessible explanations of the features of this utility function see Michael Bergman, "The CRRA Utility Function" (n.d., working paper); and Peter P. Wakker,

"Explaining the Characteristics of the Power (CRRA) Utility Family," *Health Economics*, 2008, 17, 1329–1344.

23. However, one should be extremely cautious in assuming that more and more options will consistently induce managers to undertake more risk. As Ross pointed out quite forcefully: "The common folklore that giving options to agents will make them more willing to take risks is false. In fact, no incentive schedule will make all expected utility maximizers more or less risk averse." See Stephen A. Ross, "Compensation, Incentives, and the Duality of Risk Aversion and Riskiness," *Journal of Finance*, 2004, 69, 207–225, especially p. 207. This result is largely due to the variety of utility functions that characterize individuals. Nonetheless, in most practical incentive contracts for executives, it does seem that adding more ESOs to the compensation mix increases a willingness to accept risks.

24. The following studies develop formal executive stock option valuation models in which the power utility function plays a key role: Manuel Ammann and Ralf Seiz, "Valuing Employee Stock Options: Does the Model Matter?" *Financial Analysts Journal*, 2004, 60:5, 21–37; Don M. Chance and Tung-Hsiao Yang, "Expected Utility Valuation of Executive Stock Options in a Binomial Framework: A Comparative Analysis" (July 2004, working paper); Nalin Kulatilaka and Alan J. Marcus, "Valuing Employee Stock Options," *Financial Analysts Journal*, November–December 1994, 46–56.

25. Lisa K. Meulbroek, "The Efficiency of Equity-Linked Compensation: Understanding the Full Cost of Awarding Executive Stock Options," *Financial Management*, summer 2001, 5–44. See p. 6.

26. Lambert, R., D. Larcker, and R. Verrecchia. "Portfolio Considerations in Valuing Executive Compensation." *Journal of Accounting Research*, 1991, 29, 129–149; Kulatilaka and Marcus, "Valuing Employee Stock Options," see esp. pp. 52–53.

27. See Hall and Murphy, "Stock Options for Undiversified Executives"; Hall and Murphy, "The Trouble With Stock Options"; and Hall and Murphy, "Optimal Exercise Prices for Executive Stock Options."

Chapter 5

1. Lucian Bebchuk Lucian and Jesse Fried, *Pay Without Performance: The Unfulfilled Promise of Executive Compensation* (Cambridge, MA: Harvard University Press, 2006).

2. Stephen F. O'Byrne and S. David Young emphasize this concentration of pay linked to performance running mainly through equity and ESO holdings in their "Top Management Incentives and Corporate Performance," *Journal of Applied Corporate Finance*, Fall 2005, 17:4, 105–114.

3. Brian J. Hall and Jeffrey B. Liebman, "Are CEOs Really Paid Like Bureaucrats?" *Quarterly Journal of Economics*, 1998, 112, 653–691. See p. 654.

4. Ibid., see p. 655.

5. The following discussion of Richard Fuld at Lehman and the outcomes for financial executives in the crisis of 2007–2009 is adapted from Robert W. Kolb, *The Financial Crisis of Our Time* (Oxford: Oxford University Press, 2011), 253–257.

6. Quoted in Andrew Clark and Elana Schor, "Lehman Brothers Chief Executive Grilled by Congress over Compensation," *Manchester Guardian,* October 6, 2008,

http://www.guardian.co.uk/business/2008/oct/06/creditcrunch.lehmanbrothers/print, accessed February 25, 2010.

7. *Wall Street Journal,* "Congress Grills Lehman Brothers' Dick Fuld: Highlights of the Hearing," October 6, 2008. Emphases as reported in source.

8. Clark and Schor, "Lehman Brothers Chief Executive Grilled by Congress over Compensation," *Manchester Guardian,* October 6, 2008, http://www.guardian.co.uk/.

9. Lucian A. Bebchuk, Alma Cohen, and Holger Spamann, "The Wages of Failure: Executive Compensation at Bear Stearns and Lehman 2000–2008" (November 22, 2009, working paper).

10. In general, as BCS report, Lehman and Bear had similar results. In both firms, the executives in the second through fifth spots did quite well in the aggregate, although not nearly as well as the respective CEOs.

11. Note that this is not the calculation of BCS, although it relies on their numbers of shares. Further, this figure is not inflation-adjusted, and it is not certain how many shares Fuld held through 2008, but this provides a reasonable estimate of his losses on his shares in 2008.

12. Rüdiger Fahlenbrach and René Stulz, "Bank CEO Incentives and the Credit Crisis," July 2009, Fisher College of Business WO 2009-03-013, working paper. See p. 8.

13. Ibid., see p. 16.

14. Mark Anderson and Volkan Muslu, "What Do CEOs Realize from Option Pay?" (April 2010, working paper).

15. J. Carr Bettis, John M Bizjak, and Michael L Lemmon, "Exercise Behavior, Valuation, and the Incentive Effects of Employee Stock Options," *Journal of Financial Economics,* 2005, 76:2, 445–470.

16. Tristan Boyd, Philip Brown, and Alex Szimayer, "What Determines Early Exercise of Employee Stock Options in Australia?" *Accounting and Finance,* 2007, 47, 165–185.

17. Steven Huddart and Mark Lang, "Employee Stock Option Exercises: An Empirical Analysis," *Journal of Accounting & Economics,* 1996, 21, 5–43.

18. Zacharias Sautner and Martin Weber, "Subjective Stock Option Values and Exercise Decisions" (September 20, 2005, working paper). See also Zacharias Sautner and Martin Weber, "How Do Managers Behave in Stock Option Plans? Clinical Evidence from Exercise and Survey Data," *Journal of Financial Research,* summer 2009, 32:2, 123–155.

19. Xudong Fu and James A. Ligon, "Exercises of Executive Stock Options on the Vesting Date," *Financial Management,* autumn 2010, 1097–1125.

20. Jennifer N. Carpenter and Barbara Remmers, "Executive Stock Option Exercises and Inside Information," *Journal of Business,* 2001, 74:4, 513–534. See p. 515.

21. Steven Huddart and Mark Lang, "Information Distribution Within Firms: Evidence From Stock Option Exercises," *Journal of Accounting & Economics,* 2003, 34:1–3, 3–31.

22. David Aboody, John Hughes, Jing Liu, and Wei Su, "Are Executive Stock Option Exercises Driven by Private Information?" *Review of Accounting Studies,* 2008, 13:4, 551–570.

23. Joel S. Sternberg and H. Doug Witte, "Inside Information and the Exercise of Employee Stock Options" (n.d., working paper).

24. Huddart and Lang, "Information Distribution Within Firms."

25. David C. Cicero, "The Manipulation of Executive Stock Option Exercise Strategies: Information Timing and Backdating," *Journal of Finance*, December 2009, 64:6, 2627–2663; and Robert Brooks, Don M. Chance, and Brandon N. Cline, "Private Information and the Exercise of Executive Stock Options" (October 2007, working paper).

26. Eugene F. Fama, Lawrence Fisher, Michael C. Jensen, and Richard Roll, "The Adjustment of Stock Prices to New Information," *International Economic Review*, February 1969, 10:1, 1–21. Since 1969, this basic technique has been elaborated, refined, and been used in many hundreds, or even several thousand, of studies of how security prices respond to new information.

27. J. Carr Bettis, John M. Bizjak, and Michael L. Lemmon, "Managerial Ownership, Incentive Contracting, and the Use of Zero-Cost Collars and Equity Swaps by Corporate Insiders," *Journal of Financial and Quantitative Analysis*, 2001, 36:3, 345–370.

28. Eli Ofek and David Yermack, "Taking Stock: Equity-Based Compensation and the Evolution of Managerial Ownership," *Journal of Finance*, June 2000, 55, 1367–1384.

29. John E. Core, Wayne R. Guay, and David F. Larcker, "Executive Equity Compensation and Incentives: A Survey," *Federal Reserve Bank of New York Economic Policy Review*, 2003, 9, 27–50. See also John E. Core, Wayne R. Guay, and Randall S. Thomas, "Is U.S. CEO Compensation Broken?" *Journal of Applied Corporate Finance*, 2005, 17:4, 97–104.

30. Bengt Holmstrom and Steven N. Kaplan, "The State of U.S. Corporate Governance: What's Right and What's Wrong?" *Journal of Applied Corporate Finance*, 2003, 15, 8–20. See p. 13.

31. Michael C. Jensen and Kevin J. Murphy, "Remuneration: Where We've Been, How We Got to Here, What Are the Problems, and How to Fix Them" (2004, working paper), see p. 11.

32. Lucian A. Bebchuk and Jesse M. Fried, "How to Tie Equity Compensation to Long-Term Results," *Journal of Applied Corporate Finance*, winter 2010, 22:1, 99–106. See also Lucian A. Bebchuk and Jesse M. Fried, "Pay Without Performance: Overview of the Issues," *Journal of Corporation Law*, summer, 2005, 647–673.

Chapter 6

1. There is an additional constraint on the CEO's risk taking, and that is the CEO's reputation. Undertaking a very risky project that fails might damage the CEO's reputation, which might well impair future job prospects. In addition, CEOs are often thought to suffer from hubris, so the fear of embarrassment might also act as a constraint.

2. Jennifer Carpenter, "Does Option Compensation Increase Managerial Risk Appetite?" *Journal of Finance*, 2000, 55, 2311–2331. This stream of literature also extends back to R. Lambert, D. Larcker, and R. Verrecchia, "Portfolio Considerations in Valuing Executive Compensation," *Journal of Accounting Research*, 1991, 29, 129–149.

3. Carpenter, "Does Option Compensation Increase Managerial Risk Appetite?" See p. 2327.

4. Yisong S. Tian, "Too Much of a Good Incentive? The Case of Executive Stock Options," *Journal of Banking & Finance*, 2004, 28, 1225–1245.

5. Ibid., see p. 1227.

6. Tom Nohel and Steven Todd, "Stock Options and Managerial Incentives to Invest," *Journal of Derivatives Accounting*, 2004, 1:1, 29–46.

7. Neil Brisley, "Executive Stock Options: Early Exercise Provisions and Risk-Taking Incentives," *Journal of Finance*, 2006, 61:5, 2487–2509.

8. John M. Barron and Glen R. Waddell, "Work Hard, Not Smart: Stock Options in Executive Compensation," *Journal of Economic Behavior & Organization*, 2008, 66, 767–790; Gerald T. Garvey and Amin Mawani, "Executive Stock Options and Dynamic Risk-Taking Incentives," *Managerial Finance*, 2007, 33:4, 281–288.

9. Sunil Dutta, "Managerial Expertise, Private Information, and Pay-Performance Sensitivity," *Management Science*, 2008, 54:3, 429–442.

10. Antonio E. Bernardo, Hongbin Cai, and Jiang Luo, "Motivating Entrepreneurial Activity in a Firm," *Review of Financial Studies*, 2009, 22:3, 1089–1118.

11. John E. Core, Wayne R. Guay, and David F. Larcker, "Executive Equity Compensation and Incentives: A Survey," *Federal Reserve Bank of New York Economic Policy Review*, 2003, 9, 27–50. See p. 44.

12. Shivaram Rajgopal and Terry Shevlin, "Empirical Evidence on the Relation Between Stock Option Compensation and Risk Taking," *Journal of Accounting & Economics*, 2002, 33:2, 145–171.

13. Wayne R. Guay, "The Sensitivity of CEO Wealth to Equity Risk: An Analysis of the Magnitude and Determinants," *Journal of Financial Economics*, 1999, 53, 43–71.

14. Ibid., see p. 43.

15. Peter Wright, Mark Kroll, Peter Davis, and William T. Jackson, "The Influences of the Chief Executive Officer's Stock and Option Ownership on Firm Risk Taking: An Examination of Resource Allocation Choices," *Academy of Strategic Management Journal*, 2007, 6, 47–68.

16. Cynthia E. Devers, Gerry McNamara, Robert M. Wiseman, Mathias Arrfelt, "Moving Closer to the Action: Examining Compensation Design Effects on Firm Risk," *Organization Science*, July–August 2008, 19:4, 548–566. See p. 548.

17. Ibid., see p. 561.

18. Jeffrey L. Coles, Naveen D. Daniel, and Lalitha Naveen, "Managerial Incentives and Risk Taking," *Journal of Financial Economics*, 2006, 79, 431–468.

19. Yenn-Ru Chen and Bong Soo Lee, "A Dynamic Analysis of Executive Stock Options: Determinants and Consequences," *Journal of Corporate Finance*, 2010, 16, 88–103.

20. Randolph B. Cohen, Brian J. Hall, and Luis M. Viceira, "Do Executive Stock Options Encourage Risk-Taking?" (March 2000, working paper).

21. William Gerard Sanders and Donald C. Hambrick, "Swinging for the Fences: The Effects of CEO Stock Options on Company Risk Taking and Performance," *Academy of Management Journal*, 2007, 50:5, 1055–1078. See p. 1055.

22. Peter Tufano, "Who Manages Risk? An Empirical Examination of Risk Management Practices in the Gold Mining Industry," *Journal of Finance*, September 1996, 51:4, 1097–1137.

23. Rajgopal and Shevlin, "Empirical Evidence on the Relation Between Stock Option Compensation and Risk Taking."

24. Daniel A. Rogers, "Does Executive Portfolio Structure Affect Risk Management? CEO Risk-Taking Incentives and Corporate Derivatives Usage," *Journal of Banking & Finance*, 2002, 26, 271–295.

25. Zhiyong Dong, Cong Wang, and Fei Xie, "Do Executive Stock Options Induce Excessive Risk Taking?" *Journal of Banking & Finance*, 34, 2010, 2518–2529.

26. Matthew T. Billett, David C. Mauer, and Yilei Zhang, "Stockholder and Bondholder Wealth Effects of CEO Incentive Grants" *Financial Management*, summer 2010, 463–487.

27. Hernan Ortiz-Molina, "Top Management Incentives and the Pricing of Corporate Public Debt," *Journal of Financial and Quantitative Analysis*, 2006, 41:2, 317–340. See p. 317.

28. George J. Benston and Jocelyn D. Evan, "Performance Compensation Contracts and CEOs' Incentive to Shift Risk to Debtholders: An Empirical Analysis," *Journal of Economics and Finance*, spring 2006, 30:1, 70–92.

29. Paul Brockman, Xiumin Martin, and Emre Unlu, "Executive Compensation and the Maturity Structure of Corporate Debt," *Journal of Finance*, June 2010, 65:3, 1123–1161.

30. Bo Becker, "Wealth and Executive Compensation," *Journal of Finance*, 2006, 61:1, 379–397.

31. Ulrike Malmendier and Geoffrey Tate, "Who Makes Acquisitions? CEO Overconfidence and the Market's Reaction," *Journal of Financial Economics*, 2008, 89, 20–43.

32. Juan Bautista Delgado-García, Juan Manuel de la Fuente-Sabaté, and Esther de Quevedo-Puente, "Too Negative to Take Risks? The Effect of the CEO's Emotional Traits on Firm Risk," *British Journal of Management*, 2010, 21, 313–326.

33. Institute of International Finance, "Compensation in Financial Services: Industry Progress and the Agenda for Change" (March 2009).

34. U.S. Department of the Treasury, "Guidance on Sound Incentive Compensation Policies," Federal Register, June 25, 2010, vol. 75, no. 122, 36395–36414. See p. 36396.

35. Andrew Ross Sorkin, *Too Big to Fail* (New York: Viking, 2009), 596.

36. Alex Blumberg, "Self-Fulfilling Prophecy: The Bailout of Frannie and Freddie," NPR (blog), March 29. 2011, http://www.npr.org/blogs/money/2011/04/21/134863767/self-fulfilling-prophecy-the-bailout-of-fannie-and-freddie.

37. As testimony of concern by the Fed and Treasury see Board of Governors of the Federal Reserve System, *Incentive Compensation Practices: A Report on the Horizontal Review of Practices at Large Banking Organizations* (Washington, DC: Board of Governors of the Federal Reserve System, October 2011); and U.S. Treasury Dept., "Guidance on Sound Incentive Compensation Policies."

Chapter 7

1. F. Guidry, A. J. Leone, and S. Rock, "Earnings-Based Bonus Plans and Earnings Management by Business-Unit Managers," *Journal of Accounting & Economics*, 1999, 26:1–3, 113–142.

2. Matthew Valle and Robert M. Pavlik, "Predicting the Investment Decisions of Managers Under the Influence of Stock Option Incentives," *Journal of Management Research*, December 2009, 9:3, 133–141.

3. James A. Hall and Stephen L. Liedtka, "Financial Performance, CEO Compensation, and Large-Scale Information Technology Outsourcing Decisions," *Journal of Management Information Systems*, summer 2005, 22:1, 193–221. See especially pp. 215–216.

4. Shivaram Rajgopal and Terry Shevlin, "Empirical Evidence on the Relation Between Stock Option Compensation and Risk-Taking," *Journal of Accounting & Economics*, 2002, 33:2, 145–171. See especially p. 145.

5. Jeffrey L. Coles, Naveen D. Daniel, and Lalitha Naveen, "Managerial Incentives and Risk Taking," *Journal of Financial Economics*, 2006, 79, 431–468.

6. John Paul Broussard, Sheree A. Buchenroth, and Eugene A. Pilotte, "CEO Incentives, Cash Flow, and Investment," *Financial Management*, summer 2004, 33:2, 51–70.

7. Yixin Liu and David C. Mauer, "Corporate Cash Holdings and CEO Compensation Incentives," *Journal of Financial Economics*, 2011, 102, 183–198.

8. Efraim Benmelech, Eugene Kandel, and Pietro Veronesi, "Stock-Based Compensation and CEO (Dis)incentives," *Quarterly Journal of Economics*, November 2010, 1769–1820. See especially p. 1770.

9. Valle and Pavlik, "Predicting the Investment Decisions of Managers Under the Influence of Stock Option Incentives," see especially p. 133.

10. Tom Nohel and Steven Todd, "Stock Options and Managerial Incentives to Invest," *Journal of Derivatives Accounting*, 2004, 1:1, 29–46. See especially p. 29.

11. Janikan Supanvanij, "Does the Composition of CEO Compensation Influence the Firm's Advertising Budgeting?" *Journal of American Academy of Business*, September 2007, 7:2, 117–123.

12. David H. Erkens, "Do Firms Use Time-Vested Stock-Based Pay to Keep Research and Development Investments Secret?" *Journal of Accounting Research*, September 2011, 49:4, 861–894. See p. 861.

13. Coles, Daniel, and Naveen, "Managerial Incentives and Risk Taking"; Zhiyong Dong, Cong Wang, and Fei Xie, "Do Executive Stock Options Induce Excessive Risk Taking?" *Journal of Banking & Finance*, 34, 2010, 2518–2529.

14. Katharina Lewellen, "Financing Decisions When Managers Are Risk Averse," *Journal of Financial Economics*, 2006, 82:3, 551–589.

15. Kathleen M. Kahle and Kuldeep Shastri, "Firm Performance, Capital Structure, and the Tax Benefits of Employee Stock Options," *Journal of Financial and Quantitative Analysis*, 2005, 40:1, 135–160. See especially p. 135.

16. John R. Graham, Mark H. Lang, and Douglas A Shackelford, "Employee Stock Options, Corporate Taxes, and Debt Policy," *Journal of Finance*, 2004, 59:4, 1585–1618. See p. 1586.

17. Kahle and Shastri, "Firm Performance, Capital Structure, and the Tax Benefits of Employee Stock Options," see p. 159.

18. Ilona Babenko, Michael Lemmon, and Yuri Tserlukevich, "Employee Stock Options and Investment," *Journal of Finance*, June 2011, 66:3, 981–1009. See pp. 981 and 986.

19. John McCormack and Judy Weiker, "Rethinking 'Strength of Incentives' for Executives of Financial Institutions," *Journal of Applied Corporate Finance*, summer 2010, 22:3, 65–72. McCormack and Weiker also focus on the risk-shifting from

financial institutions to the broader public and explain how equity compensation for managers can incentivize this behavior.

20. Matthew T. Billett, David C. Mauer, and Yilei Zhang, "Stockholder and Bondholder Wealth Effects of CEO Incentive Grants" *Financial Management*, summer 2010, 463–487.

21. Hernan Ortiz-Molina, "Top Management Incentives and the Pricing of Corporate Public Debt," *Journal of Financial and Quantitative Analysis*, 2006, 41:2, 317–340. See p. 317.

22. Ibid., see p. 319.

23. See Paul Brockman, Xiumin Martin, and Emre Unlu, "Executive Compensation and the Maturity Structure of Corporate Debt," *Journal of Finance*, 65:3, June 2010, 1123–1161. Hernan Ortiz-Molina finds broadly confirming results in "Executive Compensation and Capital Structure: The Effects of Convertible Debt and Straight Debt on CEO Pay," *Journal of Accounting & Economics*, 2007, 43:1, 69–93.

24. Sudheer Chava, Praveen Kumar, and Arthur Warga, "Managerial Agency and Bond Covenants," *Review of Financial Studies*, 2010, 23:3, 1120–1148. See especially p. 1145.

25. Sudheer Chava and Amiyatosh Purnanandam, "CEOs Versus CFOs: Incentives and Corporate Policies" *Journal of Financial Economics*, 2010, 97, 263–278.

26. Richard A. Lambert, William N. Lanen, and David F. Larcker, "Executive Stock Option Plans and Corporate Dividend Policy," *Journal of Financial and Quantitative Analysis*, December 1989, 24:4, 409–425.

27. For the role of ESOs in the management of earnings dilution, see Daniel A. Bens, Venky Nagar, Douglas J. Skinner, and M. H. Franco Wong, "Employee Stock Options, EPS Dilution, and Stock Repurchases," *Journal of Accounting & Economics*, 2003, 36:1–3, 51–90; and Asjeet S. Lamba and Vivek M. Miranda, "The Role of Executive Stock Options in On-Market Share Buybacks," *International Review of Finance*, 2010, 10:3, 339–363.

28. George W. Fenn and Nellie Liang, "Corporate Payout Policy and Managerial Stock Incentives," *Journal of Financial Economics*, 2001, 60:1, 45–72. See p. 45.

29. Ibid.; Kathleen M. Kahle, "When a Buyback Isn't a Buyback: Open Market Repurchases and Employee Options," *Journal of Financial Economics*, 2002, 63:2, 235–261; and Chinmoy Ghosh, John P. Harding, Özcan Sezer, and C. F. Sirmans, "The Role of Executive Stock Options in REIT Repurchases," *Journal of Real Estate Research*, January–March 2008, 30:1, 27–44.

30. David Aboody and Ron Kasznik, "Executive Stock-Based Compensation and Firms' Cash Payout: The Role of Shareholders' Tax-Related Payout Preferences," *Review of Accounting Studies*, 2008, 13, 216–251.

31. Ilona Babenko, "Share Repurchases and Pay-Performance Sensitivity of Employee Compensation Contract," *Journal of Finance*, February 2009, 64:1, 117–150. See p. 117.

32. Charles J. Cuny, Gerald S. Martin, and John J. Puthenpurackal, "Stock Options and Total Payouts," *Journal of Financial and Quantitative Analysis*, April 2009, 44:2, 391–410.

33. Jie Cai and Anand M. Vijh, "Incentive Effects of Stock and Option Holdings of Target and Acquirer CEOs," *Journal of Finance*, 2007, 62:4, 1891–1933. See p. 1891.

34. Shane Heitzman, "Equity Grants to Target CEOs prior to Acquisitions" (2006, working paper). See p. 1.

35. Eliezer M. Fich, Jie Cai, and Anh L. Tran, "Stock Option Grants to Target CEOs During Private Merger Negotiations," *Journal of Financial Economics*, 2011, 101, 413–430.

36. Sudip Datta, Mai Iskandar-Datta, and Kartik Raman, "Executive Compensation and Corporate Acquisition Decisions," *Journal of Finance,* 2001, 56:6, 2299–2336.

37. Kristina Minnick, Haluk Unal, and Liu Yang, "Pay for Performance? CEO Compensation and Acquirer Returns in BHCs" (n.d., working paper).

38. Datta, Iskandar-Datta, and Raman, "Executive Compensation and Corporate Acquisition Decisions."

39. Melissa A. Williams, Timothy B. Michael, and Ramesh P. Rao, "Bank Mergers, Equity Risk Incentives, and CEO Stock Options," *Managerial Finance*, 2008, 34:5, 316–327. See p. 316.

40. William Gerard Sanders, "Behavioral Responses of CEOs to Stock Ownership and Stock Option Pay," *Academy of Management Journal*, 2001, 44:3, 477–492.

41. Scott Fung, Hoje Jo, and Shih-Chuan Tsai, "Agency Problems in Stock Market–Driven Acquisitions," *Review of Accounting and Finance*, 2009, 8:4, 388–430. See p. 388.

42. Cai and Vijh, "Incentive Effects of Stock and Option Holdings of Target and Acquirer CEOs," see p. 1891.

43. H. Mehran, G. E. Nogler, and K. B. Schwartz, "CEO Incentive Plans and Corporate Liquidation Policy," *Journal of Financial Economics*, 1998, 50:3, 319–349.

44. Peter Tufano, "Who Manages Risk? An Empirical Examination of Risk Management Practices in the Gold Mining Industry," *Journal of Finance*, September 1996, 51:4, 1097–1137. See p. 1097.

45. Ibid., see p. 1130.

46. John D. Knopf, Jouahn Nam, and John H. Thornton, Jr., "The Volatility and Price Sensitivities of Managerial Stock Option Portfolios and Corporate Hedging," *Journal of Finance*, 2002, 57:2, 801–813. See p. 801.

47. See Daniel A. Rogers, "Does Executive Portfolio Structure Affect Risk Management? CEO Risk-Taking Incentives and Corporate Derivatives Usage," *Journal of Banking & Finance*, 2002, 26, 271–295; Rajgopal and Shevlin, "Empirical Evidence on the Relation Between Stock Option Compensation and Risk Taking"; and Alexei Tchistyi, David Yermack, and Hayong Yun, "Negative Hedging: Performance-Sensitive Debt and CEOs' Equity Incentives," *Journal of Financial and Quantitative Analysis*, June 2011, 46:3, 657–686.

48. David Aboody, Mary E. Barth, and Ron Kasznik, "Do Firms Understate Stock Option-Based Compensation Expense Disclosed Under FAS 123?" *Review of Accounting Studies*, 2006, 11, 429–461.

49. Eli Bartov, Partha Mohanram, and Doron Nissim, "Managerial Discretion and the Economic Determinants of the Disclosed Volatility Parameter for Valuing ESOs," *Review of Accounting Studies*, 2007, 12, 155–179; Leslie Hodder, William J. Mayhew, Mary Lea McAnally, and Connie D. Weaver, "Employee Stock Option Fair-Value Estimates: Do Managerial Discretion and Incentives Explain Accuracy?" *Contemporary Accounting Research*, winter 2006, 23:4, 933–975; and Kevin C. K. Lam and Yaw M. Mensah, "Disclosure of the Fair Value of Executive Stock Options Granted to Top Executives" (September 2007, working paper).

50. Hodder et al., "Employee Stock Option Fair-Value Estimates," see p. 967.

51. Lam and Mensah, "Disclosure of the Fair Value of Executive Stock Options Granted to Top Executives," see p. 1.

52. Marilyn F. Johnson and Ram Natarajan, "Executive Compensation Contracts and Voluntary Disclosure to Security Analysts," *Managerial Finance*, 2005, 31:7, 3–26.

53. William J. Donoher, Richard Reed, and Susan F. Storrud-Barnes, "Incentive Alignment, Control, and the Issue of Misleading Financial Disclosures," *Journal of Management*, August 2007, 33:4, 547–569. For the importance of strong corporate governance in resolving disclosure problems, see also Jodie Nelson, Gerry Gallery, and Majella Percy, "Role of Corporate Governance in Mitigating the Selective Disclosure of Executive Stock Option Information," *Accounting and Finance*, 2010, 50, 585–717.

54. Venky Nagar, Dhananjay Nanda, and Peter Wysocki, "Discretionary Disclosure and Stock-Based Incentives," *Journal of Accounting & Economics*, 2003, 34:1–3, 283–309. See p. 283.

Chapter 8

1. Daniel Bergstresser and Thomas Philippon, "CEO Incentives and Earnings Management," *Journal of Financial Economics*, 2006, 80:3, 511–529. See p. 513. For a detailed treatment of Enron's malfeasance, see Gary Giroux, "What Went Wrong? Accounting Fraud and Lessons from the Recent Scandals," *Social Research*, winter 2008, 75:4, 1205–1238. Giroux also explores the effect of earnings management at Enron.

2. For clarity, the example of RIM's earnings miss has no relationship to earnings management. It is just an anecdote to illustrate how strongly the market can react to a negative earnings surprise.

3. See Douglas J. Skinner and Richard G. Sloan, "Earnings Surprises, Growth Expectations, and Stock Returns or Don't Let an Earnings Torpedo Sink Your Portfolio," *Review of Accounting Studies*, 2002, 7:2–3, 289–312; and Eli Bartov, Dan Givoly, and Carla Hayn, "The Rewards to Meeting or Beating Earnings Expectations," *Journal of Accounting & Economics*, 2002, 33:2, 173–204. Others have also documented the incentives that managers have to avoid negative earnings surprises. See, for example, Dawn A. Matsumoto, "Management's Incentives to Avoid Negative Earnings Surprises," *Accounting Review*, July 2002, 77:3, 483–514.

4. For documentation of the effect of a negative-earnings surprise on the manager's bonus, see Steve R. Matsunaga and Chul W. Park, "The Effect of Missing a Quarterly Earnings Benchmark on the CEO's Annual Bonus," *Accounting Review*, July 2001, 76:3, 313–332.

5. In their study of incentives at Fannie Mae, Bebchuk and Fried make a similar point even more explicitly: "We do not know, nor do we want to speculate, whether the dilution and perversion of incentives produced by Fannie Mae's compensation arrangements in fact affected the executives' decision-making about accounting or anything else prior to their departures. Raines and Howard may have acted throughout their service with the utmost dedication to Fannie Mae and its shareholders. Our claim is merely that Fannie Mae's pay arrangements, which are typical of pay arrangements given to public company executives, did not strengthen the managers' incentives to enhance shareholder value but rather weakened and distorted them. As we discuss below, there is empirical evidence that, in the aggregate, pay arrangements at

public companies have influenced executives to inflate earnings." Lucian A. Bebchuk, and Jesse M. Fried, "Executive Compensation at Fannie Mae: A Case Study of Perverse Incentives, Nonperformance Pay, and Camouflage," *Journal of Corporation Law*, 2005, 30, 807–822. See p. 808.

6. Christopher Cox, "Accounting Irregularities at Fannie Mae," testimony before the U.S. Senate Committee on Banking, Housing and Urban Affairs, June 15, 2006.

7. Bebchuk and Fried, "Executive Compensation at Fannie Mae," see p. 810.

8. Ibid., see p. 817. Bebchuk and Fried explain other benefits that accrued to Raines and Howard after their forced departures, including a retirement benefit of $114,000 per month for the lifetime of Raines and his wife. See p. 818.

9. For a detailed explanation of the role of Fannie Mae in the financial crisis, see Robert W. Kolb, *The Financial Crisis of Our Time* (Oxford: Oxford University Press, 2011). Chapter 1 explains the role of GSEs in housing finance, while pp. 110–117 focus on Fannie Mae and Freddie Mac in some detail.

10. Paul M. Healy, "The Effect of Bonus Schemes on Accounting Decisions," *Journal of Accounting & Economics*, 1985, 7:1–3, 85–107.

11. Robert W. Holthausen, David F. Larcker, and Richard G. Sloan, "Annual Bonus Schemes and the Manipulation of Earnings," *Journal of Accounting & Economics*, 1995, 19, 29–74. See p. 29.

12. Sarah McVay, Venky Nagar, and Vicki Wei Tang, "Trading Incentives to Meet the Analyst Forecast," *Review of Accounting Studies*, 2006, 11, 575–598.

13. Daniel Bergstresser and Thomas Philippon, "CEO Incentives and Earnings Management," *Journal of Financial Economics*, 2006, 80:3, 511–529; and Xiaomeng Zhang, Kathryn M. Bartol, Ken G. Smith, Michael D. Pfarrer, and Dmitry M. Khanin, "CEOs on the Edge: Earnings Manipulation and Stock-Based Incentive Misalignment," *Academy of Management Journal*, 2008, 51:2, 241–258. See p. 241.

14. Lin Peng and Ailsa Röell, "Executive Pay and Shareholder Litigation" (August 2006, working paper), see p. 1.

15. As further examples of literature finding an important link between incentive compensation in general and ESOs in particular, as stimulants to earnings management, see Eli Bartov and Partha Mohanram, "Private Information, Earnings Manipulations, and Executive Stock-Option Exercises," *Accounting Review*, 2004, 79:4, 889–920; Mark P. Bauman and Kenneth W. Shaw, "Stock Option Compensation and the Likelihood of Meeting Analysts' Quarterly Earnings Targets," *Review of Quantitative Financial Accounting*, 2006, 26, 301–319; Qiang Cheng and Terry Warfield, "Equity Incentives and Earnings Management," *Accounting Review*, 2002, 80:2, 441–476; Qiang Cheng, Terry Warfield, and Minlei Ye, "Equity Incentives and Earnings Management: Evidence from the Banking Industry," *Journal of Accounting, Auditing, & Finance*, 2011, 26, 317–349; Marcia Millon Cornett, Alan J. Marcus, and Hassan Tehranian, "Corporate Governance and Pay for Performance: The Impact of Earnings Management," *Journal of Financial Economics*, 2008, 87, 357–373; Don Warren, Mary Zey, Tanya Granston, and Joseph Roy, "Earnings Fraud: Board Control vs. CEO Control and Corporate Performance—1992–2004," *Managerial and Decision Economics*, 2011, 32, 17–34; and Margaret Weber, "Sensitivity of Executive Wealth to Stock Price, Corporate Governance and Earnings Management," *Review of Accounting and Finance*, 2006, 5:4, 321–354. By contrast, some studies find little or no association between incentive compensation

and earnings manipulation: Merle Erickson, Michelle Hanlon, and Edward L. Maydew, "Is There a Link Between Executive Equity Incentive and Accounting Fraud?" *Journal of Accounting Research*, March 2006, 44:1, 118–143. Still other studies find a contingent relationship between ESOs and earnings fraud. For example, Joseph P. O'Connor, Jr., Richard L. Priem, Joseph E. Coombs, and K. Matthew Gilley, "Do CEO Stock Options Prevent or Promote Fraudulent Financial Reporting?" *Academy of Management Journal*, 2006, 49, 485–500, find that CEO duality and whether directors also held stock options influenced the relationship between the CEOs option holding and earnings manipulation. However, at least one study finds little relationship between equity incentives and misreporting: Christopher S. Armstrong, Alan D. Jagolinzer, and David F. Larcker, "Chief Executive Officer Equity Incentives and Accounting Irregularities," *Journal of Accounting Research*, May 2010, 48:2, 225–271.

16. Natasha Burns and Simi Kedia, "The Impact of Performance-Based Compensation on Misreporting," *Journal of Financial Economics*, 2006, 79:1, 35–67. See pp. 34–35. See also Natasha Burns and Simi Kedia, "Executive Option Exercises and Financial Misreporting," *Journal of Banking & Finance*, 2008, 32, 845–857.

17. Jap Efendi, Anup Srivastava, and Edward P Swanson, "Why Do Corporate Managers Misstate Financial Statements? The Role of Option Compensation and Other Factors," *Journal of Financial Economics*, 2007, 85:3, 667–708. See p. 667.

18. Without attempting to provide an exhaustive list, some additional studies confirming the ESO-earnings manipulation link are: Terry Baker, Denton Collins, and Austin Reitenga, "Stock Option Compensation and Earnings Management Incentives," *Journal of Accounting, Auditing & Finance*, 2003, 18:4, 557–582; Walid Ben-Amar and Franck Missonier-Piera, "Earnings Management by Friendly Takeover Targets," *International Journal of Managerial Finance*, 2008, 4:3, 232–243; Mary Lea McAnally, Anup Srivastava, and Connie D. Weaver, "Executive Stock Options, Missed Earnings Targets, and Earnings Management," *Accounting Review*, January 2008, 83:1, 185–216; and Steven Balsam, Huajing Chen, and Srinivasan Sankaraguruswamy, "Earnings Management Prior to Stock Option Grants" (2003, working paper). In addition, Aboody and Kasznik find that managers make opportunistic disclosures to maximize their stock-option compensation: David Aboody and Ron Kasznik, "CEO Stock Option Awards and the Timing of Corporate Voluntary Disclosures," *Journal of Accounting & Economics*, 2000, 29:3, 73–100.

19. Shane A. Johnson, Harley E. Ryan, Jr., and Yisong S. Tian, "Managerial Incentives and Corporate Fraud: The Sources of Incentives Matter," *Review of Finance*, 2009, 13, 115–145. See p. 142.

20. David Yermack, "Good Timing: CEO Stock Option Awards and Company News Announcements," *Journal of Finance*, 1997, 52:2, 449–476. Others confirmed the basic results of Yermack as well. See Keith W. Chauvin and Catherine Shenoy, "Stock Price Decreases Prior to Executive Option Grants," *Journal of Corporate Finance*, 2001, 7, 53–76; and Aboody and Kasznik, "CEO Stock Option Awards and the Timing of Corporate Voluntary Disclosures."

21. Yermack, "Good Timing," see p. 449.

22. Ibid., see p. 475.

23. The following studies address springloading explicitly: Lucian A. Bebchuk, Yaniv Grinstein, and Urs Peyer, "Lucky CEOs and Lucky Directors," *Journal of Finance*,

December 2010, 65:6, 2363–2401; William Hughes, "Stock Option 'Springloading': An Examination of Loaded Justifications and New SEC Disclosure Rules," *Journal of Corporation Law*, 2008, 33:3, 777–796; M. P. Narayanan, Cindy A. Schipani, and H. Nejat Seyhun, "The Economic Impact of Backdating of Executive Stock Options," *Michigan Law Review*, June 2007, 105, 1597–1641; and Rik Sen, "The Returns to Springloading" (February 2008, working paper).

24. Erik Lie, "On the Timing of CEO Stock Option Awards," *Management Science*, May 2005, 51:5, 802–812. See p. 802.

25. Randall A. Heron and Erik Lie, "Does Backdating Explain the Stock Price Pattern Around Executive Stock Option Grants?" *Journal of Financial Economics*, 2007, 83:2, 271. See the discussion on pp. 272–273. Actually, the exact rules are a little more complicated than the text suggests. Heron and Lie provide details.

26. Ibid., see p. 271. See also, Randall A. Heron, Erik Lie, and Tod Perry, "On the Use (and Abuse) of Stock Option Grants," *Financial Analysts Journal*, 2007, 63:3, 17–27.

27. Randall A. Heron and Erik Lie, "What Fraction of Stock Option Grants to Top Executives Have Been Backdated or Manipulated?" *Management Science*, April 2009, 55:4, 513–525. See p. 513. Perhaps not surprisingly, backdating gave rise to a cottage industry of research that revealed many additional aspects of the practice and its effects. The following papers are related to backdating, although their findings are not reflected individually in the text's analysis: John Bizjak, Michael Lemmon, and Ryan Whitby, "Option Backdating and Board Interlocks," *Review of Financial Studies*, 2009, 22:11, 4821–4847; Cynthia E. Devers, Albert A. Cannella, Jr., Gregory P. Reilly, and Michelle E. Yoder, "Executive Compensation: A Multidisciplinary Review of Recent Developments," *Journal of Management*, 2007, 33:6, 1016–1072; Dan Dhaliwal, Merle Erickson, and Shane Heitzman, "Taxes and the Backdating of Stock Option Exercise Dates," *Journal of Accounting & Economics*, 47, 2009, 27–49; Yi Feng and Yisong S. Tian, "Option Expensing and Executive Compensation," September 4, 2007, working paper; Carola Frydman and Dirk Jenter, "CEO Compensation," *Annual Review of Financial Economics*, 2010, 2, 75–102; Richard E. Goldberg and James A. Read, Jr., "Just Lucky? A Statistical Test for Option Backdating" (March 2007, working paper); Mary Lea McAnally, Anup Srivastava, and Connie D. Weaver, "Executive Stock Options, Missed Earnings Targets, and Earnings Management," *Accounting Review*, January 2008, 83:1, 185–216; Kristina Minnick and Mengxin Zhao, "Backdating and Director Incentives: Money or Reputation?," *Journal of Financial Research*, winter 2009, 32:4, 449–477; M. P. Narayanan and M. P. Nejat Seyhun, "The Dating Game: Do Managers Designate Option Grant Dates to Increase their Compensation?" *Review of Financial Studies*, September 2008, 21:5, 1907–1945; and Tjalling Van Der Goot, "Monitoring and Manipulation Around Option Grants Dates" (n.d., working paper).

28. Eric Dash and Matt Richtel, "Ex-Brocade Chief Convicted in Backdating Case," *New York Times*, August 8, 2007.

29. Philip Shiskin, "Backdating Conviction of Reyes Overturned," *Wall Street Journal*, August 19, 2009.

30. Ibid. For a further discussion of Brocade and some other firms, see Nolan McWilliams, "Shock Options: The Stock Options Backdating Scandal of 2006 and the SEC's Response" (2007, working paper).

31. Nathan Koppel, "Brocade's Gregory Reyes Sentenced (Again) for Options Backdating," *Wall Street Journal*, June 25, 2010.

32. Reuters, "Court Upholds Reyes Options Backdating Conviction," October 13, 2011, http://www.reuters.com/article/2011/10/13/brocade-reyes-idUSN1E79C1AB20111013.

33. Two prime examples of criticism from the point of view of corporate governance are Bebchuk, Grinstein, and Peyer, "Lucky CEOs and Lucky Directors"; and Jesse M. Fried, "Option Backdating and Its Implications," *Washington & Lee Law Review*, 2008, 65, 853–886. Explicitly ethical criticism has been provided by Avshalom M. Adam and Mark S. Schwartz, "Corporate Governance, Ethics, and the Backdating of Stock Options," *Journal of Business Ethics*, 2009, 225–237; and Norman D. Bishara and Cindy A. Schipani, "Strengthening the Ties that Bind: Preventing Corruption in the Executive Suite," *Journal of Business Ethics*, 2009, 88, 765–780.

34. "Reyes' backdating scheme was simplified by the unusual method authorizing him to issue his own option grants. Reyes was given authority to issue option grants as the sole member of a Compensation Committee that acted as the Administrator' of the plan." The entire quotation is from McWilliams, "Shock Options," p. 20. McWilliams quotes the internal quotation from the SEC *Complaint* in the matter.

Chapter 9

1. Equilar, *An Analysis of Voting Results and Performance at Russell 3000 Companies* (Redwood City, CA: Equilar, Inc., 2011).

2. Gretchen Morgenson documents the minute amounts that have been "clawed back" since the financial crisis, suggesting that the amounts recovered are fairly trivial, perhaps amounting to only an asterisk. See Gretchen Morgenson, "Clawbacks Without Claws," *New York Times*, September 10, 2011.

3. J. A. Brickley, S. Bhagat, and R. C. Lease, "The Impact of Long-Range Managerial Compensation Plans on Shareholder Wealth," *Journal of Accounting & Economics*, 1985, 7, 115–129; R. A. DeFusco, R. R. Johnson, and T. S. Zorn, "The Effect of Executive Stock Option Plans on Stockholders and Bondholders," *Journal of Finance*, 1990, 45, 617–627; M. Gerety, C-K. Hoi, and A. Robin, "Do Shareholders Benefit from the Adoption of Incentive Pay for Directors?" *Financial Management*, 2001, 30, 45–61; K. J. Martin and R. S. Thomas, "When Is Enough, Enough? Market Reaction to Highly Dilutive Stock Option Plans and the Subsequent Impact on CEO Compensation," *Journal of Corporate Finance*," 2005, 11, 61–83; and Matthew T. Billett, David C. Mauer, and Yilei Zhang, "Stockholder and Bondholder Wealth Effects of CEO Incentive Grants," *Financial Management*, summer 2010, 463–487.

4. Seppo Ikäheimo, Anders Kjellman, Jan Holmberg, and Sari Jussila, "Employee Stock Option Plans and Stock Market Reaction: Evidence from Finland," *European Journal of Finance*, 2004, 10:2, 105–122; and Hideaki Kiyoshi Kato, Michael Lemmon, Mi Luo, and James Schallheim, "An Empirical Examination of the Costs and Benefits of Executive Stock Options: Evidence from Japan," *Journal of Financial Economics*, 2005, 78:2, 435–461.

5. One well-regarded effort to create an overall "governance index" is Paul A. Gompers, Joy L. Ishii, and Andrew Metrick, "Corporate Governance and Equity

Prices," *Quarterly Journal of Economics,* February 2003, 118: 1, 107–155. There are numerous competing attempts to create the ideal index of good governance.

6. Steven T. Petra and Nina T. Dorata, "Corporate Governance and Chief Executive Officer Compensation," *Corporate Governance*, 2008, 8:2, 141–152.

7. Jay C. Hartzell and Laura T. Starks, "Institutional Investors and Executive Compensation," *Journal of Finance*, 2003, 58:6, 2351–2374.

8. Marianne Bertrand and Sendhil Mullainathan, "Are CEOs Rewarded for Luck? The Ones Without Principals Are," *Quarterly Journal of Economics*, 2001, 116:3, 901–932.

9. Vidhi Chhaochharia and Yaniv Grinstein, "CEO Compensation and Board Structure," *Journal of Finance*, February 2009, 64:1, 231–261.

10. Richard M. Cyert, Sok-Hyon Kang, and Praveen Kumar, "Corporate Governance, Takeovers, and Top-Management Compensation: Theory and Evidence," *Management Science*, 2002, 48:4, 453–469.

11. Jerry Sun, Steven F. Cahan, and David Emanuel, "Compensation Committee Governance Quality, Chief Executive Office Stock Option Grants, and Future Firm Performance," *Journal of Banking & Finance*, 2009, 33, 1507–1519.

12. Lucian A. Bebchuk, "The Myth of the Shareholder Franchise" (March 2007, working paper); and Lucian A. Bebchuk, "The Case for Increasing Shareholder Power," *Harvard Law Review,* January 2005, 118, 833–917.

{ BIBLIOGRAPHY }

Note: The working papers cited are in the author's possession but may be obtained by the reader from the Social Science Research Network, www. ssrn.com.

Aboody, David, Mary E. Barth, and Ron Kasznik. "Do Firms Understate Stock Option-Based Compensation Expense Disclosed Under SFAS 123?" *Review of Accounting Studies*, 2006, 11, 429–461.

Aboody, David, Nicole Bastian Johnson, and Ron Kasznik. "Employee Stock Options and Future Firm Performance: Evidence from Option Repricings." *Journal of Accounting & Economics*, May 2010, 50:1, 74–92.

Aboody, David, John Hughes, Jing Liu, and Wei Su. "Are Executive Stock Option Exercises Driven by Private Information?" *Review of Accounting Studies*, 2008, 13:4, 551–570.

Aboody, David, and Ron Kasznik. "CEO Stock Option Awards and the Timing of Corporate Voluntary Disclosures." *Journal of Accounting & Economics*, 2000, 29:3, 73–100.

———. "Executive Stock-Based Compensation and Firms' Cash Payout: The Role of Shareholders' Tax-Related Payout Preferences." *Review of Accounting Studies*, 2008, 13, 216–251.

Abowd, John M. and David S. Kaplan, "Executive Compensation: Six Questions that Need Answering," *Journal of Economic Perspectives*, 1999, 13:4, 145–168.

Acharya, Viral V., Kose John, and Rangarajan K. Dundaram. "On the Optimality of Resetting Executive Stock Options." *Journal of Financial Economics*, 2000, 57, 65–101.

Adam, Avshalom M., and Mark S. Schwartz. "Corporate Governance, Ethics, and the Backdating of Stock Options." *Journal of Business Ethics*, 2009, 85, 225–237.

Adams, Renee, Benjamin E. Hermalin, and Michael S. Weisbach. "The Role of Boards of Directors in Corporate Governance: A Conceptual Framework and Survey." *Journal of Economic Literature*, 2010, 48:1, 58–107.

Amman, Manuel, and Ralf Seiz. "Valuing Employee Stock Options: Does the Model Matter?" *Financial Analysts Journal*, 2004, 60:5, 21–37.

Anderson, Mark, and Volkan Muslu. "What Do CEOs Realize from Option Pay?" April 2010, working paper.

Angel, James J., and Douglas M. McCabe. "The Ethics of Managerial Compensation: The Case of Executive Stock Options." *Journal of Business Ethics*, 2008, 78, 225–235.

Armstrong, Christopher S., Alan D. Jagolinzer, and David F. Larcker. "Chief Executive Officer Equity Incentives and Accounting Irregularities." *Journal of Accounting Research*, May 2010, 48:2, 225–271.

Arya, Anil, and Brian Mittendorf. "Offering Stock Options to Gauge Managerial Talent." *Journal of Accounting & Economics*, 2005, 40:1–3, 189–210.

Arya, Avinash, and Huey-Lian Su. "Stock Option Repricing: Heads I Win, Tails You Lose." *Journal of Business Ethics*, 2004, 50:4, 297–312.

Babenko, Ilona. "Share Repurchases and Pay-Performance Sensitivity of Employee Compensation Contract." *Journal of Finance*, February 2009, 64:1, 117–150.

Babenko, Ilona, Michael Lemmon, and Yuri Tserlukevich. "Employee Stock Options and Investment." *Journal of Finance*, June 2011, 66:3, 981–1009.

Baker, H. Kent, and Ronald Anderson, eds. *Corporate Governance: A Synthesis of Theory, Research, and Practice.* Hoboken, NJ: John Wiley & Sons, 2011.

Baker, Terry, Denton Collins, and Austin Reitenga. "Stock Option Compensation and Earnings Management Incentives." *Journal of Accounting, Auditing & Finance*, 2003, 18:4, 557–582.

Balsam, Steven. *Executive Compensation: An Introduction to Practice and Theory.* Washington, DC: WorldatWork Press, 2007.

Balsam, Steven, Huajing Chen, and Srinivasan Sankaraguruswamy. "Earnings Management Prior to Stock Option Grants." 2003, working paper.

Balsam, Steven, and Setiyono Miharjo. "The Effect of Equity Compensation on Voluntary Executive Turnover." *Journal of Accounting & Economics*, 2007, 43:1, 95–119.

Balsam, Steven, and Qin Jennifer Yin. "Explaining Firm Willingness to Forfeit Tax Deductions Under Internal Revenue Code Section 162(m): The Million-Dollar Cap." *Journal of Accounting and Public Policy*, 2005, 24, 300–324.

Barnard, Chester I. *The Functions of the Executive: 30th Anniversary Edition.* Cambridge, MA: Harvard University Press, 1971.

Barron, John M., and Glen R. Waddell. "Work Hard, Not Smart: Stock Options in Executive Compensation." *Journal of Economic Behavior & Organization*, 2008, 66, 767–790.

Bartov, Eli, Dan Givoly, and Carla Hayn. "The Rewards to Meeting or Beating Earnings Expectations." *Journal of Accounting & Economics*, 2002, 33:2, 173–204.

Bartov, Eli, and Partha Mohanram. "Private Information, Earnings Manipulations, and Executive Stock-Option Exercises." *Accounting Review*, 2004, 79:4, 889–920.

Bartov, Eli, Partha Mohanram, and Doron Nissim. "Managerial Discretion and the Economic Determinants of the Disclosed Volatility Parameter for Valuing ESOs." *Review of Accounting Studies*, 2007, 12, 155–179.

Bauman, Mark P., and Kenneth W. Shaw. "Stock Option Compensation and the Likelihood of Meeting Analysts' Quarterly Earnings Targets." *Review of Quantitative Financial Accounting*, 2006, 26, 301–319.

Bebchuk, Lucian A. "The Case for Increasing Shareholder Power." *Harvard Law Review*, January 2005, 118, 833–917.

———. "The Myth of the Shareholder Franchise." March 2007, working paper.

Bebchuk, Lucian A., Alma Cohen, and Holger Spamann. "The Wages of Failure: Executive Compensation at Bear Stearns and Lehman 2000–2008." November 22, 2009, working paper.

Bebchuk, Lucian A., and Jesse M. Fried. "Executive Compensation as an Agency Problem." *Journal of Economic Perspectives*, 2003, 17:3, 71–92.

———. "Executive Compensation at Fannie Mae: A Case Study of Perverse Incentives, Nonperformance Pay, and Camouflage." *Journal of Corporation Law*, 2005, 30, 807–822.

———. "How to Tie Equity Compensation to Long-Term Results." *Journal of Applied Corporate Finance*, winter 2010, 22:1, 99–106.

———. "Pay Without Performance: Overview of the Issues." *Journal of Corporation Law*, summer 2005, 647–673.

———. *Pay Without Performance: The Unfulfilled Promise of Executive Compensation.* Cambridge, MA: Harvard University Press, 2006.

———. "Stealth Compensation via Retirement Benefits." 2004, working paper.

Bebchuk, Lucian A., Yaniv Grinstein, and Urs Peyer. "Lucky CEOs and Lucky Directors." *Journal of Finance*, December 2010, 65:6, 2363–2401.

Bebchuk, Lucian A., and Robert J. Jackson, Jr. "Executive Pensions." *Journal of Corporation Law*, 2005, 30, 823–855.

Bebchuk, Lucian A., and Michael S. Weisbach. "The State of Corporate Governance Research." *Review of Financial Studies*, 2010, 23:3, 939–961.

Becht, M., P. Bolton, and A. Röell. "Corporate Governance and Control." In *Handbook of the Economics of Finance*, edited by George M. Constantinides, Milton Harris, and René M. Stulz. Amsterdam: North Holland, 2003.

Becker, Bo. "Wealth and Executive Compensation." *Journal of Finance*, 2006, 61:1, 379–397.

Ben-Amar, Walid, and Franck Missonier-Piera. "Earnings Management by Friendly Takeover Targets." *International Journal of Managerial Finance*, 2008, 4:3, 232–243.

Benmelech, Efraim, Eugene Kandel, and Pietro Veronesi. "Stock-Based Compensation and CEO (Dis)incentives." *Quarterly Journal of Economics*, November 2010, 1769–1820.

Bens, Daniel A., Venky Nagar, Douglas J. Skinner, and M. H. Franco Wong. "Employee Stock Options, EPS Dilution, and Stock Repurchases." *Journal of Accounting & Economics*, 2003, 36:1–3, 51–90.

Benston, George J., and Jocelyn D. Evan. "Performance Compensation Contracts and CEOs' Incentive to Shift Risk to Debtholders: An Empirical Analysis." *Journal of Economics and Finance*, spring 2006, 30:1, 70–92.

Bergman, Michael. "The CRRA Utility Function." No date, working paper.

Bergstresser, Daniel, and Thomas Philippon. "CEO Incentives and Earnings Management." *Journal of Financial Economics*, 2006, 80:3, 511–529.

Berle, Adolph, and Gardiner Means. *The Modern Corporation and Private Property.* New York: Macmillan, 1933.

Bernardo, Antonio E., Hongbin Cai, and Jiang Luo. "Motivating Entrepreneurial Activity in a Firm." *Review of Financial Studies*, 2009, 22:3, 1089–1118.

Bertrand, Marianne, and Sendhil Mullainathan. "Are CEOs Rewarded for Luck? The Ones Without Principals Are." *Quarterly Journal of Economics*, 2001, 116:3, 901–932.

———. "Enjoying the Quiet Life? Corporate Governance and Managerial Preferences." *Journal of Political Economy*, 2003, 111, 1043–1075.

Bettis, J. Carr, John M Bizjak, and Michael L Lemmon. "Exercise Behavior, Valuation, and the Incentive Effects of Employee Stock Options." *Journal of Financial Economics*, 2005, 76:2, 445–470.

———. "Managerial Ownership, Incentive Contracting, and the Use of Zero-Cost Collars and Equity Swaps by Corporate Insiders." *Journal of Financial and Quantitative Analysis*, 2001, 36:3, 345–370.

Billett, Matthew T., David C. Mauer, and Yilei Zhang. "Stockholder and Bondholder Wealth Effects of CEO Incentive Grants." *Financial Management*, summer 2010, 463–487.

Bishara, Norman D., and Cindy A. Schipani. "Strengthening the Ties that Bind: Preventing Corruption in the Executive Suite." *Journal of Business Ethics*, 2009, 88, 765–780.

Bizjak, John, Michael Lemmon, and Ryan Whitby. "Option Backdating and Board Interlocks." *Review of Financial Studies*, 2009, 22:11, 4821–4847.

Black, Fischer, and Myron Scholes. "The Pricing of Options and Corporate Liabilities." *Journal of Political Economy*, 1973, 81:3, 637–654.

Board of Governors of the Federal Reserve System. *Incentive Compensation Practices: A Report on the Horizontal Review of Practices at Large Banking Organizations.* Washington, DC: Board of Governors of the Federal Reserve System, October 2011.

Boatright, John R. "Fiduciary Duties and the Shareholder-Management Relation: Or, What's So Special About Shareholders?" *Business Ethics Quarterly*, 1994, 4, 393–407.

———. "From Hired Hands to Co-Owners: Compensation, Team Production, and the Role of the CEO." *Business Ethics Quarterly*, October 2009, 19:4, 471–496.

Boorstin, Daniel. *Cleopatra's Nose.* New York: Vintage Books, 1995.

Boyd, Tristan, Philip Brown, and Alex Szimayer. "What Determines Early Exercise of Employee Stock Options in Australia?" *Accounting and Finance*, 2007, 47, 165–185.

Brenner, Menachem, Rangarajan K. Sundaram, David Yermack. "Altering the Terms of Executive Stock Options." *Journal of Financial Economics*, 2000, 57, 103–128.

Brickley, J. A., S. Bhagat, and R. C. Lease. "The Impact of Long-Range Managerial Compensation Plans on Shareholder Wealth." *Journal of Accounting & Economics*, 1985, 7, 115–129.

Brisley, Neil. "Executive Stock Options: Early Exercise Provisions and Risk-Taking Incentives." *Journal of Finance*, 2006, 61:5, 2487–2509.

Brockman, Paul, Xiumin Martin, and Emre Unlu.. "Executive Compensation and the Maturity Structure of Corporate Debt." *Journal of Finance*, 65:3, June 2010, 1123–1161.

Brooks, Robert, Don M. Chance, and Brandon N. Cline. "Private Information and the Exercise of Executive Stock Options." April 2012, working paper. Forthcoming in *Financial Management*.

Broussard, John Paul, Sheree A. Buchenroth, and Eugene A. Pilotte. "CEO Incentives, Cash Flow, and Investment." *Financial Management*, summer 2004, 33:2, 51–70.

Burns, Natasha, and Simi Kedia. "Executive Option Exercises and Financial Misreporting." *Journal of Banking & Finance*, 2008, 32, 845–857.

———. "The Impact of Performance-Based Compensation on Misreporting." *Journal of Financial Economics*, 2006, 79:1, 35–67.

Cai, Jie, and Anand M Vijh. "Incentive Effects of Stock and Option Holdings of Target and Acquirer CEOs." *Journal of Finance*, 2007, 62:4, 1891–1933.

Callaghan, Sandra Renfro, P. Jane Saly, and Chandra Subramaniam. "The Timing of Option Repricing." *Journal of Finance*, 2004, 59:4, 1651–1676.

Campbell, Cynthia J., and Charles E. Wasley. "Stock-Based Incentive Contracts and Managerial Performance: The Case of Ralston Purina Company." *Journal of Financial Economics*, 1999, 51, 195–217.

Carpenter, Jennifer. "Does Option Compensation Increase Managerial Risk Appetite?" *Journal of Finance*, 2000, 55, 2311–2331.

Carpenter, Jennifer N., and Barbara Remmers. "Executive Stock Option Exercises and Inside Information." *Journal of Business*, 2001, 74:4, 513–534.

Carter, Mary Ellen, and Luann J. Lynch. "The Consequences of the FASB's 1998 Proposal on Accounting for Stock Option Repricing." *Journal of Accounting & Economics*, 2003, 35:1, 51–72.

———. "The Effect of Stock Option Repricing on Employee Turnover." *Journal of Accounting & Economics*, 2004, 37:1, 91–112.

———. "An Examination of Executive Stock Option Repricing." *Journal of Financial Economics*, 2001, 61:2, 207–225.

Carter, Mary Ellen, Luann J. Lynch, and Irem Tuna. "The Role of Accounting in the Design of CEO Equity Compensation." *Accounting Review*, 2007, 82:2, 327–357.

Chance, Don M. "Expensing Executive Stock Options: Sorting Out the Issues." September 2004, working paper.

Chance, Don M., Raman Kumar, and Rebecca B. Todd. "The 'Repricing' of Executive Stock Options." *Journal of Financial Economics,* 2000, 57, 129–154.

Chance, Don M., and Tung-Hsiao Yang. "At-the-Money Stock Options, Incentives, and Shareholder Wealth." April 2008, working paper.

———. "Expected Utility Valuation of Executive Stock Options in a Binomial Framework: A Comparative Analysis." July 2004, working paper.

Chauvin, Keith W., and Catherine Shenoy. "Stock Price Decreases Prior to Executive Option Grants." *Journal of Corporate Finance*, 2001, 7, 53–76.

Chava, Sudheer, Praveen Kumar, and Arthur Warga. "Managerial Agency and Bond Covenants." *Review of Financial Studies*, 2010, 23:3, 1120–1148.

Chava, Sudheer, and Amiyatosh Purnanandam. "CEOs Versus CFOs: Incentives and Corporate Policies." *Journal of Financial Economics*, 2010, 97, 263–278.

Chen, Mark A. "Executive Option Repricing, Incentives, and Retention." *Journal of Finance*, 2004, 59:3, 1167–1199.

Chen, Yenn-Ru, and Bong Soo Lee. "A Dynamic Analysis of Executive Stock Options: Determinants and Consequences." *Journal of Corporate Finance*, 2010, 16, 88–103.

Cheng, Qiang, and Terry Warfield. "Equity Incentives and Earnings Management." *Accounting Review*, 2002, 80:2, 441–476.

Cheng, Qiang, Terry Warfield, and Minlei Ye. "Equity Incentives and Earnings Management: Evidence from the Banking Industry." *Journal of Accounting, Auditing, & Finance*, 2011, 26, 317–349.

Cheung, Joe, Charles Corrado, J. B. Chay, and Do-Sub Jung. "Hurdle Rate: Executive Stock Options." *Australian Journal of Management*, June 2006, 31:1, 29–40.

Chhaochharia, Vidhi, and Yaniv Grinstein. "CEO Compensation and Board Structure." *Journal of Finance*, February 2009, 64:1, 231–261.

Chidambaran, N. K., and Nagpurnanand R. Prabhala. "Executive Stock Option Repricing, Internal Governance Mechanisms, and Management Turnover." *Journal of Financial Economics*, 2003, 69:1, 153–189.

Choe, Chongwoo. "Maturity and Exercise Price of Executive Stock Options." *Review of Financial Economics*, 2001, 10, 227–250.

Choudhary, Preeti, Sivaram Rajgopal, and Mohan Venkatachalam. "Accelerated Vesting of Employee Stock Options in Anticipation of FAS 123-R." July 2007, working paper.

Cicero, David C. "The Manipulation of Executive Stock Option Exercise Strategies: Information Timing and Backdating." *Journal of Finance*, December 2009, 64:6, 2627–2663.

Clark, Andrew, and Elana Schor. "Lehman Brothers Chief Executive Grilled by Congress over Compensation." *Manchester Guardian online*. Accessed February 25, 2010.

Cohen, Randolph B., Brian J. Hall, and Luis M. Viceira. "Do Executive Stock Options Encourage Risk-Taking?" March 2000, working paper.

Coles, Jeffrey L., Naveen D. Daniel, and Lalitha Naveen. "Managerial Incentives and Risk Taking." *Journal of Financial Economics*, 2006, 79, 431–468.

Coles, Jeffrey L., Michael Hertzel, and Swaminathan Kalpathy. "Earnings Management Around Employee Stock Option Reissues." *Journal of Accounting & Economics*, 2006, 41:1–2, 173–200.

Core, John E., Wayne R. Guay, and David F. Larcker. "Executive Equity Compensation and Incentives: A Survey." *Federal Reserve Bank of New York Economic Policy Review*, 2003, 9, 27–50.

Core, John E., Wayne R. Guay, and Randall S. Thomas. "Is U.S. CEO Compensation Broken?" *Journal of Applied Corporate Finance*, 2005, 17:4, 97–104.

———. "Is U.S. CEO Compensation Inefficient Pay Without Performance?" *Michigan Law Review*, 2005, 103 1142–1185.

Cornell, Bradford, and Wayne R. Landsman. "Accounting and Valuation: How Helpful Are Recent Accounting Rule Changes?" *Journal of Applied Corporate Finance*, 2006, 18:4, 44–52.

Cornett, Marcia Millon, Alan J. Marcus, and Hassan Tehranian. "Corporate Governance and Pay for Performance: The Impact of Earnings Management." *Journal of Financial Economics*, 2008, 87, 357–373.

Cox, Christopher. "Accounting Irregularities at Fannie Mae." Testimony before the U.S. Senate Committee on Banking, Housing and Urban Affairs, June 15, 2006.

Cox, John C., Stephen A. Ross, and Mark Rubinstein. "Option Pricing: A Simplified Approach." *Journal of Financial Economics*, 1979, 7, 229–263.

Craig, Susanne. "Goldman Sachs Gives Blankfein a Big Raise." *New York Times*, January 28, 2011.

Cringely, Robert X. "The Triumph of the Nerds: The Rise of Accident Empires." 1996.

Crystal, Graef. "Alexander is Prime Example of CEO Americanus." Bloomberg.com, December 17, 2003.

———. "Steve Jobs Takes a 5 Million-Share Bite of Apple." Bloomberg.com, April 8, 2003.

Cuny, Charles J., Gerald S. Martin, and John J. Puthenpurackal. "Stock Options and Total Payouts." *Journal of Financial and Quantitative Analysis*, April 2009, 44:2, 391–410.

Cyert, Richard M., Sok-Hyon Kang, and Praveen Kumar. "Corporate Governance, Takeovers, and Top-Management Compensation: Theory and Evidence." *Management Science*, 2002, 48:4, 453–469.

Dai, Min, and Yue Kuen Kwok. "A Tale of Three Options: Reload, Shout and Lookback Features." No date, working paper.

Daily, Catherine. S., S. Trevis Certo, and Dan R. Dalton. "Executive Stock Option Repricing: Retention and Performance Reconsidered." *California Management Review*, 2002, 44:4, 8–23.

Dalton, Dan R., and Catherine M. Daily. "Director Stock Compensation: An Invitation to a Conspicuous Conflict of Interests?" *Business Ethics Quarterly*, 2001, 11:1, 89–108.

Dash, Eric, and Matt Richtel. "Ex-Brocade Chief Convicted in Backdating Case." *New York Times*, August 8, 2007.

Datta, Sudip, Mai Iskandar-Datta, and Kartik Raman. "Executive Compensation and Corporate Acquisition Decisions." *Journal of Finance,* 2001, 56:6, 2299–2336.

DeFusco, R. A., R. R. Johnson, and T.S. Zorn. "The Effect of Executive Stock Option Plans on Stockholders and Bondholders." *Journal of Finance*, 1990, 45, 617–627.

Delgado-García, Juan Bautista, Juan Manuel de la Fuente-Sabaté, and Esther de Quevedo-Puente. "Too Negative to Take Risks? The Effect of the CEO's Emotional Traits on Firm Risk." *British Journal of Management*, 2010, 21, 313–326.

Devers, Cynthia E., Albert A. Cannella, Jr., Gregory P. Reilly, and Michelle E. Yoder. "Executive Compensation: A Multidisciplinary Review of Recent Developments." *Journal of Management*, 2007, 33:6, 1016–1072.

Devers, Cynthia E., Gerry McNamara, Robert M. Wiseman, Mathias Arrfelt. "Moving Closer to the Action: Examining Compensation Design Effects on Firm Risk." *Organization Science*, July–August 2008, 19:4, 548–566.

Dhaliwal, Dan, Merle Erickson, and Shane Heitzman. "Taxes and the Backdating of Stock Option Exercise Dates." *Journal of Accounting & Economics*, 2009, 47, 27–49.

Dong, Zhiyong, Cong Wang, and Fei Xie. "Do Executive Stock Options Induce Excessive Risk Taking?" *Journal of Banking & Finance*, 2010, 34, 2518–2529.

Donoher, William J., Richard Reed, and Susan F. Storrud-Barnes. "Incentive Alignment, Control, and the Issue of Misleading Financial Disclosures." *Journal of Management*, August 2007, 33:4, 547–569.

Dugan, Emily. "Exclusive: Salaries for Top Executives Are Rocketing 'Out of Control.'" *The Independent,* May 15, 2011.

Dunford, Benjamin, John Boudreau, and Wendy Boswell. "Out-of-the-Money: The Impact of Underwater Stock Options on Executive Job Search." *Personnel Psychology*, 2005, 58:1, 67–101.

Dutta, Sunil. "Managerial Expertise, Private Information, and Pay-Performance Sensitivity." *Management Science*, 2008, 54:3, 429–442.

Dybvig, Philip H., and Mark Loewenstein. "Employee Reload Options: Pricing, Hedging, and Optimal Exercise." *Review of Financial Studies*, 2003, 16:1, 145–171.

Eberhart, Allan C. "Employee Stock Options as Warrants." *Journal of Banking & Finance*, 2005, 29, 2409–2433.

Efendi, Jap, Anup Srivastava, and Edward P Swanson. "Why Do Corporate Managers Misstate Financial Statements? The Role of Option Compensation and Other Factors." *Journal of Financial Economics*, 2007, 85:3, 667–708.

Elayan, Fayez A., Thomas O. Meyer, and Jingyu Li. "Accelerating Vesting of Employee Stock Options to Avoid Expense Recognition." December 2006, working paper.

Equilar, Inc. *2011 Equity Trends Report.* Redwood City, CA, 2011.

——. *An Analysis of Voting Results and Performance at Russell 3000 Companies.* Redwood City, CA, 2011.

——. *TSR Performance and CEO Pay Study.* Redwood City, CA, 2011.

Erickson, Merle, Michelle Hanlon, and Edward L. Maydew. "Is There a Link Between Executive Equity Incentive and Accounting Fraud?" *Journal of Accounting Research,* March 2006, 44:1, 118–143.

Erkens, David H. "Do Firms Use Time-Vested Stock-Based Pay to Keep Research and Development Investments Secret?" *Journal of Accounting Research,* September 2011, 49:4, 861–894.

Fahlenbrach, Rüdiger, and René Stulz. "Bank CEO Incentives and the Credit Crisis." July 2009, working paper, Fisher College of Business WO 2009-03-013.

Fama, Eugene F., Lawrence Fisher, Michael C. Jensen, and Richard Roll. "The Adjustment of Stock Prices to New Information." *International Economic Review,* February 1969, 10:1, 1–21.

Faulkender, Michael, Dalida Kadyrzhanova, N. Prabhala, and Lemma Senbet. "Executive Compensation: An Overview of Research on Corporate Practices and Proposed Reforms." *Journal of Applied Corporate Finance,* winter 2010, 22:1, 107–118.

Fee, C. Edward, and Charles J. Hadlock. "Raids, Rewards, and Reputations in the Market for Managerial Talent." *Review of Financial Studies,* winter 2003, 16:4, 1315–1357.

Feng, Yi, and Yisong S. Tian. "Option Expensing and Executive Compensation." September 4, 2007, working paper.

Fenn, George W., and Nellie Liang. "Corporate Payout Policy and Managerial Stock Incentives." *Journal of Financial Economics,* 2001, 60:1, 45–72.

Ferri, Fabrizio. "Structure of Option Repricings: Determinants and Consequences." No date, working paper.

Fich, Eliezer M., Jie Cai, and Anh L. Tran. "Stock Option Grants to Target CEOs During Private Merger Negotiations." *Journal of Financial Economics,* 2011, 101, 413–430.

Financial Accounting Standards Board. *Statement of Financial Accounting Standards No. 123, Accounting for Stock-Based Compensation.* Financial Accounting Standards Board of the Financial Accounting Foundation, October 1995.

Fried, Jesse M. "Option Backdating and Its Implications." *Washington & Lee Law Review,* 2008, 65, 853–886.

Friedman, Milton. "The Methodology of Positive Economics." in his *Essays in Positive Economics.* Chicago, University of Chicago Press, 1966.

Frydman, Carola, and Dirk Jenter. "CEO Compensation." *Annual Review of Financial Economics,* 2010, 2, 75–102.

Fu, Xudong, and James A. Ligon. "Exercises of Executive Stock Options on the Vesting Date." *Financial Management,* autumn 2010, 1097–1125.

Fung, Scott, Hoje Jo, and Shih-Chuan Tsai. "Agency Problems in Stock Market-Driven Acquisitions." *Review of Accounting and Finance,* 2009, 8:4, 388–430.

Gabaix, Xavier, and Augustin Landier. "Why Has CEO Pay Increased So Much?" *Quarterly Journal of Economics*, February 2008, 123, 49–100.

Garvey, Gerald T., Amin Mawani. "Executive Stock Options and Dynamic Risk-Taking Incentives." *Managerial Finance*, 2007, 33:4, 281–288.

Gerety, M., C-K. Hoi, and A. Robin. "Do Shareholders Benefit from the Adoption of Incentive Pay for Directors?" *Financial Management*, 2001, 30, 45–61.

Ghosh, Chinmoy, John P. Harding, Özcan Sezer, and C. F. Sirmans. "The Role of Executive Stock Options in REIT Repurchases." *Journal of Real Estate Research*, January–March 2008, 30:1, 27–44.

Giroux, Gary. "What Went Wrong? Accounting Fraud and Lessons from the Recent Scandals." *Social Research*, winter 2008, 75:4, 1205–1238.

Goldberg, Richard E., and James A. Read, Jr. "Just Lucky? A Statistical Test for Option Backdating." March 2007, working paper.

Gompers, Paul A., Joy L. Ishii, and Andrew Metrick. "Corporate Governance and Equity Prices." *Quarterly Journal of Economics*, February 2003, 118: 1, 107–155.

Graham, John R., Mark H. Lang, and Douglas A Shackelford. "Employee Stock Options, Corporate Taxes, and Debt Policy." *Journal of Finance*, 2004, 59:4, 1585–1618.

Grant, Ruth W. "Ethics and Incentives: A Political Approach." *American Political Science Review*, February 2006, 100:1, 29–39.

———. "The Ethics of Incentives: Historical Origins and Contemporary Understandings." *Economics and Philosophy*, 2002, 18, 111–139.

Grein, Barbara M., John R. M. Hand, and Kenneth Klassen. "The Stock Price Reaction to Repricing Employee Stock Options." November 2001, working paper.

Guay, Wayne R. "The Sensitivity of CEO Wealth to Equity Risk: An Analysis of the Magnitude and Determinants." *Journal of Financial Economics*, 1999, 53, 43–71.

Guidry, F., A. J. Leone, and S. Rock. "Earnings-Based Bonus Plans and Earnings Management by Business-Unit Managers." *Journal of Accounting & Economics*, 1999, 26:1–3, 113–142.

Hall, Brian J., and Thomas A Knox. "Underwater Options and the Dynamics of Executive Pay-for-Performance Sensitivities." *Journal of Accounting Research*, 2004, 42:2, 365–412.

Hall, Brian J., and Jeffrey B. Liebman. "Are CEOs Really Paid Like Bureaucrats?" *Quarterly Journal of Economics*, 1998, 112, 653–691.

Hall, Brian J., and Kevin J. Murphy. "Optimal Exercise Prices for Executive Stock Options." *American Economic Review*, 2000, 90, 209–214.

———. "Stock Options for Undiversified Executives." *Journal of Accounting & Economics*, 2002, 33:1, 3–42.

———. "The Trouble with Stock Options." *Journal of Economic Perspectives*, 2003, 17:3, 49–70.

Hall, James A., and Stephen L. Liedtka. "Financial Performance, CEO Compensation, and Large-Scale Information Technology Outsourcing Decisions." *Journal of Management Information Systems*, summer 2005, 22:1, 193–221.

Hartzell, Jay C., and Laura T. Starks. "Institutional Investors and Executive Compensation." *Journal of Finance*, 2003, 58:6, 2351–2374.

Healy, Paul M. "The Effect of Bonus Schemes on Accounting Decisions." *Journal of Accounting & Economics,* 1985, 7:1–3, 85–107.

Heen, Knut Peder. "The Billion Dollar Gaps: Revisiting Section 162(m)." February 2010, working paper

Heitzman, Shane. "Equity Grants to Target CEOs Prior to Acquisitions." 2006, working paper.

Heron, Randall A., and Erik Lie. "Does Backdating Explain the Stock Price Pattern Around Executive Stock Option Grants?" *Journal of Financial Economics*, 2007, 83:2, 271.

———. "What Fraction of Stock Option Grants to Top Executives Have Been Backdated or Manipulated?" *Management Science*, April 2009, 55:4, 513–525.

Heron, Randall A., Erik Lie, and Tod Perry. "On the Use (and Abuse) of Stock Option Grants." *Financial Analysts Journal*, 2007, 63:3, 17–27.

Hodder, Leslie, William J. Mayhew, Mary Lea McAnally, and Connie D. Weaver. "Employee Stock Option Fair-Value Estimates: Do Managerial Discretion and Incentives Explain Accuracy?" *Contemporary Accounting Research*, winter 2006, 23:4, 933–975.

Holmstrom, Bengt, and Steven. N. Kaplan. "The State of U.S. Corporate Governance: What's Right and What's Wrong?" *Journal of Applied Corporate Finance*, 2003, 15, 8–20.

Holthausen, Robert W., David F. Larcker, and Richard G. Sloan. "Annual Bonus Schemes and the Manipulation of Earnings." *Journal of Accounting & Economics*, 1995, 19, 29–74.

Huddart, Steven, and Mark Lang. "Employee Stock Option Exercises: An Empirical Analysis." *Journal of Accounting & Economics*, 1996, 21, 5–43.

———. "Information Distribution Within Firms: Evidence From Stock Option Exercises." *Journal of Accounting & Economics*, 2003, 34:1–3, 3–31.

Hughes, William. "Stock Option 'Springloading': An Examination of Loaded Justifications and New SEC Disclosure Rules." *Journal of Corporation Law*, 2008, 33:3, 777–796.

Ikäheimo, Seppo, Anders Kjellman, Jan Holmberg, and Sari Jussila. "Employee Stock Option Plans and Stock Market Reaction: Evidence from Finland." *European Journal of Finance*, 2004, 10:2, 105–122.

Ingersoll, Jonathan E., Jr. "Valuing Reload Options." *Review of Derivatives Research*, 2006, 9:1, 67–105.

Institute of International Finance. "Compensation in Financial Services: Industry Progress and the Agenda for Change." March 2009.

Jarque, Arantxa. "CEO Compensation: Trends, Market Changes, and Regulation." *Federal Reserve Bank of Richmond Economic Quarterly*, summer 2008, 94:3, 265–300.

Jensen, Michael C., and William H. Meckling. "Theory of the Firm: Managerial Behavior, Agency Costs and Ownership Structure." *Journal of Financial Economics*, October 1976, 3:4, 305–360.

Jensen, Michael C., and Kevin J. Murphy. "CEO Incentives: It's Not How Much You Pay, But How." *Harvard Business Review*, May–June 1990, 138–149.

Jensen, Michael C., Kevin J. Murphy, and Eric G. Wruck "Remuneration: Where We've Been, How We Got to Here, What Are the Problems, and How to Fix Them." 2004, working paper.

Johnson, Marilyn F., and Ram Natarajan. "Executive Compensation Contracts and Voluntary Disclosure to Security Analysts." *Managerial Finance*, 2005, 31:7, 3–26.

Johnson, Shane A., Harley E. Ryan, Jr., and Yisong S. Tian. "Managerial Incentives and Corporate Fraud: The Sources of Incentives Matter." *Review of Finance*, 2009, 13, 115–145.

Johnson, Shane A., and Yisong S. Tian. "Indexed Executive Stock Options." *Journal of Financial Economics*, 2000, 57, 35–64.

———. "The Value and Incentive Effects of Nontraditional Executive Stock Option Plans." *Journal of Financial Economics*, 2000, 57, 3–34.

Ju, Nengjiu, Hayne Leland, and Lemma W. Senbet. "Options, Option Repricing and Severance Packages in Managerial Compensation: Their Effects on Corporate Risk." December 2002, working paper.

Kahle, Kathleen M. "When a Buyback Isn't a Buyback: Open Market Repurchases and Employee Options." *Journal of Financial Economics*, 2002, 63:2, 235–261.

Kahle, Kathleen M., and Kuldeep Shastri. "Firm Performance, Capital Structure, and the Tax Benefits of Employee Stock Options." *Journal of Financial and Quantitative Analysis*, 2005, 40:1, 135–160.

Kalpathy, Swaminathan. "Stock Option Repricing and Its Alternatives: An Empirical Examination." *Journal of Financial and Quantitative Analysis*, December 2009, 44:6, 1459–1487.

Kato, Hideaki Kiyoshi, Michael Lemmon, Mi Luo, and James Schallheim. "An Empirical Examination of the Costs and Benefits of Executive Stock Options: Evidence from Japan." *Journal of Financial Economics*, 2005, 78:2, 435–461.

Knopf, John D., Jouahn Nam, and John H. Thornton, Jr. "The Volatility and Price Sensitivities of Managerial Stock Option Portfolios and Corporate Hedging." *Journal of Finance*, 2002, 57:2, 801–813.

Kolb, Robert W. "Distributive Justice." In *Encyclopedia of Business Ethics, and Society*, edited by Robert W. Kolb. Thousand Oaks: CA, Sage Publications, 2008. Vol. 3, 1216–1225.

———. *The Financial Crisis of Our Time*. Oxford: Oxford University Press, 2011.

Kolb, Robert W., and James A. Overdahl. *Futures, Options, and Swaps*, 5th ed. Hoboken, NJ: John Wiley & Sons, 2006.

Koppel, Nathan. "Brocade's Gregory Reyes Sentenced (Again) for Options Backdating." *Wall Street Journal*, June 25, 2010.

Kuang, Yu Flora, and Bo Qin. "Performance-Vested Stock Options and Interest Alignment." *British Accounting Review*, 2009, 41, 46–61.

Kulatilaka, Nalin, and Alan J. Marcus. "Valuing Employee Stock Options." *Financial Analysts Journal*, November–December 1994, 46–56.

Laffont, Jean-Jacques. *The Theory of Incentives: The Principal-Agent Model*. Princeton, NJ: Princeton University Press, 2001.

Lam, Kevin C. K., and Yaw M. Mensah. "Disclosure of the Fair Value of Executive Stock Options Granted to Top Executives." September 2007, working paper.

Lamba, Asjeet S., and Vivek M. Miranda. "The Role of Executive Stock Options in On-Market Share Buybacks." *International Review of Finance*, 2010, 10:3, 339–363.

Lambert, R., D. Larcker, and R. Verrecchia. "Portfolio Considerations in Valuing Executive Compensation." *Journal of Accounting Research*, 1991, 29, 129–149.

Lambert, Richard A., William N. Lanen, and David F. Larcker. "Executive Stock Option Plans and Corporate Dividend Policy." *Journal of Financial and Quantitative Analysis*, December 1989, 24:4, 409–425.

Lambert, Richard A., and David F. Larcker. "Stock Options, Restricted Stock and Incentives." April 2004, working paper.

Leung, Kwai Sun, and Yue Kuen Kwok. "Employee Stock Option Valuation with Repricing Features." No date, working paper.

Lewellen, Katharina. "Financing Decisions When Managers Are Risk Averse." *Journal of Financial Economics*, 2006, 82:3, 551–589.

Lie, Erik. "On the Timing of CEO Stock Option Awards." *Management Science*, May 2005, 51:5, 802–812.

Liu, Yixin, and David C. Mauer. "Corporate Cash Holdings and CEO Compensation Incentives." *Journal of Financial Economics*, 2011, 102, 183–198.

Løchte Jørgensen, Peter. "American-Style Indexed Executive Stock Options." *European Finance Review*, 2002, 6, 321–358.

Malmendier, Ulrike, and Geoffrey Tate. "Who Makes Acquisitions? CEO Overconfidence and the Market's Reaction." *Journal of Financial Economics*, 2008, 89, 20–43.

Marcoux, Alexei M. "A Fiduciary Argument Against Stakeholder Theory." *Business Ethics Quarterly*, 2003, 13:1, 1–24.

Martin, K. J., and R. S. Thomas. "When Is Enough, Enough? Market Reaction to Highly Dilutive Stock Option Plans and the Subsequent Impact on CEO Compensation." *Journal of Corporate Finance*, 2005, 11, 61–83.

Matsumoto, Dawn A. "Management's Incentives to Avoid Negative Earnings Surprises." *Accounting Review*, July 2002, 77:3, 483–514.

Matsunaga, Steve R., and Chul W. Park. "The Effect of Missing a Quarterly Earnings Benchmark on the CEO's Annual Bonus." *Accounting Review*, July 2001, 76:3, 313–332.

McAnally, Mary Lea, Anup Srivastava, and Connie D. Weaver. "Executive Stock Options, Missed Earnings Targets, and Earnings Management." *Accounting Review*, January 2008, 83:1, 185–216.

McCormack, John, and Judy Weiker. "Rethinking 'Strength of Incentives' for Executives of Financial Institutions." *Journal of Applied Corporate Finance*, summer 2010, 22:3, 65–72.

McVay, Sarah, Venky Nagar, and Vicki Wei Tang. "Trading Incentives to Meet the Analyst Forecast." *Review of Accounting Studies*, 2006, 11, 575–598.

McWilliams, Nolan. "Shock Options: The Stock Options Backdating Scandal of 2006 and the SEC's Response." 2007, working paper.

Mehran, H., G. E. Nogler, and K. B. Schwartz. "CEO Incentive Plans and Corporate Liquidation Policy." *Journal of Financial Economics*, 1998, 50:3, 319–349.

Merton, Robert C. "Theory of Rational Option Pricing." *Bell Journal of Economics and Management Science*, 1973, 4:1, 141–183.

Merton, Robert K.. "The Unanticipated Consequences of Purposive Social Action." *American Sociological Review*, Dec. 1936, 1:6, 894–904.

Meulbroek, Lisa K. "The Efficiency of Equity-Linked Compensation: Understanding the Full Cost of Awarding Executive Stock Options." *Financial Management*, summer 2001, 5–44.

Minnick, Kristina, and Mengxin Zhao. "Backdating and Director Incentives: Money or Reputation?" *Journal of Financial Research*, winter 2009, 32:4, 449–477.

Minnick, Kristina, Haluk Unal, and Liu Yang. "Pay for Performance? CEO Compensation and Acquirer Returns in BHCs." No date, working paper.

Monks, Robert G. *The Emperor's Nightingale: Restoring the Integrity of the Corporation in the Age of Shareholder Activism*: New York: Basic Books, 1999.

Morgenson, Gretchen. "Clawbacks Without Claws." *New York Times*, September 10, 2011.

Moriarty, Jeffrey. "How Much Compensation Can CEOs Permissibly Accept?" *Business Ethics Quarterly*, April 2009, 19, 235–250.

Murphy, Kevin J. "Executive Compensation." June 1999, working paper.

———. "Explaining Executive Compensation: Managerial Power Versus the Perceived Cost of Stock Options." *University of Chicago Law Review*, summer 2002, 69:3, 847–869.

———. "Performance Standards in Incentive Contracts." *Journal of Accounting and Economics*, 30, 2001, 245–278.

———. "Stock-Based Pay in New Economy Firms." *Journal of Accounting & Economics*, 2003, 34:1–3, 129–147.

Nagar, Venky, Dhananjay Nanda, and Peter Wysocki. "Discretionary Disclosure and Stock-Based Incentives." *Journal of Accounting & Economics*, 2003, 34:1–3, 283–309.

Narayanan, M. P., Cindy A. Schipani, and H. Nejat Seyhun. "The Economic Impact of Backdating of Executive Stock Options." *Michigan Law Review*, June 2007, 105, 1597–1641.

Narayanan, M. P., and H. Nejat Seyhun. "The Dating Game: Do Managers Designate Option Grant Dates to Increase their Compensation?" *Review of Financial Studies*, September 2008, 21:5, 1907–1945.

Nelson, Jodie, Gerry Gallery, and Majella Percy. "Role of Corporate Governance in Mitigating the Selective Disclosure of Executive Stock Option Information." *Accounting and Finance*, 2010, 50, 585–717.

Nohel, Tom, and Steven Todd. "Stock Options and Managerial Incentives to Invest." *Journal of Derivatives Accounting*, 2004, 1:1, 29–46.

NYDailyNews.com. "JPMorgan Chase CEO Jamie Dimon Gets Massive $16M Pay Package." February 5, 2010.

O'Byrne, Stephen F., and S. David Young. "Top Management Incentives and Corporate Performance." *Journal of Applied Corporate Finance*, fall 2005, 17:4, 105–114.

O'Connor, Joseph P. Jr., Richard L. Priem, Joseph E. Coombs, and K. Matthew Gilley. "Do CEO Stock Options Prevent or Promote Fraudulent Financial Reporting?" *Academy of Management Journal*, 2006, 49, 485–500.

Ofek, Eli, and David Yermack. "Taking Stock: Equity-Based Compensation and the Evolution of Managerial Ownership." *Journal of Finance*, June 2000, 55, 1367–1384.

Ortiz-Molina, Hernan. "Executive Compensation and Capital Structure: The Effects of Convertible Debt and Straight Debt on CEO Pay." *Journal of Accounting & Economics*, 2007, 43:1, 69–93.

———. "Top Management Incentives and the Pricing of Corporate Public Debt." *Journal of Financial and Quantitative Analysis*, 2006, 41:2, 317–340.

Oyer, Paul. "Why Do Firms Use Incentives That Have No Incentive Effects?" *Journal of Finance*, 2004, 59:4, 1619–1649.

Oyer, Paul, and Scott Schaefer. "A Comparison of Options, Restricted Stock, and Cash for Employee Compensation." September 2003, working paper.

Palmon, Oded, Sasson Bar-Yosef, Ren-Raw Chen, and Itzhak Venezia. "Optimal Strike Prices of Stock Options for Effort-Averse Executives." *Journal of Banking & Finance*, 2008, 32, 229–239.

Peng, Lin, and Ailsa Röell. "Executive Pay and Shareholder Litigation." August 2006, working paper.

Perry, Tod, and Marc Zenner. "Pay for Performance? Government Regulation and the Structure of Compensation Contracts." *Journal of Financial Economics*, 2001, 62, 453–488.

Petra, Steven T., and Nina T. Dorata. "Corporate Governance and Chief Executive Officer Compensation." *Corporate Governance*, 2008, 8:2, 141–152.

Rajgopal, Shivaram, and Terry Shevlin. "Empirical Evidence on the Relation Between Stock Option Compensation and Risk Taking." *Journal of Accounting & Economics*, 2002, 33:2, 145–171.

Rawls, John. *A Theory of Justice*. Cambridge, MA: Harvard University Press, 1971.

Reuters.com. "Court Upholds Reyes Options Backdating Conviction." October 13, 2011.

Rogers, Daniel A. "Does Executive Portfolio Structure Affect Risk Management? CEO Risk-Taking Incentives and Corporate Derivatives Usage." *Journal of Banking & Finance*, 2002, 26, 271–295.

———. "Managerial Risk-Taking Incentives and Executive Stock Option Repricing: A Study of U.S. Casino Executives." *Financial Management*, spring 2005, 34:1, 95–121.

Rose, Nancy L., and Catherine Wolfram. "Regulating Executive Pay: Using the Tax Code to Influence Chief Executive Officer Compensation." *Journal of Labor Economics*, 2002, 20, S138–S175.

Ross, Stephen A. "Compensation, Incentives, and the Duality of Risk Aversion and Riskiness." *Journal of Finance*, 2004, 69, 207–225.

Sanders, William Gerard. "Behavioral Responses of CEOs to Stock Ownership and Stock Option Pay." *Academy of Management Journal*, 2001, 44:3, 477–492.

Sanders, William Gerard, and Donald C. Hambrick. "Swinging for the Fences: The Effects of CEO Stock Options on Company Risk Taking and Performance." *Academy of Management Journal*, 2007, 50:5, 1055–1078.

Sautner, Zacharias, and Martin Weber. "How Do Managers Behave in Stock Option Plans? Clinical Evidence From Exercise and Survey Data." *Journal of Financial Research*, summer 2009, 32:2, 123–155.

———. "Subjective Stock Option Values and Exercise Decisions." September 20, 2005, working paper.

Sen, Rik. "The Returns to Springloading." February 2008, working paper.

Shiskin, Philip. "Backdating Conviction of Reyes Overturned." *Wall Street Journal*, August 19, 2009.

Sircar, Ronnie, and Wei Xiong. "A General Framework for Evaluating Executive Stock Options." *Journal of Economic Dynamics & Control*, 2007, 31, 2317–2349.

Skinner, Douglas J., and Richard G. Sloan. "Earnings Surprises, Growth Expectations, and Stock Returns or Don't Let an Earnings Torpedo Sink Your Portfolio." *Review of Accounting Studies*, 2002, 7:2–3, 289–312.

Smith, Adam. *An Inquiry into the Nature and Causes of the Wealth of Nations*. London: Methuen & Co., Ltd., 1904.

Sorkin, Andrew Ross. *Too Big to Fail*. New York: Viking, 2009.

Spicer, Jonathan. "JPMorgan CEO Dimon's 2009 salary $1.32 million." Reuters.com, March 19, 2010.

Sternberg, Joel S., and H. Doug Witte. "Inside Information and the Exercise of Employee Stock Options." No date, working paper.

Subramanian, Narayanan, Atreya Chakraborty, and Shahbaz Sheikh. "Repricing and Executive Turnover." *Financial Review*, 2007, 42, 121–141.

Sun, Jerry, Steven F. Cahan, and David Emanuel. "Compensation Committee Governance Quality, Chief Executive Office Stock Option Grants, and Future Firm Performance." *Journal of Banking & Finance*, 2009, 33, 1507–1519.

Supanvanij, Janikan. "Does the Composition of CEO Compensation Influence the Firm's Advertising Budgeting?" *Journal of American Academy of Business*, September 2007, 7:2, 117–123.

Taylor, Frederick W. *The Principles of Scientific Management*. Public Domain Books, 2004.

Tchistyi, Alexei, David Yermack, and Hayong Yun. "Negative Hedging: Performance-Sensitive Debt and CEOs' Equity Incentives." *Journal of Financial and Quantitative Analysis*, June 2011, 46:3, 657–686.

Tian, Yisong S. "Too Much of a Good Incentive? The Case of Executive Stock Options." *Journal of Banking & Finance*, 2004, 28, 1225–1245.

Tufano, Peter. "Who Manages Risk? An Empirical Examination of Risk Management Practices in the Gold Mining Industry." *Journal of Finance*, September 1996, 51:4, 1097–1137.

U. S. Department of the Treasury. "Guidance on Sound Incentive Compensation Policies." Federal Register, June 25, 2010, vol. 75, no. 122, 36395–36414.

Valle, Matthew, and Robert M. Pavlik. "Predicting the Investment Decisions of Managers Under the Influence of Stock Option Incentives." *Journal of Management Research*, December 2009, 9:3, 133–141.

Van Der Goot, Tjalling. "Monitoring and Manipulation Around Option Grants Dates." No date, working paper.

Wakker, Peter P. "Explaining the Characteristics of the Power (CRRA) Utility Family." *Health Economics*, 2008, 17, 1329–1344.

Wall Street Journal. "Congress Grills Lehman Brothers' Dick Fuld: Highlights of the Hearing." October 6, 2008.

Warren, Don, Mary Zey, Tanya Granston, and Joseph Roy. "Earnings Fraud: Board Control vs. CEO Control and Corporate Performance—1992–2004." *Managerial and Decision Economics*, 2011, 32, 17–34.

Weber, Margaret. "Sensitivity of Executive Wealth to Stock Price, Corporate Governance and Earnings Management." *Review of Accounting and Finance*, 2006, 5:4, 321–354.

Williams, Melissa A., Timothy B. Michael, and Ramesh P. Rao. "Bank Mergers, Equity Risk Incentives, and CEO Stock Options." *Managerial Finance*, 2008, 34:5, 316–327.

Wright, Peter, Mark Kroll, Peter Davis, and William T. Jackson. "The Influences of the Chief Executive Officer's Stock and Option Ownership on Firm Risk Taking: An

Examination of Resource Allocation Choices." *Academy of Strategic Management Journal*, 2007, 6, 47–68.

Wu, Ming-Cheng. "Selecting Suitable Compensation Plans of Executive Stock Options." *Applied Economics*, 2007, 39, 1185–1193.

Wu, Yan Wendy. "The Incentive Effects of Repricing in Employee Stock Options." *Review of Accounting and Finance*, 2009, 8:1, 38–53.

Yang, Jerry T., and Willard T. Carleton. "Repricing of Executive Stock Options." *Review of Quantitative Financial Accounting*, 2011, 36, 459–490.

Yermack, David. "Good Timing: CEO Stock Option Awards and Company News Announcements." *Journal of Finance*, 1997, 52:2, 449–476.

Zamora, Valentina. "Characteristics of Firms Responding to Underwater Employee Stock Options: Evidence from Traditional Repricings, 6&1 Exchanges, and Makeup Grants." *Journal of Management Accounting Research*, 2008, 20, 107–132.

Zhang, Xiaomeng, Kathryn M. Bartol, Ken G. Smith, Michael D. Pfarrer, and Dmitry M. Khanin. "CEOs on the Edge: Earnings Manipulation and Stock-Based Incentive Misalignment." *Academy of Management Journal*, 2008, 51:2, 241–258.

{ INDEX }

DATE DUE